AN ENLIGHTENMENT TORY IN VICTORIAN SCOTLAND
The Career of Sir Archibald Alison

An Enlightenment Tory in Victorian Scotland is a political and intellectual biography of Sir Archibald Alison (1792–1867), historian, social critic, criminal lawyer, and sheriff of Lanarkshire. The first author to examine the full range of Alison's writings and activities, Michael Michie reveals a significant link between the Scottish Enlightenment and Victorian conservatism.

Michie argues that Alison's conservative ideas were deeply influenced by the social and political thought of the Scottish Enlightenment. He contends that Alison was the embodiment of the High Tory appropriation of the legacy of Adam Smith particularly evident in the belief that an agrarian capitalist society was the most appropriate form for both the maintenance of order and the practice of virtue.

Developing the suggestion that a conservative interpretation of the enlightened legacy was possible for the succeeding century, Michie's study offers a useful corrective to the received wisdom that Victorian Liberalism was the true heir of the Scottish Enlightenment.

MICHAEL MICHIE is associate professor of political science, Atkinson College, York University.

AN ENLIGHTENMENT TORY IN VICTORIAN SCOTLAND

The Career of Sir Archibald Alison

Michael Michie

TUCKWELL PRESS

First printed in Great Britain in 1997 by
Tuckwell Press Limited
The Mill House
Phantassie, East Linton
East Lothian, EH40 3DG
Scotland

© McGill-Queen's University Press 1997

British Library Cataloguing in Publication Data

A catalogue record of this book is available
from the British Library

ISBN 1 86232 034 9

Published as a co-publication between
McGill-Queen's University Press and
Tuckwell Press Limited

Printed in Canada

This book was typeset by Typo Litho Composition Inc.
in 10/12 Baskerville.

For my father
John James Michie
and in memory of my mother
Catherine Johnson

Contents

Acknowledgments

In the planning and writing of this book I have been helped and inspired by a number of people. It was John Dwyer who first suggested that a study of Alison was viable and who gave me the benefit of his wide knowledge of Scottish Enlightenment sources and debates. My dissertation supervisor, Nicholas Rogers, deserves thanks; his knowledge of eighteenth- and early-nineteenth-century British social and political history was invaluable in setting my subject in a wider context, and his comments and suggestions for chapter revisions were thorough and extremely useful. David McNally gave me the benefit of his original and stimulating research on Adam Smith, Thomas Malthus, and political economy in general. I thank Douglas Hay for many fruitful suggestions for research in the area of eighteenth- and nineteenth-century criminal law. My colleagues in the Political Science Department of Atkinson College, York University, and our secretary, Louise Jacobs, have demonstrated their support and friendship through many years. I have received much encouragement from Leslie Sanders, a dear friend and colleague.

I am grateful for the financial support received from the CUEW (now CUPE) Part-time Research Fund and the Atkinson College Research Fund. Those grants enabled me to travel to Britain, where my experience of the courtesy and professionalism of the staffs of the Public Record Office (Kew), the Scottish Record Office, the National Library of Scotland, Edinburgh University Library, and the Mitchell Library, Glasgow, was entirely positive. The staffs at York University Libraries and the staff at the Robarts Library, University of Toronto, were also extremely helpful, as was Hazel O'Loughlin-Vidal of Atkinson College. This book would not have progressed far from the dissertation stage without the encouragement and advice of Peter Blaney, Philip Cercone, and Joan McGilvray of

McGill-Queen's University Press. I remain in awe of the copy-editing skills and wisdom of Marion Magee. Olga Cechmistro-Michie has given me her love, support, and time when they were most needed.

August 1996

AN ENLIGHTENMENT TORY IN VICTORIAN SCOTLAND

Introduction

In 1840 a two-volume critique of the population theories of Thomas Malthus was published in Edinburgh. It attacked political economists, landlords, and industrialists, advocated state-provided poor relief and landownership by the poor, and supported public executions and transportation as well as colonial possessions and protectionism – and it was received with some enthusiasm by the *Church of England Quarterly* and by Frederick Engels. It was written by a High Tory sheriff of Lanarkshire, a forty-eight-year-old Episcopalian whose intellectual and cultural background was the Scottish Enlightenment and whose main intellectual influence was Adam Smith.

The author was Archibald Alison, the subject of this intellectual and political biography. Alison, who was made a baronet in 1852, was also a historian (author of a best-selling account of the French Revolution) and an extremely prolific essayist for the Tory *Blackwood's Edinburgh Magazine*. In addition, Alison had written a two-volume textbook on the principles and practice of Scottish criminal law, a work that remains relevant to modern practice. This is the first overall study of Alison's work and career.

Alison represents an interesting link between the Scottish Enlightenment and Victorian conservatism, as his work reveals a consistent appropriation of eighteenth-century themes. This study therefore adds a new dimension to the analysis of Toryism in the first half of the nineteenth century. Alison wished to preserve an agrarian commercial society. His vision owed most of its inspiration to Adam Smith's "ethic of improvement" as well as to the Enlightenment notion of balancing the passions by the industrious and prudent pursuit of artificial wants. Alison's activities as criminal lawyer and sheriff-depute contribute to our knowledge of the distinctiveness of Scottish law and law enforcement, especially in a period when they were under pressure from the effects of industrialization, English encroachments, and working-class militancy. This study also provides an interesting perspective on the issue of Scottish nationalism. It shows how a prominent political figure in the middle decades of the nineteenth century could balance an intense identification with and defence of Scottish institutions and traditions and an equally intense pride in the Union and the power of the British empire.

It is surprising how little has been written about Archibald Alison when one surveys the range of his writings and activities. In literature dealing with the various areas in which Alison was active, he receives generally cursory attention and hardly any recognition that his activities extended beyond the area under examination. Whether as historian, writer on population and the poor laws, Victorian Tory, or opponent of the Chartists,[1] Alison's work and career have been neglected.[2] On the surface, he does seem easy to dismiss as a diehard High Tory hardly worth noticing compared with the forward-looking Whig inheritors of the Scottish Enlightenment. It is certainly true that many of his views were reactionary and bigoted. And he was in many respects an unattractive figure: stern, pompous, and long-winded.

However, as both a "political philosopher" – as he described himself – and a sheriff, Alison was influential enough in his own day to deserve a full-length study. His career reminds us of something that the recent emphasis on the Whig and liberal political economist inheritors of the Scottish Enlightenment has perhaps obscured: namely, that the roots of nineteenth-century conservatism can also be found in the Scottish Enlightenment. The chief legacy of the Enlightenment in the nineteenth century, it is commonly held, was an amalgam of Whig laissez-faire political economy and utilitarianism, expressed particularly in the politics and political economy of the *Edinburgh Review* group, especially Sydney Smith, Francis Horner, and Francis Jeffrey. If this assessment is accepted as the sole outcome of this movement, however, it is difficult to see how influential conservatives of the nineteenth century such as

1. See Saville, *1848*, 21. Saville's references to Scotland are few, but he does draw attention to Alison as the "most famous" Scottish sheriff during the Chartist years, a "contemporary of Palmerston at the University of Edinburgh," and a man who "displayed remarkable energy and courage in confronting angry multitudes and pacifying potentially riotous crowds."

2. However, a recent article provides an examination of Alison as conservative propagandist, focusing on his *Blackwood's* articles: Milne, "Archibald Alison."

Archibald Alison and his brother, William Pulteney Alison, could have developed their view of society.

The Alison family would certainly have been puzzled by modern debates on the nature of the Scottish Enlightenment, especially the extent to which participants have tried to characterize it as issuing predominantly from one particular intellectual tradition or the other. Since the early 1970s, when the Scottish Enlightenment became a significant area of study, a great deal of effort has gone into attempting to define its essential characteristics. In some early studies, the Enlightenment tended to be viewed, rather anachronistically, as the source of embryonic versions of sociology and historical materialism.[3] In subsequent work, although more attention was paid to the actual eighteenth-century context, the tendency was to describe the Enlightenment as growing out of either a civic humanist tradition or a natural jurisprudence tradition.

From the civic humanist perspective, the movement's leading lights such as Francis Hutcheson, David Hume, and Adam Smith are situated firmly in their social and political milieu. It is argued that the early part of the Enlightenment was shaped by the civic humanist tradition of republican Rome by way of the Renaissance. By the middle of the century, civic humanist values were giving way, at least in the minds of some thinkers, to an attempt to cope with the consequences of the spread of commerce and capitalist values. One focus of recent study has been the Moderate literati, a central group of Presbyterian divines. A relatively small group of men – Hugh Blair, William Robertson, Thomas Carlyle, Adam Ferguson, and Henry Home – are seen as the shaping force of the Enlightenment in a crucial cultural sense, based on the key institutions of this period: church, university, and clubs.[4] John Dwyer provides us with a wider focus on the same phenomenon while linking his work to that of Nicholas Phillipson and J.G.A. Pocock by showing how three discourses overlapped in these cultural circles: civic humanism, Stoicism, and a gentle sensibility.[5] Both Dwyer and R.B. Sher also stress the effort these men were making to cope with the disruptive effects of commerce and improvement on community values.

The natural jurisprudence approach, seen especially in the work of Knud Haakonssen and Peter Stein, starts from the basic assumption that

3. Bryson, *Man and Society*; Meek, "Scottish Contribution to Marxist Sociology."
4. Sher, *Church and University*.
5. Dwyer, *Virtuous Discourse*.

early modern society was characterized, above all, by a search for stability in the face of changing economic reality and that the key was to be found in law. The critical questions were why would individuals obey the law and authority, and whether there was a basis for law and social order in human nature. These questions entered the intellectual milieu of the Scottish Enlightenment (and to a large extent helped shape it) from the work of two Dutch jurists, Hugo Grotius and Samuel von Pufendorf, and a Scottish jurist, Gershom Carmichael. Haakonssen believes there were two intellectual and practical choices available to Enlightenment intellectuals by the end of the eighteenth century: one represented by the ideas of Adam Smith and John Millar, the other by the Common Sense (or Realist) philosophy of men such as Thomas Reid and James Beattie. Reid and Beattie were disturbed by what they saw as the dangerous sceptical tendency in the work of Hume in particular – but to some extent in that of Smith as well – reflected in a denial that common sense intuitions about the world were necessarily true. For Common Sense thinkers, such intuitions were true because they were divinely inspired. Religion, therefore, was the ultimate basis for knowledge of the world and for social and political cohesion.[6]

Exclusive focus on either the civic humanist or the natural jurisprudence perspective, as well as the insistence that the eighteenth-century Enlightenment represented a break with Scotland's unenlightened pre-Union past, have been criticized. Missing, it is argued, are the intellectual dimension of natural science and the element of continuity with pre-eighteenth-century traditions. Roger Emerson has suggested that, important though the civic humanist and natural jurisprudence perspectives are to an understanding of eighteenth-century Scottish culture, the values, concepts, and practice of natural science, specifically the heritage of Isaac Newton, must also be an integral element of that understanding. Emerson argues that "the Scottish Enlightenment was not so different in origin from enlightenments elsewhere. It had native and exogenous roots in the work of Scottish and foreign *virtuosi* who pursued natural and civil history and natural philosophy or science … Those men who came to maturity after 1715 applied the critical and empirical methods of the natural philosophers to moral philosophy and all its branches and sub-divisions." He concludes that "science and natural philosophy counted for more in the Scottish Enlightenment than is

6. Haakonssen, *Science of a Legislator*; Stein, "Legal Philosophy of the Scottish Enlightenment."

usually apparent in the accounts given of it."[7] Archibald Alison, when tracing his family pedigree, explicitly noted its connections to the scientific tradition of the seventeenth and eighteenth centuries.

Continuity with pre-eighteenth-century traditions is a prominent feature of recent work on the historiography of the Scottish Enlightenment. David Allan also takes issue with a number of interpretations of the genesis of the Scottish Enlightenment: that it was an "aberration" – a decisive break with a barbarous and benighted past; that its major influences were either continental (natural law and classical republicanism) or English (particularly Addisonian politeness and the Union); that it was primarily a function of the rapid growth of eighteenth-century commerce and agriculture and the attendant rise of merchant and urban classes.[8] In contrast, Allan emphasizes the work of sixteenth- and seventeenth-century humanist and Calvinist scholars in Scotland who argued "for the social utility of a deeply rational and learned moral virtue." Allan also analyses the large body of Scottish historical literature in the eighteenth century, arguing that this should not be read as embryonic sociology or historical materialism but as a literature which was very clear about its own moral and religious function and which consciously built upon its early modern predecessors.[9]

I am concerned here not to argue for a particular interpretation of the Scottish Enlightenment but rather to see what elements of that eighteenth-century movement Archibald Alison considered useful in constructing a response to the stresses and strains of British society in the early nineteenth century. If we can accept that the central concerns of eighteenth- and early-nineteenth-century Scottish intellectuals were how to preserve the traditional community while adapting it to new knowledge and commercial pressures, we have a framework for incorporating the range of modern interpretations and for understanding the eclecticism of people such as the Alisons. Alison did not always acknowledge his sources and influences, but when he did eighteenth-century names figured at least as prominently as those of his nineteenth-century contemporaries. In the writings of Adam Ferguson, Adam Smith, Thomas Reid, David Hume, and Dugald Stewart, Alison found various combinations of the approaches which made up the Enlightenment: commercial humanism and Stoicism, natural jurisprudence, and natural science. One thing

---

7. Emerson, "Science and the Scottish Enlightenment," 338, 356, 357.
8. Allan, *Virtue, Learning and the Scottish Enlightenment.*
9. Ibid., 12, 10, and chaps. 3, 4.

disturbed him about this eighteenth-century intellectual heritage, however, and that was what he saw as its facile dismissal, or at least marginalization, of religion and of the role of Divine Providence in the affairs of the world. The rationalist optimism of the Age of Reason did not go down so well with Alison the criminal lawyer and sheriff who saw in his daily contact with the world changes that he considered the deplorable effects of the French and industrial revolutions. The conservatism of the Alisons grew out of a mixture of the agrarian commercialism and civic duty of the landed gentry, the sceptical Whiggism which placed prosperity above obsession with political system, and the Common Sense philosophy which posited harmony between religion and science.

Alison was born in 1792 and educated in turn-of-the-century Edinburgh, at a time when the Scottish Enlightenment was in its waning phase. However, its ideas were still alive. Alison attended lectures on moral philosophy and political economy given by Dugald Stewart, the biographer of Thomas Reid, William Robertson, and Adam Smith and a synthesizer of the various strains of Scottish Enlightenment thought. Stewart was a lifelong friend of Alison's father, the Reverend Archibald Alison. An Episcopalian who has hitherto been known solely as an important figure in the history of British aesthetics (for his influential *Essays on Taste*), and as a disciple of the Aberdonian philosopher, Thomas Reid, the senior Alison's *Sermons* reveal him to be a practical moralist in the tradition of the Moderate literati and Adam Smith. The Reverend Mr. Alison, whose early opposition to Malthus inspired young Archibald to develop a critique of the latter's theory of population, deserves a more extended treatment than he receives in this book. This is also the case for Sir Archibald's brother, Dr. William Pulteney Alison, a physician whose work and writings in the 1830s and 1840s established the link between disease and destitution. He too was very much shaped by his Enlightenment upbringing and remained a disciple of the Common Sense inductive philosophy of Stewart and Reid.

Sir Archibald Alison, then, is not merely an interesting link between the Scottish Enlightenment and early Victorian Britain. More importantly, it was his Enlightenment upbringing that strongly influenced his particular brand of conservatism. It is not common today to stress the connections between the Enlightenment and early-nineteenth-century conservatism. While recent commentators do recognize the intertwining of Tory and Whig concerns, especially in defence of class interests, they nevertheless focus on the Whig inheritance, leading to political reform, as the only really significant legacy of the Scottish Enlightenment. "Not only was the *Edinburgh Review* a bridge between the [eighteenth and nineteenth centuries]," writes Anand Chitnis, "but a melting-pot in which the ideas of the Scottish Enlightenment continued to simmer and from which emerged, among other developments, James Mill and others who were Bentham's disciples."[10] John Robertson sees the *Wealth of Nations* as "a canonical text for British liberalism" because it assimilated "the indigenous British constitutional principles of parliamentary sovereignty into political economy."[11]

This biography of Archibald Alison suggests that Adam Smith's heritage could be extended in directions other than that of laissez-faire political economy, and that the uneven and often slow development of the industrial revolution left many – radicals and conservatives alike – hoping that a more harmonious development of modern society was still possible. An examination of the careers of the Alisons broadens our knowledge of the formation of conservative ideology, specifically its High Tory variant, in the early nineteenth century by adding a relatively neglected Scottish dimension. Just as studies of the Enlightenment's legacy tend to underplay its conservative side, accounts of the origins of Conservatism tend to neglect the influence of the Scottish Enlightenment on those origins.[12]

Aside from the Alisons' published writings, this biography uses letters and pamphlets in various collections, chiefly the Blackwood manuscript collection in the National Library of Scotland, miscellaneous letters and pamphlets in the University of Edinburgh library, and letters concerning state policy towards social unrest in the Public Record Office and the Scottish Record Office. The absence of more personal correspondence (for instance between the Alison brothers) means that details of Sir Archibald Alison the man must be gleaned from his works and business letters, from comments of contemporaries, and from his activities. Much of our knowledge of Alison is necessarily drawn from his autobiography, *Some Account of My Life and Writings*. Alison wrote some of this work in 1851–2 (probably his life to that point) and completed it in 1862. It was eventually edited by his daughter-in-law and published in 1883, some sixteen years after his death in 1867. I have tried to treat these memoirs with caution, balancing them where possible with other sources.

10. Chitnis, *The Scottish Enlightenment and Early Victorian English Society*, 128.
11. Robertson, "Legacy of Adam Smith."
12. See, for instance: Eccleshall, "English Conservatism as Ideology,"; Greenleaf, *British Political Tradition*, vol. 2; O'Gorman, *British Conservatism*; Sack, *Jacobite to Conservative*.

Chapter one situates the Alison family in the context of the Scottish Enlightenment. It traces the family and community connections from which Sir Archibald could later claim an authentic Enlightenment heritage. Alison's professional career as a criminal lawyer is examined in the second chapter. It shows his concern with patronage and security but also his consciousness of the tradition of Scottish local administration which placed great emphasis upon the professional civil servant. His writings on the Scottish criminal justice system – *Principles of the Criminal Law of Scotland* (1832) and *Practice of the Criminal Law of Scotland* (1833) – were in part designed to extol the virtues of that system and to warn against threatened adoptions from English legal practice, such as grand juries and an unpaid magistracy. Alison also had wide-ranging ideas about reforming the criminal justice system so that it would more closely fit his image of a hierarchical yet harmonious society.

Chapter three explores the conjuncture of Alison's intellectual attacks on political reform and its consequences and his active efforts as sheriff-depute of Lanarkshire after 1834 to contain working-class unrest. The theme of professionalism is prominent here also, as one of Alison's main concerns throughout his tenure was to achieve the establishment of a county police force, so that the law enforcement efforts of the state would not have to rely on the selfish interests of the local aristocracy and commercial groups.

Alison considered his task as a "political philosopher" was to point out and suggest solutions to the social consequences of industrialization. The rapid growth of cities and their attendant evils had been observed by Smith (and by Alison's father) in the previous century. By the 1830s, however, in Alison's words, "the zone of tall chimneys, sickly faces, brick houses, and crowded jails ... span[ned] across the whole of England and part of Scotland." This "change of manners" – by which Alison meant the consequences of increased population, poverty, and crime – could only be halted by a concerted campaign to restore the balance between agriculture and industry. Chapter four, then, has as its focus Alison's *Principles of Population and Their Connection to Human Happiness*, published in 1840. Conceived as a critique of Malthus's theory, this work went beyond Malthus to attack the whole approach of political economy towards the problems of industrialization. Alison's solutions were state-provided poor relief, greater emphasis on transportation and emigration, and, most importantly for his overall scheme, landownership by the poor.

The fifth chapter looks at Alison's literary career and his most successful publishing venture: the ten-volume *History of Europe from the Commencement of the French Revolution in 1789 to the Restoration of the Bourbons in 1815* which appeared between 1833 and 1842. Alison kept up an exhaustive correspondence with his publisher to ensure that he could closely supervise the progress of the many volumes and editions of his massive narrative. The *History* is in large part a chronicle of the conflicts resulting from the French Revolution, but its overall inspiration came from eighteenth-century philosophical history in the tradition of Hume, Gibbon, and Robertson. The work was written as an intervention into the debates around the 1830 revolution in France and the Reform Bill in Britain. Alison aimed at a professional impartiality in his use of sources while nevertheless writing a consciously conservative account of the demise of liberty stemming from "democratic ambition."

The final chapter, focusing on Alison's writing for *Blackwood's Magazine*, sets his conservatism in its nineteenth-century context. On the key issues of the early nineteenth century – finance and currency, religion and an established church, reform, free trade, and the Corn Laws – Alison consistently took a High Tory stance. This position was characterized by a far greater reliance on the regulation and protection of society by the state than Liberal Tories would support. Alison's arguments on all of these issues were consistently founded on his preoccupation with the viability of an agrarian commercial society and with the vital role of the "middling ranks" – the small landed proprietor and yeoman, the professional and the middling commercial groups – in stabilizing and balancing society. The other essential aspect of Alison's social perspective was his Scottish nationalism. This was not a radical nationalism that attacked the union with England. However, in a number of neglected but key articles, he upheld traditional Scottish society, and especially its laws and its financial system, as a prosperous and autonomous nation. It is here that we discover the foundation for Alison's "social economy" and his faith, however misplaced, in agrarian capitalism: the Scottish "ethic of improvement."

1

"Persevering Virtue"

Archibald Alison's values were formed in the Edinburgh of the late Scottish Enlightenment. His parents were connected, through family, friendship, and intellectual pursuits, to the leading scientific and literary lights of eighteenth-century Scotland. In his autobiography, Sir Archibald made a point of establishing his pedigree as descendant of a family which in the eighteenth century was intimately connected to polite learned society, not to mention respectable wealth: "I was not born of a noble or wealthy family, yet my ancestors, by both the father's and the mother's side, were such as might reasonably impose obligation and excite emulation." Four generations previously the family had been "landed proprietors"; his great-grandfather, a younger son, had gone into business.[1] The Reverend Archibald Alison's father, Patrick Alison (also a younger son), was provost of Edinburgh.

Alison's mother, Dorothea Gregory, was the daughter of Dr. John Gregory, author of *A Father's Legacy to His Daughters*. Through his mother, Alison claimed:

I could boast a descent from "the long and memorable line of the Gregorys" [Dugald Stewart's description], which, since James Gregory, the celebrated mathematician, the contemporary and rival of Sir Isaac Newton, and my great-great-grandfather, has been distinguished by many men who have attained to eminence in the physical and exact sciences. By a collateral branch I was connected through my mother with Reid, the father of the Philosophy of Mind, who

---

1. This Alison had "accumulated a considerable fortune, which he lost by undue facility in becoming security for a friend." Alison, *Some Account*, 1: 3.

was grandson of James Gregory's father. My maternal grandmother was Elizabeth, daughter of the thirteenth Lord Forbes.[2]

Alison here claimed a connection to two important strands of the Scottish Enlightenment: the scientific heritage of Newton and the moral philosophy of Reid (whose philosophical range also included natural philosophy).

One piece of the advice which Dorothea Gregory (and other young women of polite society) received from her father was that women should be encouraged to cultivate their intellect. John Dwyer notes "many of the Scottish moralists clearly regarded themselves as enlightened" in this respect. To be a proper wife or mother, a woman needed acquaintance with the arts and sciences. However, Dwyer cautions, they still believed that "women's social and moral role lay pre-eminently in their affectivity rather than their rationality."[3] Alison, and no doubt his father, shared this attitude.

Dorothea Gregory, as well as being acquainted with the Edinburgh literati, had come into contact with a far more illustrious group of literary and political figures. After her father died in 1773, she had gone to live with his friend, Elizabeth Montagu, "whose drawing-rooms in London," noted Alison, "then united the fashion and talent of England."[4] During the next ten years, as a companion to Elizabeth Montagu, Alison's mother met Johnson, Gibbon, Burke, Reynolds, Goldsmith, and Fox, and, in Paris, Voltaire, Rousseau, D'Alembert, Diderot, Helvetius, Necker, and Turgot. Despite his mother's impressive experience, Alison approvingly noted her refusal to become a bluestocking. Her learning and her acquaintance with the cream of the European Enlightenment could easily, he suggested, have equipped her for a literary career. However,

2. Ibid., 1: 2–4.

3. Dwyer, *Virtuous Discourse*, 123. Benedict, in her study of William Creech, the eighteenth-century Scottish publisher, underlines the ambivalence of male writers towards the education and culture of women. Referring to the growing female audience for literary production, Benedict notes that literature traditionally aimed at élite men was also being read by their wives – a fact which while providing some cause for male pride also implied a threat to the traditional social hierarchy. " 'Service to the Public'," 137–8.

4. Elizabeth Montagu was perhaps the most brilliant of the "literary ladies" who themselves symbolized the emergence of women into polite society: see Langford, *A Polite and Commercial People*, 109, 604, and Blain, Grundy, and Clements, eds., *Feminist Companion to Literature in English*.

she had an utter abhorrence for learned ladies, avoided all display of her information, and often repeated a favourite saying of Jeffrey's, that "he had no objection to blue stockings, provided the petticoats were long enough to conceal
them" ... having refused rank, fortune and fashion – she had voluntarily retired
at the zenith of her prospects, to share with my father the solitude and seclusion
of an English parsonage-house.[5]

Archibald Alison senior attended Glasgow College in the early
1770s.[6] There he began a lifelong friendship with Dugald Stewart, who
was in Glasgow partly in hope of obtaining an exhibition to Oxford and
partly to attend the lectures of Thomas Reid[7] on moral philosophy. As it
turned out it was Alison, not Stewart, who obtained an exhibition to Oxford. He matriculated at Balliol in 1775 and earned an LL.B. in 1784.
Stewart and Alison boarded in the same house, and, as Stewart became a
personal friend of Reid, we can assume that Alison too had more than a
passing acquaintance with the philosopher. Reid had succeeded Smith
in the chair of moral philosophy at the University of Glasgow in 1764.
Knud Haakonssen sums up the basic features of Reid's thought which
were more or less formed by the time he left King's College, Aberdeen:

They included the metaphysical and theological foundations for morals, the
methodological principles by which philosophical inquiry in general should
be conducted, the dependence of the moral sciences upon the philosophy of
mind, the notions of moral agency and moral judgement, the refutation of

5. Alison, *Some Account*, 1: 292–3. The Alisons named their first child Montagu, after
Dorothea's illustrious companion. Perhaps this was more than just a token of respect:
might it reveal Dorothea's repressed longing for a life that might have been?

6. For the biography of Alison senior in the *Dictionary of National Biography*, see
volume 1: 286–7.

7. Thomas Reid, although long considered the main philosophical influence from the
Scottish school on the nineteenth century, had a reputation – until fairly recently – as a philosopher of rather narrow concerns. These were considered to be centred around the philosophy of Common Sense, which Reid had developed out of a critique of Hume's
scepticism. Reid's early reputation, as Wood has shown ("The Hagiography of Common
Sense"), was largely due to the picture of him transmitted to posterity by Dugald Stewart,
who was as much concerned with his own political and philosophical reputation as with an
accurate portrayal of Reid. In particular, Reid's interest and work in natural philosophy and
mathematics were marginalized by Stewart. Also, as Haakonssen notes in the introduction
to his edition of Reid's *Practical Ethics* (p. 3): "the moral philosophy [Reid] professed was
only part of a wider concern with human knowledge, aimed as much at the formation of
character as at the imparting of knowledge." Recently, then, not only has the full range of
Reid's interests been recognized, but also his relevance to twentieth-century philosophy.

moral skepticism as represented by Hume, a view of the teaching of moral philosophy as the practical inculcation of morals, [and] a concern with the connection between moral education and the proper conduct of life understood in a
Christian-Stoic perspective ... [8]

Reid gave a "public" course, part of the arts degree, and a more
advanced "private" course (which we can assume that Stewart and perhaps Alison attended). The public lectures dealt with the theoretical
principles of moral philosophy, ethics, and politics, while the private lectures covered their practical applications. Reid noted that he intended
in his private course to discuss first "the Culture of the human Mind,"
followed by the mind-body relationship, the fine arts, and eloquence.[9]

This, then, was the material which formed the first encounter of Stewart and Alison with moral philosophy. Later, when he was professor of
moral philosophy at the University of Edinburgh, Stewart would develop
his own systematic philosophy of mind. Alison developed Reid's ideas
on perception and on the fine arts into his influential *Essays on Taste*
(1790).[10] Alison's sermons, while owing a great deal to the influence of
Hugh Blair and other Moderate Edinburgh divines and to Adam
Smith's writings on ethics, also incorporated Reid's ideas on the active
powers of the mind. Further, Reid's notions of Christian-Stoic moral
behaviour would have reinforced similar ideas coming from Blair,
Smith, and perhaps Edmund Burke.

Reid's importance for the Alisons was that he tried to ensure that the
relativist and sceptical aspects of Hume's and Smith's ethics were coun-
tered, and that his Realist account of Common Sense, of human nature,
was based on a "providential naturalism." Both Hume and Smith were
alleged to have weakened the connection between religion and virtue.[11]
For Reid the foundation of morality was the duties imposed upon

8. Haakonssen, "Introduction," 21.

9. Ibid., 29. The public lectures were divided into pneumatology (moral philosophy),
which included the general theory of mind, moral psychology and epistemology, and natural theology; ethics (practical ethics) covering "Duties to God," "Duties to Ourselves," and
"Duties to Others" (natural jurisprudence); and politics concerning "the nature and Effects
of all kinds of Government."

10. Alison could conceivably have heard Reid's lectures on the fine arts at Glasgow.
However, there would have been ample later opportunity for Alison to have known Reid's
views on taste, specifically from the chapter of that title in *Essays on the Intellectual Powers of
Man* but also from Reid's general philosophy which was a philosophy of perception.

11. See Smith, *Theory of Moral Sentiments*, 132–4, where Smith questions the degree of
veneration accorded to religious devotion.

human beings by divine law. As Peter Diamond puts it, "without the piety derived from an awareness of the providential order of creation men are liable to be misled into wrong conduct by their appetites and passions, by fashion and bad examples."[12] This theme was a dominant thread in the message of the Reverend Archibald Alison's sermons. Common Sense philosophy was based upon principles which were self-evidently true because they were divinely inspired.[13]

The elder Alison established himself among the Enlightenment lite-rati when he married the daughter of Dr. John Gregory in 1784. Being an Episcopalian clergyman in Edinburgh was not the intellectual or social drawback it may have been some decades earlier, as the Moderate Presbyterian clergy passed the peak of their greatest influence in the 1790s, and R.B. Sher notes that Anglican clergy seemed to be rising in intellectual influence.[14] The origin of Alison's religious affiliation is not clear, but we do know that Episcopalianism was stronger in the north-east, from whence the Alison family hailed, than it was farther south.[15] This connection perhaps enhanced the senior Alison's relationship with the Aberdonian Thomas Reid.

To establish himself in a church living, the Reverend Mr. Alison had to rely on patronage. Patronage was a fact of social and political life in eighteenth-century Britain, and young men aspiring to careers in the professions needed good connections.[16] In the beginning Alison sought his clerical living in England and needed to convince a patron there – Sir William Pulteney – of his educational attainments and his connec-tions. In a letter to Pulteney in 1789, Alison noted that even though he

12. Diamond, "Rhetoric and Philosophy in Reid's Social Thought," 8.

13. For an interesting account of the fortunes of Common Sense philosophy in the early nineteenth century, focusing on Thomas Brown and controversies around the develop-ment of a "mental science," see Robertson, "A Bacon-Facing Generation."

14. Sher, *Church and University*, 319n83. Sher also mentions Bishop George Gleig and Sydney Smith.

15. Phillipson ("Towards a Definition of the Scottish Enlightenment," 144) notes that it was Aberdeen, "the center of the 'non-conformist' north-east" which was "strongly asso-ciated with episcopalianism and jacobitism rather than the presbyterianism and whiggery of Edinburgh and lowland Scotland."

16. "For each of Scotland's established professional positions – each clerical benefice, each appointive legal office, each university chair – there was a patron, an individual or cor-porate body legally empowered to choose a successor for the position upon the death or resignation of its previous occupant": Camic, *Experience and Enlightenment*, 204. On patron-age, see also: Emerson, "Scottish Universities," and "Lord Bute"; Dwyer and Murdoch, "Par-adigms and Politics"; Phillipson, "Faculty of Advocates."

was of sufficient standing in Balliol to take the degree of doctor of laws and had been a member of the Church of England for nearly ten years, most of his career had been spent in the country. Consequently, "I have had little opportunity of being much known to people of any great Eminence in my own profession." However, he was able to suggest the late bishop of Durham and the present bishop of Peterborough as being sufficently acquainted with his character to testify on his behalf. Alison pointed out that it was really only in London that "a person in my condition can be known to the higher clergy," but whenever he had the opportunity to leave Oxford or his parish, he was "led both by duty and inclination to Edinburgh." His connections, consequently, were all "literary" ones, and he modestly wheeled out his Scottish big guns: "if you think that the testimony of Mr Smith, Dr Robertson & Dr Blair or any other of the eminent men of this Country might be of use, I can almost flatter myself they will not deny it to me." Adam Smith had in any case "offered me letters of this kind to the Bishops of Carlyle and Peterborough" and would surely forward them if necessary.[17]

The letter must have worked. Alison was given the curacy of Kenley in Shropshire (and in gratitude named his first son after his patron). This appointment was followed by those of the vicarage of High Ercal and the rectory of Rodington. In 1791 Bishop Douglas granted him a prebend in Salisbury. Kenley though was the Alison family's home, and they lived there until 1800. In 1800 Alison became minister of the Episcopal chapel in the Cowgate, Edinburgh. His move back to Edinburgh stemmed from his belief that his sons could obtain a better education and more independent careers in Scotland.

Alison's reputation has rested almost solely on his *Essays on Taste*, whose second (1811) edition went into five printings by 1842. He is regarded as an important transitional figure in the philosophy of aesthetics, standing between Enlightenment neo-classical theories and Romanticism. He is said to have influenced writers and artists as diverse as Robert Burns, William Wordsworth, and John Constable. Building on the associationist theories of Thomas Reid, Alison argued that qualities of the mind – association and imagination – formed a complex whole,

17. Alison to Pulteney, 5 August 1789, NLS, 1055. Sir William Pulteney "had been born a Johnstone of Westerhalt and had changed his name when he married the heiress to the Earl of Bath": Lenman, *Integration, Enlightenment, and Industrialization*, 122. This may explain both why other Scots in England sought him out and why he used his influence to help fellow Scots such as Alison and Thomas Telford. Alison also asked James Beattie to write a reference for him: Macmillan, *Painting in Scotland*, 149.

part of which was the emotion of taste.[18] Alison's aesthetic theories were important elements of the moral philosophy that he passed onto his sons, as the Scottish Enlightenment culture placed so much emphasis on the connection between taste and moral instruction. Just as taste could be developed, so could the moral sense or sentiments. Imagination was also an important ingredient in the approach of Scottish moralists, although less so for Reid than for Adam Smith. Reid, as an orthodox Baconian, condemned the role of imagination in natural philosophy but saw its value for inculcating practical morality.[19] Smith made an explicit connection between imagination and sympathy: social cohesion depended on the degree to which individuals were able to imagine themselves in the situation of others.

Alison's *Sermons* were published in two volumes in 1814 and 1815 and went through several subsequent editions. The article on Alison in the *Dictionary of National Biography* suggests that the sermons were of little intrinsic interest, quoting Lord Brougham's remark to Alison's son that the sermon on autumn was " 'one of the finest pieces of composition in the language'," but then rather dismissively noting that the sermons "are in the polished style of Blair, elegant discourses, showing more study of the 'Spectator' than of the masters of theological eloquence." However, it is precisely as examples of Enlightenment discourse that the sermons are interesting, especially as they were delivered at the end of the eighteenth century. As John Dwyer and Richard Sher have argued, the work of the Moderate literati represented one important aspect of the Scottish Enlightenment, establishing a discourse which emphasized sensibility and virtue in public and private life and which was concerned with preserving the refined values of a traditional moral community in the face of increasing commercialism.[20]

Therefore, if we take into consideration his *Sermons* and his memoir of Alexander Tytler, the historian, lawyer, and literary figure, we can see the Reverend Archibald Alison himself as a product of Enlightenment culture. His range of interests was grounded in familiar Enlightenment connections: between aesthetics and morals, and between imagination and judgement. His career highlights the important religious and conservative aspects of the Scottish Enlightenment, aspects which both his sons would take into the very different world of early-nineteenth-century

18. Townsend, "Archibald Alison: Aesthetic Experience and Emotion."
19. Diamond, "Rhetoric and Philosophy in Reid's Social Thought," 65–6.
20. Dwyer, *Virtuous Discourse*; Sher, *Church and University*.

Britain. However, to the extent to which Alison's sermons *were* models of Moderate discourse, they had become somewhat old-fashioned by the turn of the century. Sher notes that with the reorientation and politicization of Scottish intellectual life by the late 1780s, the influence of the Moderates waned and their concerns and their style became increasingly irrelevant.

In his sermons, the Reverend Mr. Alison, following Reid, placed a good deal of emphasis on the cultivation of the "active propensities" of human nature to balance its "passive sensibilities."[21] Too much exposure of the "passive sensibilities to pleasure" – more likely among the affluent than among the poor – produced "diseased" dispositions.[22] One of Alison's sermons, "On the Dangers of Moral Sentiment, When Not Accompanied with Active Virtue," was concerned with the balance both within the psychology of an individual and between public and private virtues. He cautioned that every virtue had a tendency "to run into excess, – and to mark the character with some features either of folly or of guilt." Our nature's highest attainable perfection, he argued:

consists not in the dominion of any one affection or principle, however virtuous, but in the due balance of all our affections; – in the proper mixture of intellectual and of moral attainment; and in the cultivation, not only of the contemplative, but still more of the active principles of our constitution ... restraining the dominion even of the most virtuous affections ...[23]

The "religion of the Gospel" also taught this principle. The gospel was "not merely a subject of intellectual or contemplative gratitude" but "a subject of active obedience, of filial affection, and of grateful imitation." We are not "spectators only," Alison cautioned, using a common dramatic metaphor, "but we are ... called to be actors."[24]

21. See Reid: "It is evidently the intention of our Maker, that man should be an active, and not merely a speculative being": *Essays on the Active Powers of Man*, 510. An insistence on active virtue was a common notion in the Enlightenment; Hugh Blair, John Drysdale, Henry Mackenzie, James Macpherson, and others made use of it.

22. The Rev. Archibald Alison, *Sermons*, II, sermon XVI, 331.

23. Ibid., II, sermon XII, 229–30.

24. Ibid., II, sermon X, 197. It may be that Alison was echoing Adam Ferguson here. Kettler ("History and Theory," 443) suggests that Ferguson took exception to what he saw as Smith's exclusive emphasis on the spectator and wished instead to contrast it with the attitude of the actor: "Ferguson takes up Smith's suggestion ... that agents playing some parts may govern themselves by the spectator's point of view. But he reserves that mode of

In his work on the Moderates, Sher points out that Hugh Blair (along with William Robertson) "sought to reconcile Christian principles with those of the Enlightenment." Blair's sermon, *The Importance of Religious Knowledge to the Happiness of Mankind,* "emphasized the constructive function of religion as a socializing and humanizing force, tending 'to improve the social Intercourse of Men, and to assist them in co-operating for common Good'."[25]

Alison's sermons used categories of expression similar to those found in the devotional literature of the Moderates and in Adam Smith's ethical writings. For instance, the civic humanist concern with the corrupting effects of commerce and luxury was prominent in several sermons. For a long time, Alison noted, "this country has enjoyed a prosperity unexampled in the history of time." However, history revealed nations fallen after periods of prosperity and the time had come when their nation would be tested. It would now be seen, he warned, "whether wealth has brought with it its usual avengers, – and whether the selfishness of commerce, and the feebleness of luxury, have also made our hands weak, and our hearts cold." Nations and monarchs were "falling around us." The causes were not hard to see: "the corruption of their private manners; ... the injustice or oppression of their internal governments; ... the ambition or avarice of their national policy."[26] In the past those whose actions had corrupted private morals and destroyed public virtue were motivated by "simple vanity": the desire for freedom without truth and for "a base and momentary fame."[27]

Moral corruption was especially prevalent in cities. In one sermon, "On the Moral Dangers of the Society of Great Cities," Alison stressed one particular danger of the city: it plunged the individual into the "obscurity" of mingling in "the multitude of society." To Alison, closely following Smith, the contrast with rural life was clear, and it had to do with the presence or absence of the moral community:

---

conduct to situations of little moral significance and insists that there is a distinctive actor's perspective which must be developed if men are to act well." Young Archibald Alison, commenting on his father's allotment scheme for his parishioners, said that it "tended to enlist the active propensities on the side of virtue": *Some Account,* 1: 12.

25. Sher, *Church and University,* 63–4.

26. The Rev. Archibald Alison, *Sermons,* I, sermon IV, 88, 81–2. John Dwyer (*Virtuous Discourse,* 38) suggests that three overlapping vocabularies can be distinguished in Moderate literature: the ancient civic humanist and Stoic discourses and the softer modern discourse of sensibility and sociability. Alison's forms of expression tended to be confined to the first two.

27. The Rev. Archibald Alison, *Sermons,* I, sermon XIV, 292–3.

Amid the solitude of rural life, every man is an object of observation; his vices as well as his virtues are prominent; and whatever be the path he takes, he is followed by the eyes of all who surround him. When he enters, on the other hand, into the society of populous cities, he is lost in some measure in the multitude. No eye follows him with interest or affection; – no well known countenance marks, in every hour, by its expression, the joy or the sorrow his conduct may occasion.

A further consequence of such isolation amongst the multitude was the alienation from one's own conscience: "Removed from the observation of others, [an individual] is too apt to think himself removed from his own." One remedy was to "hold regular communion" with oneself; to consciously withdraw from society in order to recharge the moral batteries. Another was to seek out a moral community of Christians.[28] "The corruption of every people," Alison argued, "has begun with the great." This eighteenth-century Scottish moralist sketched a conservative doctrine he hoped would be adequate to the new century: "the fabric of society itself can only be maintained by the progressive improvement of every rank in knowledge and in virtue."[29] This message was to form the core of the political philosophy of his two sons.

Perhaps because of Alison's preoccupation with the potential for national and individual suffering in the early years of the new century, Stoic discourse with its focus on self-control and steadiness of mind was prominent in his sermons. Smith and the Moderate literati, especially Blair,[30] most likely influenced Alison in this respect. D.D. Raphael considers that "Stoic philosophy is the primary influence on Smith's ethical

28. Ibid., II, sermon XIII, 260, 263, 266. Compare Smith (*Wealth of Nations*, 2: 795): While "a man of rank and fortune" is tightly constrained by his society with regard to manners and actions, a man of low condition "is far from being a distinguished member of any great society. While he remains in a country village his conduct may be attended to, and he may be obliged to attend to it himself. In this situation and in this situation only, he may have what is called a character to lose. But as soon as he comes into a great city, he is sunk in obscurity and darkness. His conduct is observed and attended to by nobody, and he is therefore very likely to neglect it himself, and to abandon himself to every sort of low profligacy and vice." Alison's passage, while less direct in its language than Smith's, does bring out more clearly the seeming paradox of community in solitude and loneliness within crowds.

29. The Rev. Archibald Alison, *Sermons*, I, sermon IX, 187.

30. Alison's sermon, "On the Beginning of the Century," was preached a few days after Blair died. Alison reminded his congregation that Blair "has been the greatest ornament of the church of this land" for half the previous century and has "left to every church a model of piety and virtue which no age can destroy." Ibid., I, sermon I, 18.

thought" and that "it also fundamentally affects his economic theory."[31] In particular, Smith took from Stoic doctrine the notions of self-command, self-preservation and the desire to better one's condition, prudence, and the idea of the harmonious system.

Of course "the great body of mankind" was doomed to a life of obscurity, their virtues unnoticed by any "sympathizing interest"; the patience, magnanimity, and self-denial "which their condition incessantly demands" known only to themselves and God. Their natural stoicism did not need much prompting. However, the audience for Alison's sermons tended to be the affluent and the educated. They were born into a favoured existence; from the first "marked by the sympathy of innumerable spectators," their virtues constantly applauded. They were not called upon to exhibit "the austere, the passive, or the solitary virtues," but rather in public life "the intrepidity of the warrior, the uprightness of the magistrate, the independence of the statesman," in private life the beneficence of landed or the generosity of commercial wealth, and in domestic life "pure and dignified manners."[32] Such individuals, and especially the young, did not experience the "pressure … which usually hardens the human character into any degree of conscience and solidity." Without experiencing "some stroke of adversity," their hearts tended to produce "unsteadiness." Life brought serious duties to everyone, regardless of social status, and "labour, perseverance, and self-denial, must be exerted." The only discipline, Alison warned, which could lead to "honour and to virtue" was that which "inspires resolution, and habituates to self-command."[33] The affluent and the educated had a public duty, which could be carried out only by "firmness and steadiness of obedience," by "steadfastness and perseverance." Alison's ideal would seem to have been "the man of … persevering virtue."[34]

Blair, to blunt the starkness of Stoic doctrine, had introduced the more reassuring notion of Divine Providence; an idea that was also important for Reid. Alison claimed that while the rising and falling of races and nations could be observed in history, so too could one observe "the Eternal Mind that governs the whole design … a system carrying on, in which all things 'are working together for good' to the wise and to the virtuous."[35] Alison's belief that "above all the weakness or suffering

31. Raphael and MacFie, eds., "Introduction," to Smith, *Theory of Moral Sentiments*, 5.
32. The Rev. Archibald Alison, *Sermons*, I, sermon IX, 179–80.
33. Ibid., II, sermon XVI, 323, 325, 328, 331.
34. Ibid., II, sermon XVII, 340–1, 345.
35. Ibid., I, sermon I, 6.

of men, there presides one Almighty Mind, in whose extended government 'all things are working together for final good' " was very similar to his friend Dugald Stewart's description of a spontaneously unfolding benevolent design of divine origin. It certainly was the immediate inspiration for young Archibald Alison's central belief, first expressed in public shortly after 1810, in "a system of Divine superintendence."[36]

Archibald Alison read his father's sermons in Enlightenment fashion: as tracts in moral philosophy. He thought they were less impressive as theological learning than as "pieces of devotional eloquence" (an important Ciceronian quality): tracing the "analogies between natural and revealed religion," and forming not only "our taste and style of composition" but also "our principles and views of life." The elder Alison's private conversation, according to his son, revealed "the prolific powers of genius" which his son regretted were never developed. His defect was an over-optimistic estimate of human nature – "the fatal error of the age in which he lived" – acquired partly from an early but never entirely renounced interest in Rousseau and against which his lack of worldly experience was no match. The problem was in recognizing the true source of evil: his father always said "evil was learned from the corruption of the world and the influence of bad example; he could not be brought to see the force of the question, 'Who corrupted the corrupters?' In a word, 'he had not enough of the devil in him to find the devil out.' "[37] Archibald Alison, the criminal lawyer and chronicler of the French Revolution, was convinced he knew better.

Both Alison boys received their early education at home, partly because the family residence at Bruntsfield Links was too far from Edinburgh High School and partly from pedagogical principle. Archibald Alison recollected:

My father was well aware of the justice of Adam Smith's observation that the best system of education is that which combines the emulation and coercion of a public school with the attachment and superintendence of home;[38] but he

36. Ibid., I, sermon VII, 136; Stewart, *Active and Moral Powers*, 328–9; Alison, *Some Account*, 1: 56.

37. Alison, *Some Account*, 1: 44–5.

38. Alison was referring to this passage in *Theory of Moral Sentiments* (p. 222): "Do you wish to educate your children to be dutiful to their parents, to be kind and affectionate to their brothers and sisters? ... educate them in your own house ... Domestic education is the institution of nature; public education the contrivance of man. It is surely unnecessary to say, which is likely to be the wisest."

thought, and I think wisely, that these advantages were more than counterbalanced in our case by the strengthening of the constitution consequent on a residence in the country, and that twelve years of age, when we were to go to college, was soon enough to begin the practical collision of life.[39]

Education in the home was an élite notion much favoured by the Enlightenment literati, and it underscores the conservative nature of the Scottish Enlightenment. As John Dwyer[40] points out, some Scottish moralists, especially John Drysdale, placed a great deal of emphasis upon education in the home, which aimed to ensure a close relationship between children and parents so that the latter could best guide the youthful passions into polite channels. In his memoir of Alexander Fraser Tytler, we find the Reverend Mr. Alison commenting favourably on Tytler's domestic education. This had enabled Tytler to acquire "that taste in life, or that sensibility to whatever is graceful or becoming in conduct or in manners." Such taste and sensibility constituted "the most important advantage that the young derive from an early acquaintance with good society."[41]

The Alison boys were tutored at home; this schooling included French lessons from their sister Montagu[42] and long country walks with their father, conversing on every subject: "the most effectual way that ever will be devised to enlarge and strengthen the mind."[43] They were also tutored in the classics, which "early impressed me with the conviction," Sir Archibald later recollected, "that it is in such studies that the mind of liberal youth can best be exercised." The "Scotch" system of teaching the classics, according to Alison, was inferior to the English method. Although they learned scanning, they never applied it to Latin or to Greek verse, for poetry "was never thought of."[44]

39. Alison, *Some Account,* 1: 25. "Practical collision" and "coercion" may well have been a reality for the Alison boys if they had gone to the high school, for it was "widely known," a biographer of Lord Selkirk notes, "for its harshness and vulgarity." Henry Cockburn, who had attended the school in the 1780s, observed: "Nothing evidently civilized was safe. Two of the masters, in particular, were so savage, that any master doing now what they did every hour, would certainly be transported." Bumsted, ed., "Introduction," *Writings of Lord Selkirk,* 1: 7.

40. Dwyer, *Virtuous Discourse,* 81–2.

41. The Rev. Archibald Alison, "Memoir of Tytler," 516. See also Reid, *Essays on the Active Powers of Man,* 577–8: Reid argued that the pursuit of virtue depended in part upon the improvement of manners through participation in the affairs of polite society.

42. Archibald taught himself Italian in 1810, while at university.

43. Alison, *Some Account,* 1: 25.

44. Ibid., 1: 27. These observations echoed his father's comments on Tytler's early education: such early studies, especially in the classics, "awaken the minds of the young to

Landscape painting, collecting prints at auctions, and buying books were valued extracurricular activities for Archibald. Significantly, history was an early passion: the first book he bought was Hume's *History of England*, followed by Robertson's *Works*, and eventually Gibbon, Thucydides, Tacitus, and Homer; the beginning "of the large library from which in after-times the History of the French Revolution was formed."[45] As these titles indicate, Alison's historical approach was to be a philosophical one. His critique of the French Revolution emerged from a comparison with the evolution of liberty in Britain.

Archibald Alison went to the University of Edinburgh for the first time in November 1805, at the age of twelve. William had entered two years before. Classics and mathematics (at which William excelled) were early enthusiasms, but it seems that the study of political economy, which, along with his reading of history, had the greatest implications for later work, was extracurricular – at least initially. Archibald had already read *The Wealth of Nations* at home with his father. At university during the summer he also studied the works of the French economists, particularly Guillaume-François Le Trosne's *L'Ordre social.* This, he recalled, "led to the study of Malthus's Essay on Population, which had been published ten years before, and the doctrines of which were then implicitly adopted by almost all who thought on these subjects." Alison later recollected his father pointing out what he took to be the fundamental flaw in Malthus's scheme: the latter's proposition that population tended to outstrip subsistence erroneously blamed Providence for the causes of human corruption. His father's criticism of Malthus formed the basis of all Archibald Alison's subsequent work on population. The outcome was Alison's first draft, in autumn 1808, of "an Essay on Population containing all the fundamental views which were afterwards developed in my work on that subject."[46]

Alison attended Dugald Stewart's lectures on political economy, but he was more impressed by what Stewart had to say on moral philosophy. "I was somewhat disappointed," he later wrote, "with Mr. Stewart's lectures on political economy, and began to suspect that he either had not gone to the bottom of the subject, or was not gifted with an original

---

a new sense of the beauties of nature, and of the charms of poetical imitation." The Reverend Mr. Alison noted that Tytler went to England to further his classical knowledge: "Memoir of Tytler," 516–17.

45. Alison, *Some Account*, 1: 31.

46. Ibid., 1: 39.

mind." Alison was particularly disturbed, "convinced as I was of the false positions and deplorable consequences of the Malthusian philosophy ... to find its leading principles represented as axioms which could not be controverted."[47] Alison's reaction to Stewart's political economy was in complete contrast to that of Henry Cockburn, who was to become an influential Whig lord advocate and to clash with Alison on several occasions, most notably around the anglicization of the Scottish criminal justice system. Cockburn considered Stewart to have "unfolded the elements and the ends of that noble science, and so recommended it ... that even his idler hearers retained a permanent taste for it."[48]

Alison took complete notes of the lectures he attended and wrote them out at night. These notes came to "over 26 bound quarto volumes." He added very little if any commentary but claimed in good Stoic fashion that the exercise of writing in itself produced good habits "of steady application, the feeling of duty not to fall behind – a feeling invaluable in the business of life." This "faculty of ready composition" later helped him keep up his advocate's business as well as a prodigious output of articles for *Blackwood's Magazine* and the volumes of his massive *History of Europe*.

In his autobiography, Alison discussed the comparative merits and purposes of the English and Scottish systems of education (although he had experience only of the latter). At the age of eighteen, about to begin his legal training, Alison considered that he had many deficiencies which could have kept him out of the English universities. For instance, he knew nothing of Greek composition or the composition of Latin verse and was "indifferent proficient in writing Latin prose." The health of the classics in Scottish universities was to be one of the areas of dispute between reformers and traditionalists in the nineteenth-century debates over education. "The weakness of the classics," notes R.D. Anderson, referring to the 1826 Royal Commission on Scottish Universities, "was increasingly seen as a defect at a time when they enjoyed much social prestige and when the revival of Greek was a major intellectual movement."[49] Alison struggled to make up for any deficiencies. He claimed he

47. Ibid., 1: 35–51.

48. Cockburn, *Memorials*, 169–70.

49. "Classics and mathematics," notes Anderson (*Education and Opportunity*, 32), "were studied for more than one year, but the starting-point was so low that there was no question of competing with the levels of attainment found in England, based as these were on far more effective school training; besides, the classics in Scotland were seen as preliminary subjects, to be dropped once the main work in philosophy began."

"had already read part at least of all the principal classical authors both in Greek and Latin … was master of French and Italian, and had read their leading writers." He was proficient in mathematics, had taken courses in natural philosophy, moral philosophy, and chemistry, and, unlike many of his English counterparts, had not contracted "a *distaste* for the classical languages; I could not write Latin, but I had *not learned to dislike to read it.*" Alison concluded:

the Scotch and English systems of education are intended for different ends, and each is excellent in its way. The Scotch, [is] intended chiefly for the education of the middle class who have their fortune to make, … the English, being intended mainly for the training of the great and the affluent whose fortune is made, is calculated to give what is desired for them, finish and grace to the mind.[50]

While Alison described himself as part of "the middle class who have their fortune to make," his admiration for "finish and grace" was clear. It is probable that he considered himself to have acquired the latter qualities through his education at home and his exposure to polite society.

Less is known about the intellectual development of Archibald's brother. After studying medicine at Edinburgh University, William Pulteney Alison became an M.D. in 1811.[51] His choice of profession may have been influenced by contact with his uncle, James Gregory, professor of the practice of medecine at Edinburgh from 1790. Gregory, like William's father, was an adherent of Thomas Reid's philosophy of Common Sense and was interested in the connection between natural philosophy and the philosophy of mind.[52] Whatever the earlier influence, Alison did become a philosophical disciple of Dugald Stewart

50. Alison, *Some Account*, 1: 54–5. Lyon Playfair made a very similar observation in 1889: "The old English universities have not the same function as the Scottish and Irish universities. The former teach men how to spend a thousand a year with dignity and intelligence, while the latter aim at showing men how to make a thousand a year under the same conditions." Harvie, referring mainly to the second half of the nineteenth century, suggests that "Scottish secondary and higher education didn't always reach its own high claims, but it was, in terms of access and relevance, much superior to the non-system south of the border": *Scotland and Nationalism*, 47–8.

51. William Alison would have taken courses from the following list: anatomy and surgery, chemistry, medical practice (the three most well-attended courses), medical theory, clinical lectures, midwifery, Materia medica, and botany. For a discussion of the general experience of medical education at Edinburgh during the later eighteenth and early nineteenth centuries, see Rosner, *Medical Education*.

52. Barfoot, "James Gregory."

and apparently Stewart thought Alison should succeed him in his chair.[53] In 1817 William wrote an article in *Blackwood's* defending Stewart's (and Reid's) philosophy from an attack made in the *Quarterly Review*. Alison described the self-evident nature of Common Sense principles: "the simple circumstance of a man's being conscious that he can remember, judge, or will, is not only a sufficient proof of his possessing the powers of memory, judgment, and volition; but the only proof which the nature of the subject allows us to require."[54] In a pamphlet on the famine of 1846, Alison was still following Reid in expressing a Baconian belief in the unity of all sciences and their connection to religion: "I firmly believe, that all the sciences, when fully and fairly presented, will be found to be in strict accordance with the fundamental precepts of Religion; and the confirmation which they afford of religious truth, is probably the most useful and important result that can be derived from them."[55] Upon graduating from Edinburgh Medical School, Alison went to work in the New Town Dispensary in 1815. It was here that he first made the link between poverty and disease that dominated his later work (see below, chapter 4). Alison was a beneficiary of the second Viscount Melville's flurry of patronage appointments in 1819: Melville nominated him to the chair of medical jurisprudence at Edinburgh. In 1821 he became professor of medicine and medical theory.

Archibald Alison's friendships and acquaintances, particularly amongst the club life of Edinburgh, drew him into the broad literary culture of Enlightenment Edinburgh. His "most valued" friend from childhood on was Patrick Fraser Tytler, author of the *History of Scotland* (1828–43), son of the historian Alexander Fraser Tytler (Lord Woodhouselee), and grandson of yet another historian, William Tytler. The Tytlers' influence on both the practice of historical writing in Scotland and the literary life of Edinburgh was considerable.[56] This connection was tightened in 1825, when Alison married Elizabeth Glencairn, William Tytler's granddaughter and cousin of Patrick Tytler. As it is rare to find Alison discussing his personal life other than in the most conventional terms, a short passage in his memoirs describing the

53. For the biography of William Pulteney Alison in the *Dictionary of National Biography*, see volume 1: 290.

54. William Alison, "Remarks on the Review of Mr. Stewart's Dissertation in the *Quarterly Review*," 61.

55. William Alison, *Observations on the Famine*, 2–3.

56. See the Rev. Archibald Alison, "Memoir of Tytler"; Ash, *Strange Death of Scottish History*.

circumstances of his marriage is uncharacteristically revealing. Remarking on his eligibility as a bachelor, the difficulty of remaining a "hermit," and how marriage had detached his "mind from dangerous excitements," Alison elaborated: "My disposition led me in a peculiar manner to prize the society of elegant and superior women, and to form intimacies with persons of the other sex often above my fortune." He hastened to add that it was his heart and his imagination that were fascinated rather than his "senses," and "vice" was "not indulged."[57] A rare moment for a biographer of Alison, but hardly a vision of Byronic excess – Alison elsewhere described Byron, whom he met briefly in Italy, as wallowing in an "epicurean sty."[58]

The central importance of clubs and societies for the formation and continuation of the Scottish Enlightenment has been well established.[59] Alison was steeped in this tradition: the Oyster Club, of which his father's friend, Dugald Stewart, was a member, along with Smith, Ferguson, Robertson, Joseph Black, James Hutton, and John Playfair; Scott's Friday Club; the revived (1787) Poker Club – with Alexander Tytler, Lord Daer, Playfair, Robertson, Baron Hume, and Henry Mackenzie; the Philosophical Society (out of which came the Newtonian Club), and the Royal Society of Edinburgh. The Reverend Mr. Alison himself had attended the Friday Club along with the leading lights of Whig Edinburgh and was a member of the Royal Society.[60] In the winter of 1810–11, when he began his legal studies, young Archibald also joined a debating club, "formed by a few young men having a similar destination, who met once a-week in a room of the college to habituate themselves to public speaking." Alison called this "the 'Select Society'" and noted that its fame "rapidly increased; it soon overshadowed, and wellnigh extinguished, the 'Speculative', which was of much older standing."[61] Alison's club seems to have been named after the mid-eighteenth-century Select Society, which existed from 1754 to 1764, and to have been very much like the Juridical Society which had been formed in 1797 by the merging of the Logical Society with the original Juridical Society begun in 1773. Every meeting

57. Alison, *Some Account*, 1: 233–4.

58. Ibid., 1: 143.

59. See McElroy, *Century of Scottish Clubs*; Chitnis, *Scottish Enlightenment*; Phillipson, "Towards a Definition," 132–5; Sher, *Church and University*; Dwyer, *Virtuous Discourse*.

60. McElroy, *Century of Scottish Clubs*, 293, 307.

61. Alison, *Some Account*, 1: 55. Those attending included Patrick Tytler, John Hope, Mungo Brown, Alexander Pringle, David Anderson, and several Englishmen studying law at Edinburgh – Nathaniel Hibbert, Gilbert Heathcote, W.H. Hyett, and Charles Brownlow.

night the Juridical Society first discussed a "Law Question" and then a "Speculative Question."[62]

Another influence on the young Archibald was travel. The Alison brothers, accompanied by Patrick Tytler and another friend, John Hope, undertook a tour of Europe from April to December of 1814, visiting the scenes of the French Revolution and observing the allied armies in Paris. This visit, a kind of "working" version of the Grand Tour, and a subsequent one to France, Switzerland, and Italy were to furnish Alison with a great deal of material for both his *History* and his *Population*. Immediately, however, it resulted in his first publication, an account of his travels in France, written in collaboration with his travelling companions and with Patrick's brother, Alexander, who had made a similar trip. It had unexpected success, going into a second printing in less than three months.[63]

As a young man growing up in Edinburgh in the first decade of the nineteenth century, Archibald Alison inevitably found himself in a Whig cultural environment. One key aspect of his development was the social and political awareness acquired in clubs and societies which, as we will see, were becoming politicized by the early years of the nineteenth century. Alison said that he then took a liberal line in arguing for Catholic emancipation and parliamentary reform, which he was later to oppose, but took a conservative position with regard to "an Established Church" and the necessity of war with France. He put his liberal views down to "the want of practical acquaintance with men ... in which professional and official duty afterwards gave me much experience." His youthful and ardent temperament, he claimed, led him to overestimate the good side of human nature, and he came to see that the existence of evil was caused not so much by "erroneous political institutions" as by the "corrupt and selfish principles of our natures."[64]

In this intellectual environment, it is not surprising that Archibald Alison's political opinions were initially liberal, even though he had early on taken a non-liberal line with regard to Malthus. For a few years following 1816, Alison frequented the Whig Society in Edinburgh, along with Francis Jeffrey, George Cranstoun, Henry Cockburn, John Murray, Macvey Napier, W.H. Playfair, and others. Prominent English Whigs often attended in summer. Alison found "considerable cleverness, much

62. McElroy, *Century of Scottish Clubs*, 231.
63. Alison, *Some Account*, 1: 72–99, 111–13.
64. Ibid., 1: 58.

fun, and great *bonhomie* and joviality in this society," but although he agreed with many of the Whigs' opinions, eventually certain "peculiarities in their mode of life and manner of thinking" caused him to withdraw.[65]

Sir Archibald Alison's later evaluation of his father revealed not only his own desire to distance himself from what he saw as the excessively naive optimism of the eighteenth century, but also the change in sensibility from the last generation of the Enlightenment proper to a generation brought up in the shadow of European war, industrialization, and rapid social change. While young Archibald adopted much of his father's civic humanist and Stoic approach, the political distance between father and son needs emphasizing. The impact of the discovery of poverty and the changing vision of the city was the key to this distance and indeed to the distance between the Scottish Enlightenment at its height and the early nineteenth century. In its attempts to counter the growing effects of industrialism and urbanism, early-nineteenth-century conservatism, and especially its High Tory version, represented by people such as Sir Archibald, could build on the élitist and paternalist elements of the Scottish Enlightenment. Young Archibald Alison, taking the French Revolution to be a cataclysmic warning of the dangers of political reform, would stretch the rather milder warnings of his father, against the corruption of manners and aristocratic governments, and of Smith, against the rationalist "man of system," into a full-blown crusade against the evils of "democratic innovation."

Archibald Alison, like his father and Dugald Stewart, supported the balanced constitution. However, young Archibald took a much more conservative view of that balance. One aspect of this difference was the degree of participation allowed to the "people" in the balanced constitution. Sir Archibald's view of governing required only that the people "watch" for corruption and tyranny. The more important determinant of political differences was the response to the impact of economic dislocation. Whigs and Tories could agree on the "balance" of social ranks and constitutional arrangement. Where they were coming to differ – although the split tended to be in Tory ranks, between Liberal Tories and High Tories – was on economic questions: free trade or protection, and government intervention to relieve poverty. Ultimately, political economy came to be the touchstone for attitudes towards social and economic problems.

65. Ibid., 1: 126.

Alison's account of his shift from Whig to Tory sympathies is not entirely satisfactory as it places so much emphasis on personal antipathies, and so little on why he took some political positions rather than others. Still, his account of his estrangement is interesting as it confirms how much both intellectual life and party politics were dominated by the legal profession at this time. Discussing the decline of the Scottish Enlightenment in the early years of the nineteenth century, A.C. Chitnis notes the "increasing party politicisation" of the institutions, particularly the clubs. Politicization of the law as well became a marked phenomenon in the early 1800s.[66]

Alison's experience confirms this judgement. He charged the Whigs with being too exclusive, a fault for which he saw the Tory party as partly to blame:

During the thirty years preceding, promotion at the Scotch Bar had been in the hands of the Tory party, and they had made in many cases an indifferent, in all, too exclusive a use of their patronage. Their object was in general to select not the ablest, but the most accommodating men – not those of original thought, but those of marketable abilities. This is the general and inherent fault of aristocratic government all over the world, which so often banishes genius to the other side: property is ever jealous of the rival power of mind. *Pliant ability is what it desires ...* The surrender of independence of thought which it requires had recently driven some of the most eminent men in the country into the ranks of Opposition.[67]

Consequently most legal business, Alison argued, was in the hands of the Whig advocates, leaving virtually no Tories competent to be appointed to the bench. Alison claimed that even the Tory home secretary, Robert Peel, was forced to appoint six Whig lawyers. Whig exclusivity had become so great, according to Alison, that the Whig leaders "came to imagine that they were really leaders of thought as well as of legal practice." A complacency ensued, and others who came to surpass them in intellectual and literary achievement were either only reluctantly recognized, as in the case of Walter Scott, or were ignored or ridiculed, as were John Gibson Lockhart and John Wilson, respectively.[68] Alison's

66. Chitnis, *Scottish Enlightenment,* 238, 242–3. See also Sher, *Church and University,* 315–16.

67. Alison, *Some Account,* 1: 127. See also Phillipson, *Scottish Whigs,* chap. 1.

68. Alison's judgement, rendered of course after thirty or so years as a devout Tory, was that this Whig "coterie" had produced nothing more celebrated than Francis Jeffrey's collected essays: well crafted but over-rated. Moreover, he thought that their influence was based not on the originality of their views but on their propagation of others' ideas: in

account accords, in its general outline, with Nicholas Phillipson's assessment of law and politics in the early years of the century. The latter notes that even though the Tories were in power, "the cards were heavily loaded against the government": "In a professional society, personal ability mattered and it was easy to contrast the growing array of whig talent which was excluded from the bench with the second-rate abilities of the existing [Tory] judges." Phillipson's account corrects Alison's on two points: it was not Peel (who was not even home secretary in 1811) but Henry Dundas, first Viscount Melville, who reversed the traditional policy of excluding Whigs from the bench; and Scott, who managed to stay to some extent above party politics, was "revered alike by whig and tory."[69]

Alison's evaluation of Edinburgh politics and his relation to it shows him emphasizing the values of independence and originality. It would be hard to argue that Alison's career and intellectual production, prodigious though the latter was, exhibited these values. However, we must read this as his attempt to make an intellectual and personal space for himself. Wishing to uphold the values of a class – the landed gentry – to which he did not belong and faced with the need to make his way in a society so dependent on patronage and connection, Alison chose to make a virtue of "professional" values. As sheriff, for instance, he would argue insistently for a professional (and independent) police force. He also argued for the originality of his views on social and political questions while exhibiting the same "pliant ability" in serving the governing class which he deplored in the aristocracy. In this he had a lot in common with Edmund Burke. As Christopher Reid says of Burke: "His need to proclaim the value of his own efforts sometimes comes into conflict with the more deferential attitudes expected of one of his class." Burke above all valued his own industriousness and Alison too seems to have felt that sheer quantity of production must in some way compensate for the disadvantages of his "middling" rank. "Feeling himself to be an outsider in an English political establishment which remained primarily aristocratic in character, he was peculiarly sensitive about his own position." This is Reid writing about Burke, but it could so easily describe Archibald Alison.[70]

---

politics, those of Fox and Grey; in political economy, Smith, Malthus, and Ricardo; and in "matters of taste" (which included the lamentable elevation of Dryden over Pope), Holland House and Lansdowne House. Here Alison lumps Smith together with Malthus and Ricardo, one of the few times, so far as I can tell, that he mentions David Ricardo. Ironically, however, his *Population,* written against Malthus, owes a great deal of its argument to Smith.

69. Phillipson, *Scottish Whigs,* 25, 26.
70. Reid, *Edmund Burke,* 84.

2

"Laborious Lawyer"

In his study of church and university in the Scottish Enlightenment, Richard Sher notes the rise of "a new breed of literary lawyers" in the early years of the nineteenth century. Sir Archibald Alison is one in a long list of such men.[1]

Alison thought of himself as a professional man "possessed of no fortune but what he could make at the Bar" and the product of an educational system intended to enable the middle class to make its "fortune."[2] Having to make one's own living in a range of occupations which could eventually provide the lifestyle of a gentleman seems to have been Alison's main criterion for defining the "middle class." The term "class" in its modern sense did not become common until the early nineteenth century, however. Until then, social differentiation and stratification were indicated by the use of "rank," "order," "estate," "degree," or "sort" (or, in a transitional usage, the plural "classes"). While these terms had been in use since the sixteenth century, the first two were especially common in the eighteenth.[3] Nineteenth-century conservatives probably tended to use "rank" or "order," which suggested an hierarchical or organic society, more often than radicals, for whom "class" connoted the divisiveness and

1. Sher, *Church and University*, 315–16.
2. Alison, *Some Account*, 1: 261, 54.
3. Williams, *Keywords*, 52–3. See also Nenadic, "Urban Middle Class," and Wallech, "'Class versus Rank'." Wallech's main argument (pp. 410–11) is: "The history of the emergence of 'class' saw the erosion of that calculus identified by 'rank' and the substitution of a 'species' of roles involved in production. The concepts developed by the authors of political economy imparted new meaning to a system of social division that became rooted in the word 'class'."

exploitation of industrial capitalism. Thus we find Alison using "rank" and "order(s)" far more often than "class."4

While the Alisons were clearly part of the urban environment, it must be remembered that links between town and country were close. The Alison boys grew up in country vicarages, and in Edinburgh many of Alison's legal clients must have been landed gentry. When Archibald Alison took up his position as sheriff of Lanarkshire, he moved his family into Possil House which, although only three miles from Glasgow, was a mansion standing in a thirty-acre estate.

Alison's ideal society was an agrarian commercial one, strongly influenced by his reading of Adam Smith. The "middling rank" was crucial to this social vision. Smith's "middling ranks," amongst whom were to be found the most virtuous members of society, were made up of the lesser gentry and small proprietors and members of the "inferior professions." Men of commerce might be included depending on the closeness of their ties to the land. Alison was often ambivalent about the moral worth of the commercial classes. His historical analysis of the rise of freedom, examined below in chapter 5, was centred firmly and solely on the small farmers or "yeomanry." When he was describing the social structure in the 1830s and 1840s, even though he did not trust the civic virtue and capacity for disinterested service of manufacturers and merchants, he nonetheless included them in "the useful orders." The "middling and useful orders of society" then – as opposed to the "feudal proprietors" and "manufacturing rabble" – were "the inferior nobility, the gentry, the merchants, manufacturers, lawyers, higher tradesmen, and farmers."

Among Alison's criteria for analysing society was the distinction between those groups who were "useful" and those who were idle, parasitic, or dangerous. "Manners" were also a very important criterion for Alison, and he appears to have drawn a line between those who were "genteel," that is, possessing manners, and the rest of society. Modern usage has diluted the term "manners," and it is necessary to remind ourselves of the power this term carried for a Scot such as Alison, brought up in Enlightenment culture. The historical sociology of the Scottish school placed as much stress upon manners as upon constitutions and legal arrangements for guaranteeing social cohesion and social order.

4. Smail has a useful discussion of the conflict between a traditional "corporate" discourse and a newer "industrial" discourse: "New Languages for Labour and Capital."

Alison's experience suggests that for him professionalism provided a means of coping with the transition from the predominantly landed society of the eighteenth century to the more socially dislocated and polarized society of industrial capitalism. To varying degrees, the professions combined the "pre-market" corporate values of service and community and the "market" values of competition and individual success. That these ostensibly conflicting values were already coexisting in eighteenth-century formulations of the social role of the "middling ranks" is clear from Adam Smith's description:

In the middling and inferior stations of life, the road to virtue and that to fortune, to such fortune, at least, as men in such stations can reasonably expect to acquire, are, happily in most cases, very nearly the same. In all the middling and inferior professions, real and solid professional abilities, joined to prudent, just, firm, and temperate conduct, can very seldom fail of success ... Men in the inferior and middling stations of life, besides, can never be great enough to be above the law, which must generally overawe them into some sort of respect for, at least, the more important rules of justice. The success of such people too, almost always depends upon the favour and good opinion of their neighbours and equals; and without a tolerably regular conduct these can very seldom be obtained.[5]

"Scotland's major social contribution to Britain over the last three centuries," writes Rosalind Mitchison, "has been the creation of the professions."[6] The rise of the professions nourished the universities in Scotland, which in turn developed a system of education peculiarly suited to

5. *Theory of Moral Sentiments*, 63. Speaking even more specifically of the professions, Smith, a professional man himself, said that while law was a "lottery" and like "many other liberal and honourable professions" was "under-recompenced," nevertheless "all the most generous and liberal spirits are eager to crowd into" such occupations. This was because of their desire for the reputation which excellence brings and the "natural confidence" which they had in both their abilities and their good fortune: "To excel in any profession in which but few arrive at mediocrity, is the most decisive mark of what is called genius or superior talents. The publick admiration which attends upon such distinguished abilities, makes always a part of their reward; ... It makes a considerable part of that reward in the profession of physick; a still greater perhaps in that of law; in poetry and philosophy it makes almost the whole." In discussing the market values of professional services, Smith also associated the price of services as much with social rank as with the cost of training. *Wealth of Nations*, 1: 123, 122.

6. Mitchison, "Nineteenth Century Scottish Nationalism," 137. For studies of the rise of the professions and of professionalism, compare Larson, *The Rise of Professionalism*, with more recent work: Holmes, *Augustan England*; Prest, *Professions in Early Modern England*.

"training and often exporting these middle-class men."[7] This assessment echoes Alison's own. In Edinburgh at least, the professions, especially the law, were closely bound up with landed wealth. Patronage and family determined an individual's chances of rising in the world. Alison found himself caught between what he saw as the stifling social control and corruption of the traditional aristocracy and the dangerously subversive tendencies of the new Whig political economy. Prizing independence and originality of thought, while wanting to protect social order and the hierarchy of ranks, Alison, as a lawyer and a sheriff, and as a writer, believed professionalism to be the solution. Personally, it rewarded his industry; socially, it gave him a position of respectability and even of power. Alison came to believe that the professional values of disinterestedness, independence, social order (all of which harmonized very well with the predominantly Stoic and civic humanist values of his upbringing) were vital to the maintenance of British society.

The legal profession in Scotland was flourishing by the mid-eighteenth century and was intimately connected to the improving landed and entrepreneurial groups. Stana Nenadic comments that "in Scottish towns of the eighteenth and early nineteenth centuries the two areas with the highest capacity for personal wealth and the highest status and power were merchants in overseas trade and legal professionals."[8] Alison embarked, somewhat reluctantly at first, upon a law career which was to propel him fairly rapidly into positions of middle-class respectability and power. Through it he was able to pursue the maintenance of social order in a society which, in his words, had seen a pronounced "change of manners" and an "extraordinary increase of crime" in the first decades of the nineteenth century. In addition, because he chose to eschew political advancement, he was able to pursue a literary career through which he could attempt to explain the "change of manners" that was threatening

7. Mitchison, "Nineteenth Century Scottish Nationalism," 137.
8. Nenadic, "Urban Middle Class," 114. McLaren's study of Aberdeen reinforces this picture. He notes ("Patronage and Professionalism," 133) that in the "consulting" professions, lawyers had attained a fairly high degree of professionalism by the 1780s, certainly when compared with their medical counterparts. "By and large," in Aberdeen, "lawyers were much more clearly identified with the leading city families from whom many were recruited. The close-knit family and business relationships of the eighteenth-century city ensured in itself a professional standard, but as well as this a long-standing professional body – the Society of Advocates in Aberdeen, which drew members from throughout the north-east – exerted a degree of control over the behaviour of its members."

to transform the relatively virtuous, hierarchical world of Enlightenment Scotland.

While Alison's motives in attempting both to save his society from its own wickedness and to enlighten it with his accounts of historical change and social economy were sincere, there was also a strong element of self-promotion in his endeavours. His status in society, while not precarious, had been uncertain. Patronage and connections were vital for advancement, and success in the world required a good deal of initiative for someone, no matter how well educated, who had not been born into the "natural" governing class. Party politics made a law career particularly insecure, and opportunities had to be created and grasped. The position of sheriff-depute of Lanarkshire provided Alison with the power to assist the British state in protecting the social order against threats from below. It also enabled him to move in the social circles which confirmed his sense that that social order was virtuous and just. Alison's career followed one fairly typical path that an educated "middling" member of Edinburgh society could take; one particular way of trying to keep conservative Enlightenment values alive in a rapidly changing world.

In 1808, when Alison produced the first draft of what was to become his *Principles of Population*, his father's response was to recommend his son take up a law career. The process by which the choice of career was made is itself an interesting illustration of the career options an educated Edinburgh man of "middling" rank considered available to his son. Initially, the elder Alison had planned that Archibald should be a civil engineer, as a result of his son's interest in mathematics and of his own friendship with a rising young Scots engineer, Thomas Telford.[9] This design was replaced by the idea of Archibald being a banker: his father's sister was married to a cashier of the Royal Bank ("ultimate heir to the immense fortune of Mr. Gilbert Innes of Stow"), a connection that seemed propitious. However, upon reading his son's essay on population, he strongly recommended the law as a career.

That the elder Alison did not, despite his own scholarly pursuits and his son's literary bent, recommend an academic career is not surprising.

9. Thomas Telford, "perhaps the greatest of all civil engineers," started as a mason apprenticed in the service of the Duke of Buccleuch. He followed successive building booms south to London and Portsmouth. In England, like the Reverend Mr. Alison, he enjoyed the patronage of Sir William Pulteney, who helped him become a surveyor of public works in Shropshire. "Like the architect Robert Adam, Telford returned to Scotland with a reputation made outside it": Lenman, *Integration, Enlightenment, and Industrialization*, 121–2.

Such positions were extremely hard to get and subject to rigorous political patronage. Generally, according to Roger Emerson, as the eighteenth century progressed "the arrangements by which professors were recruited changed very little; merit was never the sole criterion of a candidate's worth even when he was examined as so many were. These arrangements resulted in the appointment of men who had the approval and support of one or more powerful group within the community."[10] The Reverend Mr. Alison could conceivably have appealed to Sir William Pulteney, who had some patronage influence with regard to Scottish universities: he had established the chair of agriculture at Edinburgh in 1790.[11] However, even Pulteney's influence may not have been enough in the context of only a few hundred posts, to which access by the end of the eighteenth century, as Emerson demonstrates, "had become more effectively organized and controlled by the political managers."[12] It is also quite possible that Alison's Church of England affiliation might have told against him here.

The law must have seemed a more promising option. For practical men, politics and the law were the dominant occupations, embracing "the country's improvers and enlightened men." Although there was "a surfeit of ambitious young men" in law, career openings were probably less rigidly controlled than in the church and the universities. Charles Camic sums up the views of a number of authorities concerning entering a career in the law:

After going through an unexacting sequence of courses in philosophy and jurisprudence, an apprenticeship of highly uncertain rigour, or a combination of the two, a prospective lawyer wrote or commissioned a thesis, underwent examination by committees from the Faculty of Advocates ... and, if successful, was then admitted to the Faculty upon payment of a hefty fee. He was thereafter entitled to plead cases before Scotland's principal courts and could directly go about building up his own legal practice; no biding time until an established position became available was necessary ... however, ... unless one was sufficiently well connected to draw an ample clientele early on, the private practice of law in so small a country did not generally bring adequate financial and social returns for many hard years.[13]

10. Emerson, "Scottish Universities," 456–7.
11. Withers, "Improvement and Enlightenment."
12. Emerson, "Scottish Universities," 456.
13. Camic, *Experience and Enlightenment*, 200, 201. See also Emerson, "Scottish Universities," 457. Phillipson ("Faculty of Advocates," 156) notes that the "heirs of the elite of men

Archibald Alison's career decision and its consequences fitted fairly closely the pattern Camic describes. Young Archibald had indeed considered law as one of several options, although harbouring some doubts on account of "a dread of the slow progress usually made in that line."[14] In the end, his father's opinion prevailed, and Archibald Alison embarked on a law career.

There is no study of the Scottish bar in this period to match that by Daniel Duman of the English bar. However, conditions within the profession, especially with regard to advancement, were no doubt similar enough north and south of the border that we can use Duman's profile as a framework to help assess Alison's experience. Discussing professional advancement, Duman explains that "connections and patronage could be powerful forces especially in the opening stages of a legal career," although a young lawyer also needed talent and, perhaps just as importantly, an aptitude for hard, often grinding work.[15] Two of the most important avenues for advancement noted by Duman were: being the son of a professional man, who could secure business for his offspring through personal and business influence; and help from within the profession by attorneys and solicitors acting as patrons, "'who by employing young men early, give them not merely fees, but courage, practice, and the means of becoming known to others.'"[16]

Alison's early law career could well have provided an illustration for Duman's study. He was called to the bar in December 1814 "and from the first obtained a respectable and ere long a considerable share of business." Business came from members of his father's congregation,

---

of rank and property" tended to seek opportunities in England at the turn of the nineteenth century. It was lawyers, rather than the business community, who became the new local élite. The latter bypassed use of the Court of Session, considering it to be so totally bound up with the intricacies of feudal law. The Faculty of Advocates had much to gain from the maximum possible number of new entrants because entry money was used to maintain its library: Pinkerton, "Cockburn and the Law," 104.

14. Alison, *Some Account*, 1: 40.

15. Duman, *English and Colonial Bars*, 93–4, 112. Some Scottish evidence exists. Archibald Russell advised John Hill Burton, then practising in an advocate's office in Aberdeen, to "think twice before you *speak* of practicing in *Edinburgh* as an advocate. You are not aware of the various obstacles that oppose a young man's success at the bar; it must be by superior talents and great industry that one could expect to rise and the competition is such as would appal most – no one need think of making 10 the first 10 years." Russell to Burton, 18 February 1830, NLS, 9391, ff. 39–40.

16. Duman is quoting Thomas Talfourd, a well-known legal authority and member of parliament: *English and Colonial Bars*, 90–1.

"several of whom were highly respectable agents, who gave me briefs, and to some of whom I soon became standing counsel." A considerable portion of this work came his way from the lawyer J.H. Mackenzie, son of the author of *The Man of Feeling,* Henry Mackenzie. Alison would prepare court papers for Mackenzie and eventually got to present some of these under his own name, which he says were received favourably by judges, thus establishing his reputation.

Henry Cockburn's entry into the profession, which occurred fourteen years before Alison's, is another example of the relative ease with which young men could become advocates and of the more difficult means for advancement.[17] A young advocate who had connections to landed property, and who could set out written arguments based on the often tortuous structure of Scottish land law, could flourish before the Court of Session. Cockburn had connections: his father's cousin was Henry Dundas, first Viscount Melville. Unfortunately, he did not shine in written argument, and work ceased to come his way. There were two main alternatives: criminal law or a political appointment. Cockburn chose the latter (apparently with some desperation, as it was a Tory appointment). He lasted three years, until his Whig principles could bear it no longer. For the next ten years, Cockburn had to rely on criminal work for his livelihood; work that was boring and poorly paid. One could succeed with an aptitude for hard slogging, as Alison displayed, or with a particular flair – in Cockburn's case a skill before juries. Indeed, Alison marvelled at Cockburn's "oratorical powers" which were "unbounded with juries," but added that he was "indolent, and averse to *continued* labour." Walter Scott's experience as a lawyer at the end of the eighteenth century provides further illustration. Scott obtained a good deal of business from his father and brother, making up about half his income in his first five years. However, Scott was not particularly interested in advocacy, preferring to write, and as this became known in the profession he lost work.[18]

In less than three years Alison found himself ahead of most of his contemporaries, earning £500–£600 a year.[19] Scott, for instance, earned

---

17. The following section relies on Pinkerton, "Cockburn and the Law," 104–7.

18. Stevenson, "Scott at the Bar," 77.

19. Alison, *Some Account,* 1: 107–8. An unknown Scottish author, writing to John Hill Burton in 1846, and *probably* describing a junior advocate's salary, noted that salary was "£200 the first year with a rise of 10 each year till it reaches £300 which is the maximum": Letter to John Hill Burton, 1846, NLS, 9393, ff. 94–5. It appears that Alison's was a respectable

only £228 in his eleventh year in practice; Francis Jeffrey only £240 in his ninth year.[20] Alison regarded his salary as hard won. The work was almost entirely writing papers (as high fees in pleading and debates were reserved for senior counsel). Fifty or sixty octavo pages of print might bring only two or three guineas. On some occasions, he wrote the equivalent of seventy octavo pages in a day.[21] The pace and intensity of this work in fact remained a feature of his professional career as sheriff and writer.

Taking account of young Alison's desire to be a writer (and his father's appraisal of his talent) perhaps the choice of a law career was doubly appropriate, if a university post was out of the question. Making a living as a professional author in eighteenth-century Scotland was next to impossible because of a very small market and a lack of wealthy patronage. There had always been a close connection between law and literature in the Enlightenment. Nicholas Phillipson shows how the Edinburgh literati, especially when organized in the Select Society, "found themselves, unexpectedly leading a highly aristocratic society, deeply preoccupied with the role of public men in a modern society and with the possibilities of improving its politics, economy, manners and literature ... Polite learning as well as inherited rank and position had become associated with civic leadership." Almost a third of the Select Society's members were lawyers, and some, particularly Henry Home (Lord Kames), were celebrated for combining legal and literary careers.[22] Indeed, the Reverend Mr. Alison celebrated this combination in his memoir of Alexander Tytler.

However, during the Scottish Enlightenment, clergymen had generally been more prominent than lawyers as literary figures (the elder

---

income: discussing the profession "circa 1850," Duman notes that "while the most successful junior barristers earned £2,000 per annum, the average annual income for the junior bar was from £500–£1,200": *Judicial Bench in England,* 110.

20. Johnson, *Sir Walter Scott,* 248. Stevenson notes ("Scott at the Bar," 80): "Although he was not interested in the practice of the law, Scott was not averse to using the legal profession to gain for himself prestige and wealth."

21. There were compensations: vacations amounting to nearly seven months a year(!) and friendship with a number of "distinguished families," especially their daughters. In his autobiography Alison discussed the differences he saw between English and Scottish lawyers. The former generally displayed a lively conversational style because they spent a great deal of time arguing in court, whereas the latter spent much more time writing pleas. Alison, *Some Account,* 1: 108–9; 2: 221.

22. Phillipson, "Lawyers, Landowners," 186.

Alison was a late example of this pattern). It was not until the late eighteenth and early nineteenth centuries that "a new breed of literary lawyers" emerged; the "two prototypes" were Henry Mackenzie and John Millar.[23] Alison's desire to be a writer caused him eventually to pass up a promising political advancement to solicitor-general and lord deputy in favour of a dual career of sheriff and literary figure.

Alison had been practising civil law for eight years when at the end of 1822, he was advised by Sir William Rae, the lord advocate, that if he would accept the office of advocate-depute, Rae would recommend him for solicitor-general "at the next move." This offer of the advocate-depute position had not come out of the blue. Rae had clearly been considering Alison as his protégé for some time: he had repeatedly indicated (as had his predecessor, Allan Maconochie) "that if I would go a few circuits, and evince a disposition to cultivate criminal practice, I would be appointed to the first vacant situation of Advocate-General." Alison admitted that he had been tardy in not actively pursuing such a move, "the first step in official promotion ... partly from a dislike to criminal business on the side of the prisoner," partly from being extremely busy with civil cases, and partly from a reluctance to give up the opportunities to travel in Europe that his civil business had afforded him. The prospect of an eventual "gown" was too tempting, however, and Alison received his appointment on 15 February 1823.[24]

The criminal justice system in Scotland had evolved through the eighteenth century under pressure of economic and social changes from a locally administered face-to-face system that favoured "compromises and compensations" to one controlled by paid magistrates and central government. The latter was a more impersonal system principally concerned with making the world safe for the commercial classes. The police forces, as well as paid officials, became crucial in preventing and prosecuting offences against property and the person.[25] Alison accepted those changes as progressive and argued that a more professional system was a more humane system.

23. Sher, *Church and University*, 315. Sher's list, which includes Sir Archibald Alison, is an impressive one: Walter Scott, Francis Jeffrey, Henry Brougham, Robert Louis Stevenson, Francis Horner, Macvey Napier, Sir James Mackintosh, Henry Cockburn, Malcolm Laing, John Hill Burton, Alexander and Patrick Tytler, John Wilson, John Gibson Lockhart, Sir William Hamilton, et al.

24. Alison, *Some Account*, 1: 213–14.

25. Lenman and Parker, "Crime and Control in Scotland," 17.

The office of advocate-depute involved a great deal of responsibility and, confirming Alison's fears, virtually no time off. Scotland had only three advocate-deputes at that time. They were responsible for a wide range of duties: weighing evidence in criminal cases more serious than police offences; deciding whether those committed should go to trial or be released; deciding if and how evidence might be amended; preparing all the indictments against the accused; and, not least, conducting all such trials in person. The lord advocate and the solicitor-general did not interfere with cases or indictments unless these were extremely serious or "of a political tendency."

Thus the three Advocate-Deputes were, practically speaking, the grand jury, coroner, Attorney-General, and counsel on the Crown side in all cases, all over Scotland. The advantage of this system ... was, that it intrusted the administration of criminal law to a small number of professional men, who, from the great amount of business constantly put through their hands, soon became familiar with their duties and acquainted with its niceties; who worked daily, and liberated accused persons, against whom there was not sufficient evidence, within a few days of their committal, instead of awaiting the distant decision of a grand jury; and who, being few in number, universally known, and obliged to conduct the trials in person, could not escape responsibility for any part of their proceedings.[26]

Alison immediately took on a very heavy work load. As no indictments had been drawn up for almost four months on the North Circuit, there was a large number of cases in arrears. Alison worked "like a galley-slave" between his civil business and official duties. A load of sixty cases was heavy for a novice with little experience of criminal justice, or of jury trial in civil cases (only recently introduced in Scotland), but Alison's forte was persistence and steady application (especially in view of the promised promotion), and he reported "no great difficulty."[27]

The utility of having professional counsel as opposed to unpaid local notables was one of the main arguments Alison used in a pamphlet he wrote in 1824. The pamphlet, his first serious foray into legal and political controversy, was a criticism of the imposition of English practices on the Scottish justice system. For some time before Alison became an

26. Alison, *Some Account*, 215–16. Alison notes that there were already over 2500 individuals committed for serious offences in Lanarkshire at the time of his appointment.

27. Ibid., 1: 216. For an account of the introduction of civil juries, see Phillipson, *Scottish Whigs*. Alison drew the indictment in the famous Burke and Hare case, 24 December 1828: *Some Account*, 1: 272n.; "Sir Archibald Alison," 38.

advocate-depute, the Scottish criminal justice system had been heavily criticized. Many anglophile Whigs, Henry Cockburn foremost among them, considered that the Scottish system exhibited too many authoritarian features and should be liberalized by incorporating certain English practices.

Cockburn had been one of the foremost advocates (and beneficiaries) of the introduction of civil juries in 1815.[28] He followed up this reform with a series of three articles for the *Edinburgh Review* in 1821, 1823, and 1824.[29] The first, framed as a review of Jeremy Bentham's work on packing juries, argued for the use of a ballot and the right to challenge jurors in criminal cases. By 1823, when the second article appeared, the right of challenge for prisoner and prosecution had been established, and the Court of Justiciary had lost its right to name the forty-five people from whom the jury was empanelled.[30] Not long after, the judge's selection of the jury ceased. Cockburn's main target was the office of lord advocate and the almost unlimited power – discretionary and political – he thought it represented. However, he had no notion of recommending the introduction of private prosecutions along English lines although he did favour the English practice of grand juries because they would constrain the lord advocate.

The immediate context of the Cockburn-Alison exchange was "the controversies surrounding the Borthwick case in 1822 and 1823,"[31] where "Lord Advocate Rae had twice to face in the House of Commons charges of abusing his powers for political purposes."[32] In his memoirs, Alison argued that Scottish criminal justice had been under attack in the 1820s "with a view to the introduction of the more popular systems of grand juries and the unpaid magistracy of England."[33] In 1823 Alison was asked by his friend John Hope, now the solicitor-general, to write a pamphlet defending the criminal justice system in Scotland.

---

28. Michael Fry describes the introduction of civil juries as "the sole major legislative innovation" of the early years of the second Viscount Melville's management. At the time, Melville expressed great caution about any changes, especially English-inspired ones, to the Scottish system. The Jury Court was given wider powers in 1819 but was merged into the Court of Session in 1830. *Dundas Despotism*, 329–30.

29. Cockburn, "Nomination of Scottish Juries" (1821 and 1823); "Office of Lord Advocate."

30. Miller, *Cockburn's Millennium*, 234.

31. Hay and Snyder, *Policing and Prosecution in Britain*, 33n103.

32. Normand, "Public Prosecutor in Scotland," 355.

33. Alison, *Some Account*, 1: 221.

Alison's pamphlet, *Remarks on the Administration of Criminal Justice in Scotland and the Changes Proposed to be Introduced into It,* was published anonymously in 1825. It included statistical results of criminal commitments and prosecutions in England and Scotland as well as a comparison of provisions in English and Scottish law "for the restraining of crime and the prevention of delay or injustice in criminal proceedings." Alison concluded that both tests "proved favourable to the Scotch institutions, and exhibited in striking colours the superior wisdom and expedition of the Scotch criminal proceedings to those of the neighbouring country."[34]

Alison opened his argument by remarking on the English propensity to "innovate upon the customs of other states." He considered a recent remark that the English were " 'always disposed to make other states happy by the force of the cudgel' " to be "more truly applicable to their plans of foreign legislation in time of peace, than to their benevolent hostilities in time of war."[35] He hastened to add that this was not a judgement of English legislation and customs as such – on the contrary, the Union had benefited Scotland immeasurably. Still, he asked whether the details of English law could be "applied to a people whose physical and moral circumstances are so very different as those of Scotland undeniably are." The Scottish mode of enforcing civil rights and redressing wrongs was surely, he suggested, better adapted to its own situation than any from outside could be.

The criminal law of Scotland, Alison complained, "is regarded as a mass of absurdity and oppression ... the English members [of parliament] are led to consider the most perfect branch of our institution, ... as a relic of barbarism."[36] The reality was that increasing attempts were being made in parliament to "effect a total change in the CRIMINAL INSTITUTIONS of this country, and to assimilate them gradually" to the English ones. The specific object of the bills was "to enlarge the powers of Justices of the Peace – to substitute Grand Juries for a public prosecutor – and to have juries chosen by ballot, or some equivalent method."[37] To help defeat this plan Alison needed not only to show how the Scottish system was a product of its own circumstances (drawing upon his Enlightenment four-stage view of history and social development) but

34. Ibid., 1: 221–2.
35. Alison, *Administration of Criminal Justice,* 1.
36. Ibid., 4.
37. Ibid., 5.

also to show the areas in which Scottish criminal law was superior to English criminal law and why, consequently, the proposed changes would be harmful.

Alison argued that the Scottish landholding "class" could not act together to carry out local administration, mainly because most of the land was divided amongst a very few "great proprietors" too thinly scattered about the country to make local co-operation possible. Therefore no justice could be administered in Scotland, Alison argued, without the local jurisdictions and county courts. Sheriffs-depute and sheriffs-substitute combined knowledge of local jurisdiction with the expertise of practising lawyers "who are acquainted with the subsisting state of the law in the Supreme Courts, and thus the obvious danger of a discrepancy between the decisions in different counties is prevented."

Alison went further than merely claiming that the administration of Scottish law was different from that of England; he wished to show that it was superior. This was the first of several attempts by Alison to present Scottish experience as providing exemplary ways of coping with the problems besetting the larger British society. One superior feature was the Scottish system of public prosecution, which Alison believed allowed for a more disinterested application of the law. The Scottish system was largely conducted by public officials not only trained in the law but also possessed of a wealth of practical experience. In contrast, the English system relied on essentially untrained country gentlemen. Overall, then, in Scotland the rights of the accused and of prisoners were better protected, and the danger of an increase in the criminal population by "contamination" was far less. In addition, Alison claimed that Scotland's justice system was more lenient than that of England.[38]

Cockburn replied – also anonymously – in the *Edinburgh Review* of January 1825. He did not know Alison was the author of the pamphlet, suggesting it had been "got up by some one (probably more than one) personally connected with the administration of the system." One great merit of the pamphlet, Cockburn thought, was that it provided "the distinct, and almost the official, answer to the objections that have been stated to our penal policy."[39] Cockburn's general objection to Alison's position was that it posed unrealistic alternatives: the English system was bad, therefore the Scottish one was good. Cockburn protested that a

38. Ibid., 32, 49, 54.
39. Cockburn, "Criminal Law of Scotland," 451.

more sensible approach might be to adopt what was valuable from England while retaining the worthwhile aspects of the Scottish system.

Cockburn's reply focused on what he saw as the authoritarian and often draconian nature of Scots criminal law. His main attack was directed at several aspects of it already criticized in his earlier articles: the authoritarian and political role of the lord advocate; the unfair onus on the accused to apply for legal protection and the latter's vulnerablity in the absence of an English-style grand jury; the power of the Scottish courts to declare an act to be criminal; and the Scottish practice of judges, precluded by law from consulting with other lawyers, reviewing their own cases. Alison's replies to these objections, Cockburn claimed, besides being simply mistaken, tended to rely on the force of tradition and paternalistic benevolence.[40] For instance, Alison claimed the lord advocate's powers were not necessarily as co-extensive as his duties and, besides, cases of party political bias involving the lord advocate's position had never occurred. Further, Alison said, the lord advocate had to apply for a warrant before jailing an accused ("he always gets it," replied Cockburn). Judges could make law, Alison argued, because Blackstone described them as repositories of the law. To the latter, Cockburn protested that Alison confused "judicial determination, operating as a law, and a direct exercise of legislative power." In the past, wrote Cockburn, judges needed to open up new principles, but now "the proper provinces of the judicial and the legislative powers" were "distinctly marked."[41]

To Alison's argument that there were not enough country gentlemen to go round, and certainly not to carry out the arduous duties of a jury, Cockburn suggested the pamphlet's author(s) should stop pandering to the prejudices and pecuniary nature of Scottish lairds and country gentlemen and, instead, "train them to the knowledge and the exercise of public virtues." Cockburn agreed that the power of English magistrates to keep an accused in jail was an "evil." However, he claimed that in political cases, the opposite was true: the English practice was more lenient, Scottish practice more draconian. His overall suggestion, then, was to keep the advantages – responsibility and professionalism – of the public prosecutor, but introduce the grand jury as a check on the lord advocate, in the interests of the accused.[42]

40. Ibid., 461.
41. Ibid., 461.
42. Ibid., 460, 458.

In this anonymously conducted exchange, Alison and Cockburn were speaking of course from different political perspectives and as holders of different views of liberty and democracy. Alison's view that one of the strengths of the Scottish justice system was its professional sheriff courts was a reasonable one. One modern scholar has described the court system of Alison's time as efficient and as the core of "a relatively modern form of local government."[43] While the Union deprived Scotland of proper access to legislative reform, it also by default strengthened the power and prestige of the Scots law and legal establishment. As a result, notes David Lieberman, this "enhanced the institutional importance of Scottish courts."[44] Alison was defending this historic power of the courts as a bulwark of ruling-class power in Scotland, not to mention as an avenue for his own power and prestige.

However, it was not so much the sheriff courts that were under attack as the office of the lord advocate and, by extension, public prosecution. Alison's desire for an agrarian commercial society that was paternalist and hierarchical meant that he ignored, or even saw as an asset, the authoritarian and paternalist aspects of the Scottish social and legal structure. Cockburn's desire to see a further opening up of trade and commerce to market forces and a greater incorporation of Scotland into the sphere of British commercial power, and thus a liberalization of the Scottish legal system, could have inclined him towards private prosecution. However, his patrician Whig instincts coupled with his experience of the professionalism of the Scots system led him towards a compromise based around checks and balances: the lord advocate in tandem with grand juries.

Scotland had frequently been cited in debates about the introduction of public prosecutions in England. However, the Scottish system was often portrayed in a negative way in attacks on the political motives of public prosecutors, attacks which had occurred several times from the 1790s to the early 1820s. There were also more general reasons for the failure to introduce public prosecutions into England. First, "for many of the English upper and middle class, public prosecution still, in the nineteenth century, had resonances of the connotations of oppression that the reviled police and courts of France had in the eighteenth." Second, past experience of state tyranny in England itself acted as a powerful negative example for parliamentarians.[45] English perception of an

---

43. Whetstone, "Scottish Sheriffdoms," 71.
44. Lieberman, "Lord Kames," 219.
45. Hay and Snyder, *Policing and Prosecution in Britain*, 33, 34.

authoritarian Scottish political system combined with a traditional English view of Scots "backwardness" could only have reinforced this climate of opinion against public prosecution.

While it could be argued that Alison was actually more sensitive to the relationship between law and society than Cockburn and that he was able to use Enlightenment ideas for conservative and nationalist purposes, he may not have got the better of the exchange. Cockburn was probably able to present Alison's nationalist arguments as authoritarian and anti-liberty, suitable only for a small society still in need of "improvement." Even though Cockburn himself was not enamoured of private prosecutions, this exchange may well have delivered another blow to the cause of public prosecution in England.

Alison's law career proceeded with the expectation of his superiors as well as himself that he was destined for a "gown" and perhaps the bench. However, party politics and the patronage which accompanied it intervened. The Duke of Wellington's ministry fell in November 1830 and as a result Lord Advocate Rae and all the crown counsel in Scotland resigned. Alison's hope for political advancement, "almost within my reach, … was suddenly and apparently for ever blasted." He felt, in addition, that he had been unfortunate in remaining advocate-depute for an unusually long time because Rae had remained as lord advocate for seven years, declining "seven gowns, any one of which was at his disposal, from a desire to secure that of Chief Baron, which he did not get." Consequently, this "stopped the promotion among the whole Crown counsel, and left me Advocate-Depute in 1830, when I should have been Lord Advocate or on the Bench."[46]

Adding financial worries to dashed hopes, two writers' firms for which he had been counsel failed; his professional income was "at once diminished by above a thousand a-year; and that, too, when I was married, was under heavy life insurances, and had recently expended all the money I had made at the Bar on the purchase of a town and a country house." Moreover, the considerable time he had put into his official duties had "impeded my advance in general business, and a check in it, during the critical years from thirty to thirty-seven, is not easily recovered."[47]

Alison was at a turning point in his life; the political upset would throw him "decidedly and permanently into the career for which my

46. Alison, *Some Account*, 1: 295–6.
47. Ibid., 1: 295. Alison was, however, retained, at a fee of 200 guineas, as counsel for the Conservatives in Aberdeen in the first elections under the Reform Act: *Some Account*, 1: 310.

tastes and qualities were more peculiarly adapted." He claimed, of
course with the wisdom of hindsight, that his assessment of his life and
prospects became more realistic:

I cast aside as no longer an object of desire what was unattainable. I ceased to
dream of being Lord Advocate and of shining in Parliament, the secret object of
my former ambition. I still aimed at distinction, but it was to be gained, as
I hoped, by intellectual strength, not political power. I have no reason to regret
the change. The laborious lawyer has been converted into the successful author;
the cramped political partisan into the independent social thinker; the life
emoluments of office into an early competence derived from honest exertion.[48]

Law *and* literature were now to be the means to Alison's daily bread
and the latter, he hoped, to his intellectual renown. Alison was to some
extent making a virtue out of necessity; however, we also see his constant
emphasis on independence, his desire to escape from patronage and to
be a social commentator above party, his concern to elucidate the
broader contours of social progress. These kinds of career calculations
were not at all uncommon, especially on the part of the literary lawyers.
Walter Scott (although more secure than Alison at a similar stage of his
life, having a fixed income of £1000 per year) obtained a position as a
principal clerk of the Court of Session so that he did not have to be
dependent on literature for his "ordinary expenses."[49]

Almost immediately, Alison's two avocations were combined. He
resolved to write a text on criminal law and thereby turn his eight years
of legal experience to advantage. Alison must have been conscious of
the rapid expansion of the bar at this time and saw a growing market for
new texts.[50] Blackwood was interested; Alison was to receive two hun-

48. Ibid., 1: 297, 298.
49. Quayle, *Ruin of Scott*, 28.
50. Alison, *Some Account*, 1: 298. Duman ("Pathway to Professionalism," 619) describes
the expansion of the English bar in the late eighteenth and nineteenth centuries as "a population explosion of unprecedented dimensions." Between 1785 and 1840, the overall rate
of increase was 480 per cent – "more than twice that of the population of England and
Wales during the identical period." Between 1830 and 1840 (Alison's texts were published
in 1832 and 1833) the English bar increased from 1129 to 1835. One must be cautious in
generalizing from the English experience, but secondary material on the Scottish legal profession in the early nineteenth century is scarce. It is probable that the same phenomenon
occurred north of the border, given Scotland's rapid industrialization in this period. Alison
himself noted the "vast increase of business, arising from the extension of population and
from transactions in all parts of the empire": *Some Account*, 1: 300.

dred guineas for the first edition of "a work on the Principles and Practice of Criminal Law, in two volumes octavo."[51] Alison's aim in this work
was to supply general principles for the basic practice of law. Once again
he considered his work to be methodologically innovative. While it
seems as if professionalization and standardization in Scots law had proceeded earlier and more thoroughly than in England, nevertheless Alison was right in perceiving a need to bring his branch of the profession
up to date.

Elementary legal texts seemed to Alison to be dense and confusing;
the reader became lost in detail, unable to discern the relative importance of what he was reading. He adopted the plan, "of which Heinec-
cius had given an example in his Institutes and Pandects of the Civil
Law, of giving the principle on every subject in a single proposition, and
deducing from it a variety of cases of which the particulars were given in
the paragraph which followed."[52]

Principles of the Criminal Law of Scotland was published in 1832, followed
the next year by *Practice of the Criminal Law of Scotland.* In the preface to
Principles, Alison noted that while Baron Hume's work – *Commentaries on
the Law of Scotland Respecting Crimes* – should remain the foundation of
Scots criminal jurisprudence, there was a need for a text more specifically addressed to the everyday business of the court. Recent developments, he argued, had made a more timely text imperative:

The change of manners has consigned to oblivion a great variety of crimes and
cases which occupy a conspicuous place in [Hume's] elaborate Commentaries;
while the same causes, joined to the vast increase of criminal business, has
brought prominently forward a complete new set of delinquencies, of which little is to be found in the records prior to the last twenty years ... such has been
the extraordinary increase of crime of late years, that probably a greater number
of cases have been tried since the Peace in 1814 than from the institution of the
Court of Justiciary down to that time.

51. Alison, *Some Account,* 1: 299.
52. Ibid., 1: 300–1. The rapid increase of legal business "has rendered it impossible for
judges in whose minds principle has become matured to give it to the world, except in
detached fragments in the decision of particular cases." The young lawyers, whose task it
had become to write legal texts, wrote each on a separate subject. They did not choose some
cases which could illuminate principle and discard others. Even if they had done this, however, Alison thought that judges would have balked at being instructed in the law by their
juniors.

Alison's contribution was to add to the decisions already contained in Hume and Burnett: "above a thousand cases, in which I had been myself engaged, but of which no reports had been published."[53] The introduction to *Practice* was very similar to Alison's pamphlet of eight years before: a sketch of the working of Scots criminal law compared with that of England. It was designed to show "the wisdom of the ancient Scottish Legislature" with regard to "the liberty of the subject, and the interest of the prisoners," and to once again caution against transplanting English customs and practices.[54]

With regard to punishment, Alison argued that Scottish practice paid due attention to "the mistaken or virtuous intentions from which such dangerous ebullitions frequently proceed" and thereby achieved a more humane and enlightened procedure "than the laws of some other states." He drew his illustrations from the cases – reported in Hume and Burnett – of the trials of radicals in 1793 and 1794. In 1793, "the contagion of the French Revolution … infected a large proportion of our manufacturing classes, and the evident peril of the country induced the Court to inflict some punishments which are now justly regarded as too severe." It was not that the sentences given to Muir, Gerrald, Skirving, and Margarot were not "competent" – by which Alison meant justified in law. Those who argued that the aims of the radicals in the 1790s were the same as those which many more people advocated in 1831, and that a plan of reform brought forward by government in 1831 could not have been sedition in 1793, were mistaken. The aims, in fact, were not the same, "for annual parliaments and universal suffrage formed not part of the Reform Bill of 1831." What mattered in judging such cases was the "*mode* of bringing forward the measure, the *means* proposed to be adopted, and the temper of the times when it is broached. It is not seditious to advocate universal suffrage and annual parliaments, but it is seditious to do so in a way calculated to excite rebellion, or effect the objects by the weapons of actual violence." Thus, these men were rightly convicted and their sentence of transportation was technically "competent." However, in Alison's view, it need not, even in 1793, have been imposed. The "infection" of revolutionary ideas was but an outcome of a moment in time – not an endemic disease – and a less harsh sentence would have been equally efficient in terms of coercion and decidedly

53. Ibid., 1: 302.
54. Ibid., 1: 302; Alison, *Practice of the Criminal Law*, vii.

less risky in terms of legitimation.[55] His view was to be far harsher once he had become sheriff and embroiled with the cotton spinners and Chartists.

Alison judged his work on criminal law a success. He claimed that within two years of its publication "it was constantly quoted in all the criminal courts of the kingdom; ... it has steadily maintained its ground, and is now habitually referred to, except where subsequent statute or decision has made an alteration, as a standard authority." The plan of the work was adopted in several similar texts in Britain, and Alison "had the satisfaction of learning that this attempt to reduce legal intricacy to definite principles has been appreciated both in Germany and America, where my work is not only frequently quoted, but forms part of the course of legal education." The value of Alison's volumes is supported by sources other than his own reports. His obituary in the *Scottish Law Magazine* noted that his texts "are to this day used as a hand-book, and recognised as an authority in all the Sheriff Courts of the country." And more recently J. Irvine Smith states, in his introduction to a 1989 reprinting of Alison's work, that "most of the Principles ... and part of the Practice remain relevant to modern practice."[56]

Alison had strong opinions on reforming the criminal justice system, in Britain generally as well as in Scotland. "Manners" and the nature of crimes had changed. In "the progress of society," Alison wrote, "the offences flowing from violent passion gradually diminish, but those arising from the love of gain are continually on the increase."[57] The legitimating efforts of the state should be backed up by its coercive efforts. Alison's ideas focused on reformation of criminals and support for transportation. Here we draw on his discussion in *Principles of Population*, a work dealt with more fully in chapter 4, as well as three major articles published in *Blackwood's* on crime and transportation. In addition, he

55. Alison, *Principles of the Criminal Law*, 583, 588. Also, in Alison's opinion, these verdicts were additional proof of the mistake of entrusting the punishment of sedition to statute law rather than to common law, the latter having far greater flexibility.

56. Alison, *Some Account*, 1: 301, 310; "Sir Archibald Alison," 38; Smith, "Introduction." Smith concludes that "Alison's two books, along with Hume, remain the principal statement of how Scotland at common law has defined crime; of what at common law she devised as her characteristic system for its prosecution." He lists twenty-eight modern examples "where Alison has been founded on by the Bench." Crowther ("Response: North of the Border," 101n) finds Alison's text still the most useful source for comparisons between Scottish and English criminal law in the nineteenth century.

57. Alison, *Population*, 2: 133.

expressed essentially the same views to the Select Committee on Transportation in 1856.

Alison argued that the criminal justice system had traditionally seen its first, and most often only, task as deterring through terror, which had resulted in "the destruction, either physical or moral, of the criminal." The problem had been to combine adequate deterrence to others with reformation of the offender. Alison believed the efforts of the philanthropic reformers – Samuel Romilly, James Mackintosh, Robert Peel, and John Jebb in particular – to be eminently justified with regard to the abuses of the old justice system, which, "with its uncertain punishments and frequent opportunities to escape, afforded in fact a bounty on the commission of crime."[58] Yet the humane principles of the reformers had not succeeded in reducing the amount of crime. In fact, as Alison never tired of repeating, crime had increased, and especially so during the years "when the leniency of its administration had been at its maximum." The main error of the reformers was their belief that education and religion could reform criminals. Alison's reply was, first, that statistics showed a far higher percentage of crimes committed by the educated than by the uneducated and, second – his familiar explanation – that moral exhortation could not compete with the strength of material desires. His conclusion was that it was only by "the active, not the intellectual powers, the desires, not the understanding, that the great majority of men" were governed. Consequently, only equally strong counterdesires – artificial wants which promoted frugality and virtue – would provide a solution. Alison thought it made sense to remove criminals whose offences stemmed from living in crowded cities in close proximity to other criminals to a rural setting and to separate them from each other. The lower orders were hardly to be blamed for yielding to temptations any more than for falling victim to typhus. Therefore it was "reasonable that a small portion of the vast profits which individuals or the state make by their labour, should be devoted to correct the mental diseases which that labour had induced."[59] Reformation of offenders also removed the centres of "contagion," that is, the hardened criminals released from jail.

58. For a discussion which places the early-nineteenth-century debates over reform of the criminal justice system in the context of class conflict and competing conceptions of "social life," see McGowen, "Image of Justice and Reform."

59. Alison, *Population*, 2: 135.

The means for implementing this solution was transportation. It removed the criminal from corrupting surroundings, and it provided a life of labour which could be both reforming and useful. Alison gathered from Cunningham's *Two Years in New South Wales* and from parliamentary returns that "out of 18,531 convicts transported to New South Wales prior to 1821, *six thousand* had gained their liberty, and realized property to the amount of *fifteen hundred thousand pounds*."[60] In response to the often-voiced opinion that criminals did not regard transportation as a very severe form of punishment, Alison replied that, on the contrary, a punishment which removed people from promise of a relatively speedy return to their old habits, and which guaranteed a life of "unvarying" labour, was indeed regarded with horror. He pointed to his own experience "of the wishes of such persons" as confirmation: "many act on the principle that death is better than transportation."[61] Alison thought transportation to be far better than imprisonment, which only "accumulates criminals together in circumstances where contamination is certain, and reformation impossible." As a system of deterrence, transportation is widely regarded to have failed. However, Alison's assessment of its reforming effects tends to be supported by modern historians.[62]

Alison acknowledged that over the previous twenty years, the colonies themselves were beginning to refuse convicts. He felt sure this was because they were receiving masses of hardened, untrained convicts totally out of proportion to the numbers of free immigrants. He thought that difficulty could be eased by reversing the pattern: sending only individuals who were not yet contaminated by the prison system and who were trained in useful skills, and only in numbers which would comprise small minority of the free colonial population.

60. Ibid., 2: 136.

61. But see the *Scots Times*, 12 January 1839, in which a report from Alison's Glasgow winter circuit noted that Alexander Watson, sentenced to seven years' transportation (for "stealing a worsted shirt" and "with being by habit and repute a thief and previously convicted") "thanked his lordships, as that was just what he wanted." This kind of response was precisely what critics of transportation pointed to as evidence for its decreasing effectiveness: see McConville, *History of English Prison Administration*, 187–93.

62. Shaw writes (*Convicts and the Colonies*, 359): "[Transportation] was in many cases successful in reforming the criminal, at least to the extent of removing him [*sic*] to an environment where he was more likely to be able to live honestly … In fact, transportation and assignment was the most effective reformatory punishment that was widely adopted before 1850; but at that time few accepted the principle that the aim of punishment and prison discipline should be reformation rather than the infliction of suffering." See also Ignatieff, *Just Measure of Pain*, 92.

Alison was responding to the continuing debate over transportation. Because he believed that "imprisonment had no effect whatever, either in deterring from crime, or in reforming criminals," he continued to hope that transportation would be a key component of a systematic approach to poverty and crime. However this was contrary to the trends in colonial development and in administration of the prison system. In 1849, he felt pleased that the government seemed to have realized its folly in suspending transportation and had decided to resume the practice. However, this turned out to be only a temporary expedient for dealing with long-service felons. Transportation was effectively ended in 1857, although convicts continued to be sent to Western Australia until 1867, the year Alison died.[63]

Alison thought that to complement a balanced sytem of transportation, the administration of criminal law at home should also be changed:

Imprisonment should consist of three kinds: – 1. A very short imprisonment, perhaps of a week or ten days, for the youngest criminals and a first trifling offence, intended to terrify merely. 2. For a second offence, however trivial – or a first, if considerable, and indicating an association with professional thieves – a long imprisonment of *nine months or a year,* sufficient *to teach every one a trade,* should invariably be inflicted. 3. The criminal who had been thus imprisoned, and taught a trade, should, when next convicted, be *instantly transported.*

The advantages of this change would be fewer prisoners and a cheaper prison system, and it would also provide a means of getting productive work out of younger offenders. "The prisons would become," he declared, "instead of mere receptacles of vice, great houses of industry."[64] Alison was impressed by the "great house of industry" at Pentonville, where convicts were trained before being transported. A modern assessment is that Pentonville failed as a reformatory. It was in 1849, the year Alison's article on transportation appeared, that "the special selection for Pentonville of the most fit and promising convicts ceased and,

---

63. Alison, "Transportation Question," 518; McConville, *History of English Prison Administration,* 381–5.

64. Alison, "Transportation Question," 534–7. Alison ended his discussion of punishment and reformation in *Population* (2: 139–40) by reiterating changes in the practice of criminal justice that he had earlier suggested. The focus is professionalism: commitments should be carried out by professional magistrates and not unpaid country gentlemen; those committed should immediately have their cases considered by professionals who are to conduct the prosecution.

with various other changes in the regime, the reformatory experiment was effectively abandoned."[65]

Alison's approach to crime and punishment was a curious mixture of the old and the new.[66] His belief in the efficacy of public executions and his religious conviction that human wickedness was at the root of criminal behaviour would seem to have given him an allegiance to the traditional social order of deference and tolerance within a draconian framework. Yet Alison had much in common with the philanthropic reformers. He and they shared an "environmentalist" approach to the causes of crime; seeing crime as a "form of social envy" – Alison noted the decrease of offences "flowing from violent passion" and the increase of those "arising from the love of gain."[67] Alison thought the reformers' efforts to rationalize and make the criminal justice system less brutal and less uncertain were just and humane. He approved of a prison being like Buxton's "well-ordered manufactory" – in Alison's words, "a house of industry." He also generally shared with the reformers a deep sense of unease over what Michael Ignatieff calls "the whole social crisis of a period" and the need for "a larger strategy of political, social, and legal reform designed to reestablish order on a new foundation."[68]

However, Alison did not accept the reformers' rationale for or methods in reorganizing the prison system. It is questionable whether they and their middle-class supporters really believed, in the face of mounting evidence to the contrary, that penitentiaries deterred or reformed. As Ignatieff suggests, the "failure" of the penitentiaries to do what they were ostensibly designed to do was less important than their "success" in

65. Alison, "Transportation Question," 531; McConville, *History of English Prison Administration*, 209.

66. An almost exact contemporary of Alison's, Alexander Thomson of Banchory, nephew of the Scottish political economist, Robert Hamilton, published *Punishment and Prevention* in 1857. Despite considerable similarity between this text and Alison's published views on crime, neither author gave any indication of knowing the other's work.

67. Ignatieff, *Just Measure of Pain*, 210. Ignatieff suggests that the "new environmentalism used the perspective of associationist psychology to illuminate the idea that a criminal career could be initiated by bad social associations and economic misfortune." Not only did Alison partly accept this idea, he had learned his associationist psychology from one of its foremost practitioners – his father. Alison did not believe that economic misfortune was a major initiator of criminal activity. As he told the Poor Law commissioners in 1844 (*Poor Law Inquiry Scotland*, 20: 470): "I dare say many criminals may be on the poor roll; but I only recollect one or two cases where poverty or distress was the reason assigned for crime. I should say it is not a twentieth part of crime that arises from poverty or distress."

68. Ignatieff, *Just Measure of Pain*, 210, 215.

being seen as part of the larger social consensus around response to social crisis.[69] Alison did not believe that prisons reformed, especially not by attempts to inculcate morality and guilt through education and religion. He was more clear-sighted in his insistence that if the standard of living of poor people could be improved, "artificial wants" would help to counteract impulses to crime. Of course, some of Alison's criticism of the reformers was based on the mounting public perception – an erroneous belief – from the late 1850s that crime was increasing all the time and that the end of transportation would mean more convicts in British streets. The existence, in Alison's words, of "*les classes dangereuses*," was a widely held conviction. Alison was at one with public opinion in demanding, as Jennifer Davis puts it, "deterrence and not repentance."[70] Alison put this view forcefully to the Select Committee on Transportation in 1856, vainly trying to convince the commissioners (whose minds, he felt with justification, were made up anyway) of the value of his alternative of a balanced system of transportation.[71] Perhaps Alison's problem was that he was a local official on the front lines and not a legislator. His experience, and what was politically possible, were too often at odds.

Shortly after the publication of Alison's law texts, the political pendulum swung back to the Tories. October 1834 brought the dismissal of the Melbourne government, and Rae (reinstated as lord advocate) sent for Alison to discuss appointments in Scotland. The post of solicitor-general was, in all likelihood, Alison's for the taking, but he chose instead to apply for the recently vacated position of sheriff of Lanarkshire. This decision closed off the promotional avenue through government offices, but Alison had found what he felt was an adequate substitute:

I now saw within my grasp what had ever been the grand object of my life, as it should be of every sensible man – competence and independence. The office was worth above £1400 a-year.[72] With the fruits of my literary labours and the returns of the property I had realised, this might be expected to be raised to £2000. I had no wish for more extended means, or a higher situation. I was not

69. Ibid., 210–11.

70. Davis, "London Garrotting Panic," 196–7.

71. Alison, *Some Account*, 2: 240–4.

72. Average payments to sheriffs, as reported in the *Glasgow Chronicle*, 18 May 1838, for the years 1834, 1835, and 1836, were £1174 for Lanarkshire, compared with £660 for Ayrshire, the next highest. Alison's obituary notes that a year before he died "a movement was made in his behalf for an increase of salary. The amount he received was only £1700 – a ridiculously small sum for a man in a city like this, where incomes so much greater are gained in business." "Sir Archibald Alison," 39.

ignorant that, by leaving the Crown offices in Edinburgh – the highway to official elevation – I put myself out of the way of further advancement ... But
though the time was that to be Solicitor-General had been the great object of my
ambition, that time had passed away. The events of the last four years had inspired me with distrust in the stability of any Administration, especially one
founded on a Conservative basis. Above all, new and higher objects of ambition
had opened to my mind. Literary had come to supersede legal ambition.[73]

Alison's use of the phrase "competence and independence" is significant because these terms were commonly used by eighteenth-century
writers to denote the ideal civic virtues. Frequently they were used as
synonyms and paired with "comfort."[74]

If Alison thought that his new position would easily accommodate his literary pursuits, he was to be quickly disabused. Immediately upon taking
up his duties in December 1834 he was involved in the direction of four
contested elections. Already he was learning about the practical exigencies
of class conflict and exhibiting High Tory paranoia. It was widely perceived
that these elections would determine the fate of Peel's administration. Alison actually believed that the Liberals could easily resort to force and did
not do so only because they had a big enough majority.[75]

In the meantime, the ordinary business of the office was taxing
enough: there was an arrears of over a hundred cases. Alison also claimed
that he had to take on most of the cases normally handled by his sheriffs-
substitute, as they were too ill or too old to manage.[76] He was forced to
assume responsibility for all the work in the small-debt and criminal jury
courts. In fact, his very efficiency and success in these areas only increased
the flow of business.[77]

73. Alison, *Some Account,* 1: 334. Alison would remain sheriff until his death in 1867.

74. For a discussion of the use of "competency" in early modern America, see Vickers,
"Competency and Competition," 3–29. Vickers explains (p. 3): "To early modern readers,
[competency] connoted the possession of sufficient property to absorb the labors of a given
family while providing it with something more than a mere subsistence. It meant, in brief,
a degree of comfortable independence." For a discussion of this idea as expressed in Adam
Smith's ethics of improvement, see Dwyer, "Property and Propriety."

75. Alison, *Some Account,* 1: 340.

76. Alison exaggerated here: according to statistics in the *Glasgow Chronicle* of 18 May
1838, of a total of 14,125 cases, from ordinary actions to criminal trials, decided in Alison's
jurisdiction in the three years 1834–6, Alison decided only 468.

77. This volume of business was not a new phenomenon. Until the appointment of a res-
ident sheriff in the 1820s, "Glasgow came to have the busiest civil court in Scotland under
[James] Reddie's assessorship, and criminal cases reached record figures of over a thousand
in 1820, the year of the 'Radical War' ": Maver, "Guardianship of the Community," 255.

Cockburn gives us an interesting glimpse of Alison in court on the Glasgow winter circuit of 1838. As judge in the trial of one Thomas Riddle, sentenced to seven years' transportation for violently forcing a work mate to go on strike, Cockburn took the occasion to remark on the "criminality of violence" while acknowledging "the innocence of mere combination." After a fellow judge, Lord Medwyn, had given "a lecture ... on the same subject" to the sheriffs and magistrates, Alison "took occasion to add a long discourse" which apparently took a much harsher view of strikes and unions. Cockburn was bothered by Alison's presumption, noting that it was "the second time my friend Alison has made a long speech after the judge, a very dangerous and unusual practice, which he probably won't be allowed to repeat."[78] Their ideological differences notwithstanding, Cockburn had a very high personal opinion of Alison. A "most excellent man," Cockburn wrote in his journal, "honourable, warm-hearted and friendly, disinterested, and public-spirited; one whom ... it is impossible not to love." If Alison had a weakness, Cockburn thought, it was that he "deals in too many things, and in some of them does not deal well," particularly political economy and "pure law."[79]

In addition to regular court work, Alison was entrusted with the "general superintendence of the peace of the county," overseeing the preparation of the important criminal cases for the circuit judges, sitting on numerous committees (such as prison boards and tax commissions), and keeping up an official correspondence of five or six letters per day. However, by a rigid division of daily labour, which he had learned while at university, he was also able, he tells us, to continue writing his *History* and occasional papers for *Blackwood's* and to educate his son at home. Unlike in his years in Edinburgh, there was no time to spare for vacations.[80] While Alison's capacity for work was prodigious, we can see in Scott the same kind of ability to handle a dual career. J.G. Lockhart reported, discussing Scott's work load as clerk of session and sheriff of Selkirk, "it forms one of the most remarkable features in his history, that, throughout the most active period of his literary career, he must have devoted a large proportion of his hours, during half at least of every year, to the conscientious discharge of professional duties."[81]

78. Cockburn, *Circuit Journeys*, 9.
79. Cockburn, *Journal*, 234.
80. Alison, *Some Account*, 1: 354.
81. Lockhart, *Memoirs of Scott*, 2: 103-4.

There were compensations for the Alisons. The family moved into Possil House near Glasgow. Alison's description of it conveys his yearning for a lifestyle like that of the landed gentry and illustrates the close relationship which still existed between law and land: "Situated in a park of thirty acres studded with noble trees, some of which are elms of huge dimensions two centuries old, it had the advantage of fine gardens and perfect retirement, and was yet at a distance of only three miles from Glasgow ... The house consisted of an old mansion of a hundred and fifty years' standing, and a modern addition containing public rooms, forming together a commodious house." In addition to these more-than-comfortable surroundings, the Glasgow social circuit proved sufficiently entertaining. County society, "among the best in Scotland," provided for the Alisons a "circle which was far superior to that in Edinburgh."[82] Alison was clearly prepared, in the interests of social prestige, to overlook the "supineness" which he was convinced the wealthy too often displayed in refusing to stand up to the unruly lower orders.

Alison claimed to find in Lanarkshire a microcosm of "nearly all the elements of national strength and weakness of which I had read or written in other states" (and which he analysed in *Principles of Population*). Both higher and lower ranks displayed the energy, and the dissipation and preoccupation with personal wealth, characteristic of an opulent commercial state:

In the vast combinations of the trades-unions, arrayed under their secret and despotic committees, with whom I was ere long involved in serious conflicts, I found an example of democratic ambition on a large scale, and with a formidable organisation. In the terrors of moneyed men, of which on the occurrence of every crisis I received the most convincing proof, I perceived the truth of Mirabeau's observation, that a "capitalist is the most timid animal in existence"; and learned to appreciate the vast source of weakness which is opened in every community with the spread of commercial opulence.[83]

However "laborious" Alison may have been as a lawyer, as sheriff he was to cut quite a dashing figure and, in his dealings with the "despotic" trade unions and "timid" capitalists, he would achieve a great deal of fame or notoriety, depending on one's class allegiance.

82. Even the "mercantile circles" – "though not intellectual or literary" – were judged very interesting on a variety of topics: Alison, *Some Account,* 1: 342, 358–9.
83. Ibid., 1: 350.

3

"Riding at Them with a Squadron of Dragoons"

Archibald Alison's crusade against "democratic innovation" frequently took him into the streets against striking workers and Chartists. By 1834, when Alison arrived to take up his new post in Glasgow, the city and the county had been the heart of industrial growth in Scotland for at least twenty-five years. Glasgow's growth and prosperity was based on textiles. With the introduction of the spinning mule in 1799, "for the next three-quarters of a century the economic livelihood of Glasgow depended upon cotton textiles and related industries such as chemicals, machinery and steam engines."[1] The development of the coal and iron industries in Lanarkshire themselves spurred growth in machinery and engineering. Spinning and weaving mills were large, most employing between 1000 and 2000 people. The population of Glasgow city and suburbs grew from 84,086 in 1801, to 112,330 in 1811, to 151,368 in 1821, and had reached 208,103 by 1831.[2]

Worker resistance to the changes accompanying industrialization built upon the organizational struggles of tradesmen in the eighteenth

---

1. Cage, *Working Class in Glasgow*, 2. Alison's description of the social stratification of the Glasgow mercantile community as he found it in 1834 is interesting. Despite the predominance of textiles, at the top were still the West Indies merchants, five or six families in an exclusive social circle known as the Sugar Aristocracy. Ranked under them were the cotton magnates, only the oldest and most eminent of whom occasionally dined with the Sugar Aristocracy. Next came the "calico printers." Only the men of the families of this group were allowed to dine with the sugar or cotton lords. Making up the lowest stratum were the iron and coal masters who, though their wealth was beginning to outstrip that of the other groups, were hardly ever seen in their circles. Alison, *Some Account*, 1: 344–6.
2. Cage, *Working Class in Glasgow*, 10.

century.[3] However, from about 1812–13, the context changed. Paternalist notions of the state were giving way to market-driven assumptions about production, wages, and control. Distress following the end of the Napoleonic wars added a politicization of the relationship between capital and labour. Union organization grew apace, and so did the radical movement. The state had to respond with informers and arrests to riots and armed workers in Glasgow in 1816–17 and in the aftermath of Peterloo. The culmination, albeit unsuccessful, of this wave of radical activity was the Radical War of 1820. The government response, which included executions and transportation, effectively smashed hopes of political reform through direct action.[4]

Through the 1820s and into the 1830s, worker response to industrialization remained focused on trade unions and economic solutions (including, nonetheless, fierce industrial disputes).[5] The radical-reform movement remained primarily middle class, although there is considerable evidence of connections between trade union and radical groups.[6] For weavers, spinners, colliers, and builders, the main emphasis of organization was control, especially over entry into the trade, and conditions of work. Trade union growth prospered in the middle 1830s despite employers' efforts to break the unions. In 1834, the year Alison took up his appointment, 30,000 people in Glasgow "signed a petition protesting at the harsh sentences on the Tolpuddle men, and at a mass meeting there were demands for a Consolidated Union of Scottish Operatives."[7] The potential for full-scale conflict remained latent, but the degree of trade union organization and assertiveness meant that in periods of economic distress and employer retrenchment throughout the 1830s and into the 1840s, Glasgow and its surrounding areas would experience a

3. Fraser, *Conflict and Class*, chaps. 2, 3.
4. For an account of the Radical War of 1820, which overstates both the magnitude of the events and the degree of nationalism involved, see Ellis and Mac a' Ghobhainn, *Scottish Insurrection*. For a corrective, see Fraser, *Conflict and Class*, and Donnelly, "Scottish Rising." There has been considerable debate as to the existence of an insurrectionary tradition in Britain in the late eighteenth and early nineteenth centuries. Roger Wells makes a strong case for the "politics of insurrection" during the period 1795–1803 under the impact of the French Revolution and the Irish crisis of 1798. Whether this can be extended to support a serious threat of revolution in Britain at various points up to 1848 is more doubtful. Wells's argument that government *perception* of the potential for insurrection was "a lasting legacy of our insurrectionary period" is persuasive: *Insurrection*, 265.
5. Whatley, "Labour in the Industrialising City," 377.
6. Ibid., 386.
7. Fraser, *Conflict and Class*, 148.

substantial degree of militancy and disruption, sufficient to cause Alison and fellow officials to bolster the coercive capacity of the state.[8]

Radical political reform, somewhat dormant since 1817, revived in the late 1830s in the shape of Chartism. The 1832 Reform Act, while it increased the size of the Scottish electorate from 4,239 to 65,000, and thus increased the representation of a broader cross-section of adult males, nonetheless left numerous loopholes through which the pre-Reform landed interests could manipulate the system.[9] Reformers and radicals were rapidly disabused of any hopes that 1832 was merely the first stage of reform, at least of the constitution. Radical disillusionment and anger after 1832 did find vehicles for expression and organization: newspapers, political and trade unions, and the Anti-Corn Law League. The return to power of the Tories under Wellington, which indirectly changed the course of Alison's career, also prompted a massive reaction by middle- and working-class reformers allied against "military government." More ominous for government generally, however, was the emerging division within radical ranks between middle-class and working-class reformers. By 1836 the beginnings of what would become the Chartist movement were evident; clear signs of the determination and ability of working-class reformers to organize themselves. By 1837 such organization was sorely needed as workers began to feel the severe effects of trade depression.

Policing was an obvious, but not always enthusiastically embraced, response by government to unrest. In Scotland, the development of policing was slow in the burghs but rapid and relatively early in the rural

8. Discussing the two main approaches to the question of the "making" of the Scottish working class in the three decades prior to 1832, Whatley concludes that while T.C. Smout's "compartmentalist" perspective – stressing the overwhelmingly sectional, economic preoccupations of Scottish workers – cannot be sustained for Glasgow, he does not wish to go as far as accepting J.D. Young's "holistic" assessment of large-scale working-class unity and consciousness. Whatley argues ("Labour in the Industrialising City," 393): "On the eve of the Reform Bill ... the working class in Glasgow had not been 'made.' For a few years around 1820 a powerful and unprecedented sense of working-class unity had manifested itself. A combination of factors, however, were leading in another direction and to the breaking of that emergent class consciousness." Briefly, these factors were: "the divergence of the fortunes and aspirations of occupational groups"; the "ferocity of the employer-led campaign to obtain the upper hand within the workplace"; and "the determination of the authorities to rid the community of troublemakers, radicals or others." See also Montgomery, "Glasgow and the Struggle for Parliamentary Reform," 130–45.

9. Wilson, *Chartist Movement in Scotland*, chap. 2; Ferguson, "Reform Act (Scotland)"; Brash, "New Scottish County Electors in 1832," 137. See also the discussion below, pp. 167ff.

areas, especially after 1839.[10] Although agricultural and industrial development in Scotland lagged behind that in England, when it did "take off" it did so extremely rapidly and its consequences were felt that much more acutely. In agriculture the acceleration of improvement was not encumbered for Scottish landlords, in the way it was for some English landlords, by the existence of unwieldy and expensive acts of enclosure. The problem of vagrancy and the perceived need to control the wandering poor, as well as a desire to rationalize the high costs of enforcing law and order, were the most important reasons for the development of policing in the rural areas. In Glasgow, the Weavers' Riot of 1788 had produced the first appointment of police officials, although their mandate was a wide one, including the health and repair of the city as well as the prevention of crime – "policing" in the traditional sense, which continued well into the next century.[11]

A police force was by no means a popular response. Opposition to the proposals and demands of Alison and like-minded magistrates in the 1830s and 1840s for a county police force in Lanarkshire are discussed below. Such opposition to an organized police had existed all along: in Scotland in 1789 a police bill was withdrawn because of the outcry against paying for it.[12] Opposition also existed for broader reasons, such as the memory of Stuart attempts at absolutism, the military rule of the

10. For recent work on the history of policing in Britain, see: Miller, *Cops and Bobbies*; Philips, *Crime and Authority*; Bailey, ed., *Policing and Punishment*; Emsley, *Policing and Its Context*, and *English Police*; Steedman, *Policing the Victorian Community*; Carson, "Policing the Periphery"; Carson and Idzikowska, "Social Production of Scottish Policing"; Gallacher, "First Glasgow Police"; Maver, "Guardianship of the Community." For more on the theme of political unrest and public order, see Mather, *Public Order*; Radzinowicz, "New Departures in Maintaining Public Order"; Silver, "Demand for Order in Civil Society," and "British Elite Reactions to Domestic Crisis"; Storch, "Plague of Blue Locusts," 64; Donajgrodzki, *Social Control*; Saville, *1848*.

11. Gallacher, "First Glasgow Police," 32; Carson and Idzikowska, "Social Production of Scottish Policing," 271. Steedman comments (*Policing the Victorian Community*, 15–16): "When they acted in this way policemen were performing an administrative function, the job that a local government inspector would otherwise have done. Policemen were obliged to do this work because for most urban authorities they were the most convenient and cheap executive force to hand." Social discipline was the ultimate purpose: "In this way the discipline and punishment of people living in these communities was provided for by much more than the definition of crime and the operation of the criminal law."

12. Gallacher, "First Glasgow Police," 32. For a discussion of more general opposition to compulsory assessment for community services, fuelled by the "social gospel" ideology of Evangelicals, see Devine, "Urbanisation and the Civic Response," 190–1.

Protectorate, and awareness of French attempts at social control through the use of spies and informers.[13]

The first police force was established in Glasgow in April 1800; at first in the city only, then gradually in the suburbs (1808 in the Gorbals, 1819 in Calton, 1826 in Anderston). The degree of organization involved was not matched elsewhere in Britain until the London police were set up in 1829.[14] A police board was set up, composed of 24 commissioners elected by a minimum £10 franchise. The board provided for a superintendent of police, clerks, 3 sergeants, 9 officers, and 68 watchmen. They wore blue military-style uniforms, and their duties included street maintenance. In June of 1821, the New Police Act was passed. An attempt at a new concept of policing, it provided for more emphasis on prevention: increased surveillance to catch early indications of criminal behaviour as well as to detect radicalism amongst workers.[15] Efforts were made to establish a more effective police force, but its actual performance left a lot to be desired. For instance, there is no evidence, Geraldine Gallacher argues, "that the Glasgow police were in any way effective in controlling riots."[16] Conflicts occurred over jurisdictions between the municipal council and the new police commissioners, and between burghs. An 1819 royal commission report on Scottish burghs cited Glasgow as a special example of the adverse effects of competing authorities. This had led to "an uncoordinated system of policing,"[17] about which Sheriff Alison frequently complained.

Alison did not consider the position of sheriff-depute political because it did not depend on attachment to a particular ministry. According to him it was "official" rather than "political." Nevertheless, it was certainly political in a wider sense. Alison was the official mainly responsible for keeping the peace of the county which contained the most rapidly growing manufacturing area and the most combative working class. As such, he was on the front lines as an agent of the British state throughout the period in which working-class resentment and political organization reached their peak. His most acute administrative problem

13. Hay, "Property, Authority," 18.
14. Gallacher, "First Glasgow Police," 45, 64.
15. Ibid., 59; Maver, "Guardianship of the Community," 254.
16. Gallacher, "First Glasgow Police," 61.
17. Ibid., 66. The difficulties of co-ordinating competing jurisdictions were not peculiar to Glasgow. Philips (*Crime and Authority*, 78–9) describes similar problems in Staffordshire before 1848 where there existed, legally, "two parallel systems of policing with no common control or connection."

was to be the lack of a regular county police force; his most pressing strategic problem was to use the law as effectively as possible to contain disturbances and maintain order. In both of these tasks he was often frustrated by his superiors in Whitehall and by the local aristocracy and "burghers." All this served to confirm his opinion of the selfishness of politicians and landowners, whether Tory or Whig, and of the desirability of professional values.

Sheriff Alison embraced the values of professionalism – public virtue, disinterested service, and efficiency – which coincided so closely with the Enlightenment values of his upbringing. These values, however, came to be severely tested in the early-nineteenth-century world of class conflict and social dislocation. In his published writings Alison argued for the fundamental humanity and fairness of the professionally based Scottish justice system. As sheriff, he adopted harsh measures against working-class unrest. This chapter examines three major episodes of his involvement with striking workers and Chartists: the cotton spinners' strike and trial of 1837–8; the miners' strike and the riot at Airdrie in 1842; and the Chartist "insurrection" of 1848.

Alison's first overtly political duties were to supervise four contested elections in December 1834. Fearing that the Liberals might provoke public unrest, he was relieved when no disturbances occurred, because of the lack of a regular police force anywhere in Lanarkshire except in Glasgow, and because he had grave doubts as to the reliability of special constables "especially in a moment of excitement, in a contest with the populace."[18] Concerns about the reliability of policing were to remain for the rest of his tenure. Alison faced "obstinate resistance" from "the country gentlemen of Lanarkshire, from the duke down to the bonnet-laird … to my every effort to get a rural police established." This showed, he thought, how few individuals "in any rank" were qualified to practice self-government. The "supineness" of the government's response to entreaties for increased security was added proof of "how many sources of weakness existed under the reformed constitution, and how little even the most urgent necessities of the community are often attended to by a mixed Government, unless backed by influence or enforced by clamour."[19] The selfishness of the nobility reminded Alison of the refusal of their French counterparts in the 1780s to be taxed, "an immediate cause of the Revolution." He uttered a lament for the fate of

18. Alison, *Some Account*, 1: 341.
19. Ibid., 1: 351.

modern society: "The prodigious accumulation of wealth and capital on the one side, and of numbers and indigence on the other, which arose from the rapid congregation and almost unparalleled increase of population in the great emporium of manufacturing industry with which I was connected, brought before my eyes the principal difficulties and dangers of modern society."[20]

Alison's first attempt to suppress a "popular disturbance" in Lanarkshire brought home to him the seriousness of a lack of disinterested professionalism in law enforcement. In July 1835 he received information that Catholics planned to disrupt the Orange parade. He issued a proclamation against both the parade and any disruption of it and ordered a squadron of dragoons to be ready. On 12 July, he was informed that a "vast mob" was rioting and that the constables present were overwhelmed. Alison set off with a mounted troop and eventually surrounded the rioters, seized the leaders, "and before eight at night I had the satisfaction of returning to Glasgow with eight-and-twenty prisoners ... the principal of whom were afterwards brought to trial and transported." A tidy day's work, and an illustration for Alison of the effectiveness of the military presence. The real lesson, though, was "a demonstration [of] how dangerous it is to suppress even the most outrageous violence in one part of the population by the aid of another part. Some hundreds of special constables had been called out ... and these became so excited in consequence, that a fortnight after, another riot as serious as the former was got up in the same place, in which the Protestants were the aggressors."[21] This second riot had the same outcome as the first, but both hardened Alison's resolve to campaign for a regular county police force.

The cotton spinners' strike, along with strikes by the sawyers, the carpenters, the masons, the iron moulders, and the dyers, was precipitated by the commercial crisis of 1837. Falling prices had led the manufacturers to lower wages, and so the strikes were predominantly defensive. Alison believed that strikes were generally hopeless undertakings at the best of times and that in the midst of an economic crisis striking workers

20. Ibid., 1: 351.

21. Ibid., 1: 360–1. Radzinowicz ("New Departures in Maintaining Public Order," 70–1) notes that in England, "the general policy of the Government was to employ [the yeomanry] only in extreme need. Their presence was more unpopular than that of the regular army; ties of kindred and neighbourhood were likely to embroil yeomen in the disorders they had been mustered to calm." In addition, organizing them was expensive, and it took farm workers away from their occupations, which was especially disruptive during the harvest.

were cutting their own throats. The only outcome could be poverty and indigence. While Alison abhorred strikes, unlike some other Tories (such as Lord Ashley) who were concerned with the conditions of labour, he did believe that combinations were inevitable. Many in his own district, he was pleased to note, were drawn from the "better" class of skilled workmen. He offered, in a *Blackwood's* article and to a Parliamentary Committee on Combinations of Workmen, suggestions as to how trade unions might be regulated: for instance, shortening the hours of work, having union officials registered annually, and granting the unions (by act of Parliament) the right to sue and be sued.[22] Alison may have been willing to countenance a considerable degree of government intervention with regard to poor law relief, but when it came to threats to social order posed by striking workers, he became a devout believer in the iron law of wages and the imperatives of the market.

As the Radical-Chartist newspaper, the *Scots Times* reported, Alison testified at the cotton spinners' trial that he had initially been alerted to the potential for violence at Oakbank at the beginning of May 1837, "tumultuous assemblages" having already occurred some days before he saw them. On 8 May he saw the road leading to Oakbank "for some miles ... covered with people"; although while he was there he "saw no assaults on that day." About a hundred workers were found "in the Oakbank manufactory itself, armed with large sticks." Alison further testified he knew about 20 or 30 new hands – "nobs" or strike breakers – had been taken in at Oakbank "and saw several of them with blood upon their faces and clothes." As a result of what he saw, Alison thought it necessary to have military assistance. He "identified a proclamation which was issued, warning the people of the danger they were in by joining in riotous acts or assemblages, and the determination of the Magistrates to punish such acts." He gave instructions "at Mile-End, to get hold of some prisoners."[23]

Alison also worked with informers to trap the union leaders. After hearing of the killing of an Irish strike breaker, one Smith, he wrote to the home secretary, Lord John Russell, and received authority to offer a reward.[24] His procurator fiscal informed him that certain individuals

22. Alison, "Practical Workings of Trades' Unions"; Hill, *Toryism and the People,* 110–12.

23. *Scots Times,* 13 January 1838.

24. On 29 July, in a second exchange of correspondence, Russell wrote to Alison from Whitehall, regretting that "acts of violence and intimidation continue to be practiced in the City of Glasgow and its vicinity" and offering an additional reward of £100, together with a Queen's pardon for the murderer's accomplices. Russell to Alison, 29 July 1837, PRO, HO/103/8.

were "willing to give information if they were protected from danger." Alison "met the persons in an obscure place in Glasgow, and took their depositions," which included the information "that another individual named was to be murdered next day." Alison then went to the meeting place of the spinners' committee and arrested its members.[25] He received a great deal of notoriety from these actions (not to mention sixty or seventy threatening letters); indeed, this strike made his reputation as a scourge of the working-class movement. His conclusion was that "the stroke against the cotton-spinners' committee told with decisive effect upon all the trades who were out on strike at the time. Violence and intimidation rapidly declined in Glasgow."[26]

Alison never seemed to have doubted that he took the right course of action and that the workers convicted were guilty. Hamish Fraser has written a detailed account of the economic circumstances of the union movement at the time and of the strike and trial. He offers a convincing argument that the case against William McLean, who was convicted of killing the strike breaker John Smith, was extremely shaky. Also: "the case against the accused committee men was not a strong one. There was no attempt to try to show direct complicity and the prosecution made it clear that what was on trial was the Cotton Spinners' Association. It was a trial for twenty years of intermittent violence." It is clear, Fraser notes, that there had been violence associated with the union; "it was a violence associated with the environment in which they worked and lived and with the pressures which they felt themselves to be under."[27] In his *Principles of Population* Alison would write with some degree of sympathy of the conditions facing urban workers and the poor and was quite critical of the profit-driven imperatives of the manufacturers which played a large part in producing such conditions. Yet sympathy for the poor was one thing; sympathy for striking workers quite another. For Alison, the solution to urban poverty lay in a combination of government provision of poor relief, economic policies which would keep Britain self-sufficient in food and thereby keep the agricultural sector always predominant over the manufacturing sector, and emigration.[28] There was precious little room for combinations of workers in Alison's version of agrarian capitalism.

25. *Scots Times*, 13 January 1838.
26. Alison, *Some Account*, 1: 389.
27. Fraser, *Conflict and Class*, 158.
28. See Alison, "How to Disarm the Chartists."

While Alison's account of the 1837 strike and trial must be read with caution, it does provide a view of ruling-class perceptions of social conflict and of the kind of organization that was evolving to try to keep pace with unrest from below. Alison claimed to be beseiged with pleas from "masters and new workmen" alleging intimidation and assault by union members. Outside Glasgow, however, he had "not a single policeman" to offer them aid.[29] The authorities were forced to rely on "the precarious resource of voluntary contribution."[30] Authorities' suspicion of the loyalty and effectiveness of volunteer constables had been constant at least since the strikes of 1816.[31] Alison felt constrained by the attitude of the Whig government (which he felt owed its election to intimidation and threats anyway) and by much of public opinion which had come to regard meetings, processions, and "violent speeches" as "their birthright." In this state of affairs he decided to lie low until a serious attack on life or property occurred and he could act with confidence of popular support. Lying low was not easy for a man of Alison's temperament and convictions – an attack on a cotton mill at Oakbank in June, where some new hands were apparently wounded, was enough for him. He swore in a hundred special constables, armed them with truncheons, and when the "mob" gathered the next day, ordered the constables to meet him. "Only *one* appeared!" however. He therefore went to the barracks and called out "a troop of horse, and the sight of the vanguard of red-coats at once dispersed the assemblage. This assertion of the power of law by military display, however, excited a violent clamour."[32]

The Radical newspapers had the temerity to complain of interference with the liberty of the subject. Indeed, Alison was attacked in the Radical press for his assault on the trade union movement. At a meeting of Glasgow workers in January 1838, reported in the *Scots Times*, the secretary read a passage from the Liberal *Argus* allegedly from Alison's speech at

29. He put the number of police in Glasgow and the suburbs at 280. Further, "in the suburbs, which contained 100,000 souls, and where the principal manufactories were situated, there was either no police at all, or a very inefficient one, so broken down into minute subdivisions and separate jurisdictions that no respectable force for any common object could be collected." Alison, *Some Account*, 1: 372.

30. Ibid., 1: 370–1.

31. As Viscount Melville commented in 1816: "Officers have ... found, to their astonishment and mortification, that they could not trust those on whom they had depended for loyalty and attachment; I allude to artisans and persons of that description and that class of life." Fry (*Dundas Despotism*, 337) sees this arising from "an apparently profound alteration in attitudes, previously unsuspected by the landed elite."

32. Alison, *Some Account*, 1: 376.

the Glasgow Circuit Court. Alison apparently claimed that the authorities almost despaired of maintaining order, not because of any doubts as to the guilt of the cotton spinners, but from the power of the union, thousands strong locally, "combined with hundreds of thousands through the whole empire, by whose activity and intimidation, the arm of justice has for the last twenty years ... been so often paralyzed." Unions, argued Alison, would ultimately themselves suffer because they were "violating a law of nature." In response to this, Alex Campbell, the secretary, suggested Sheriff Alison "should go to school to learn a little of the law of nature; for here he was confounding the law of nature with the cruel conventional system under which they were placed ... human nature, bad as it might be, was not so bad as Sheriff Alison thought – it was not a law of nature that people should sit down and starve."

Alison refused an invitation to justify his conduct. In a letter to the Trades of Glasgow, he denied making the charge against trade unions in general, claiming he referred only to the Cotton Spinners' Association. If the latter felt hard done by, he said, let them give evidence about seven crimes, including murder, and two fire-raisings. If they did this, they would be "absolved of any attempt to screen the criminals."[33] The workers were unconvinced by Alison's disclaimer, and probably with good reason, given his published views in *Blackwood's Magazine* on the futility of strikes. Even property owners doubted whether Alison's actions were expedient, or indeed legal.

Alison was not alone in his desire to see a more professional system of law enforcement. (Indeed, this had been a priority for many Tory politicians since the widespread unrest following the end of the Napoleonic wars.) In the ensuing years, as Chartist activity continued, law enforcement officers in regions other than Lanarkshire continued to press the central government for a county police force. Forfarshire in 1839 provides one example of this concern as well as of the caution with which the authorities were forced to move against alleged breaches of the law. In August of that year, a local magistrate wrote to the Earl of Airlie, lieutenant of the county, about the difficulty of gathering evidence against suspected Chartists. He noted that there was clear proof that a blacksmith in Kirriemuir made pikes. However, he thought any decision to prosecute had to be made by the crown counsel. "The *mere act* of making pikes ... might not be sufficient to procure a verdict of a jury ... and the Crown Counsel are naturally anxious to avoid a defeat in any charge of the sort." The writer noted that language was being closely scrutinized:

33. *Scots Times*, 27 January 1838.

"the language which Burns[34] seems to have used is very dangerous. F. O'Connor is expected at Dundee and I have given orders to watch *his* words."[35] Four days later, the magistrate reiterated that he could do only so much in obtaining a conviction and that accuracy of reporting was crucial. For instance, a potential witness to Burns's speech noted that his information "was at *third* hand and therefore he cannot be a witness."[36]

Assessments of the intentions and strength of the Chartists[37] and of the authorities' degree of readiness led inevitably to calls for a more secure and professional policing system. The magistrate already quoted informed Airlie that it was "to be regretted that the town of Forfar affords but a scanty supply of Constables. The number actually enrolled ... cannot be very much increased (without asking Chartists to join) a *physical Local Defect* for which there is no immediate remedy." If the Chartists attempted a general rising, he warned, the number of constables might not be enough and the military would be required. Use of the military in any case seemed wise after the "late affair at Kirriemuir, tho' it ended in merely apprehending a few weavers." "We must not forget," he went on,

that the acting Chief Magistrate of the County, at the head of 50 constables, was routed, & several of the constables severely Wounded, by the Insurgents of Kirriemuir ... we have heard, that it was *said*, that even on the last occasion, the presence of the Military would *not* have been a certain protection to the Civil Officers, if the attempt to apprehend the guilty parties had taken place during the day time, when the mass of the population would have been aware of & alive to what was going on.[38]

34. See Wilson, *Chartist Movement in Scotland*, 72–3.

35. Letter to Airlie, 24 August 1839, SRO, GD 16/40/76. The Burns in question may be James Dawson Burn: see Christopher Godfrey, *Chartist Lives* (London 1987), 468–70.

36. Letter to Airlie, 28 August 1839, SRO, GD 16/40/76. Radzinowicz ("New Departures in Maintaining Public Order," 63) confirms this caution: "the preliminary steps in collecting evidence of illegal conduct were sometimes the most difficult: strict rules made the testimony of reporters on the speeches to which they had listened at Chartist meetings inadmissible, except in corroboration of evidence otherwise obtained."

37. In November 1839, the provost of Forfar replied to a request from Whitehall as to the intentions of the Chartists and the local need for augmented forces: "we know nothing of the *intentions* of the Chartists, but, so far as we can discover they have as yet done nothing hostile to the public peace. We have upwards of one hundred constables sworn in, but, in case of disturbance, we do not consider that, however zealous they might be, they would be able to quell a mob ... We do not, however, anticipate any such emergency." Lord Provost, Forfar, to Thomas Carnaby, lieutenancy clerk, Forfar, 11 November 1839, SRO, GD 16/40/76.

38. Letter to Airlie, 27 August 1839, ibid.

As an official initiative towards boosting security forces in Forfar, a prize of £100 was offered by Lord Panmure for the best essay on "a fit police for this County." One local magistrate thought this a good idea and suggested "the late Rogue Money Act will be useful towards providing *means* for accomplishing that object ... our police force will be ... made useful in putting down riotous proceedings."[39] Airlie lent his authority to the demands in a letter to the lord advocate. He was sorry to find that "so very small an addition can be made to the Constabulary force in Forfar. The Chartists must be more numerous than I had supposed them, and I fear that the most strenuous exertions of so small a body of Police would be ineffectual in quelling a serious riot." The earl himself received a letter a week later suggesting that a county police force should be set up.[40]

In Lanarkshire, Alison had more on his hands than Chartist ferment. Riots between Scots and Irish were frequent and provided him with yet another illustration of the need for more coercive power. In March 1840 his sheriff-substitute Vere reported a riot in Castlebank which involved attacks upon Irish labourers (the latter, according to Vere, having started the riot by hurling religious insults at Protestants). After what had already happened at Penrith, Vere warned, they should be prepared for the worst. Perhaps "the appearance of 150 to 200 sabres ... might (and I think would) prevent the necessity of resorting to actual violence."[41] The next day Alison wrote to the Duke of Hamilton, lord lieutenant of the county, warning that further riots were anticipated on the Caledonian Railways. The duke should get authority to call out the yeomanry or Sir Norman Lockhart's troops if the riots got as serious as they had done at Penrith and in Midlothian. Alison bemoaned the reluctance of the military authorities to allow a regular force to be stationed anywhere "but their usual barracks [which] renders the Yeomanry in the neighbourhood the only force that can be relied on upon a sudden emergency." Alison suggested that "a *conditional* power might be obtained to be deposited with Mr Vere @ Lanark or Sir N. Lockhart and only acted upon then in the event of its becoming

39. Letter to Airlie, 28 August 1839, ibid. Rogue money was an assessment collected to defray the cost of arresting, maintaining in jail, and prosecuting criminals. This in fact was the main source – albeit an illegal one – for funding most Scottish policing efforts in the early nineteenth century. Carson and Idzikowska, "Social Production of Scottish Policing," 272.

40. Airlie to lord advocate, 1 September 1839, and letter to Airlie, 6 September 1839, SRO, GD 16/40/76.

41. Vere to Alison, 5 March 1840, PRO, HO/45/1433.

necessary to have recourse to Military aid to support the Civil Power." He had appointed fifteen constables, "but if a certain collision between English or Scotch & Irish takes place I need hardly state, so inconsiderable force can be of little service and experience has long convinced me that on any serious emergency little reliance is to be placed on the Special Constables."[42]

Alison eventually (especially after his experiences with the cotton spinners) resolved to wage an active campaign for the establishment of a central police for Glasgow and vicinity. He noted in his autobiography that while the city of Glasgow police force was admirable ("it amounted to 224 men; and was not only efficient, but adequate to the wants of the district"), the suburban force was divided between different subordinate jurisdictions.[43] Each was jealous of the other and of the city authority; all were hampered by the difficulty (not resolved until 1846) of "defining the enlarged municipal entity."[44] One result was that similar offences received wildly differing sentences. Alison claimed that because the suburban police commissioners were chosen "by what amounted almost to household suffrage," they consequently feared their constituents so much that they would not institute an adequate assessment. The police force which they did provide – sixteen or eighteen men among 30,000 or 40,000 inhabitants – "inadequate even in ordinary times, was wholly unfit to meet the exigencies of disturbed periods when general distress prevailed, or formidable strikes had reduced half the working classes to compulsory destitution."[45] Alison was exasperated by what Carson and Idzikowska describe as an element of democratic control of burgh administration through the organization of police commissioners.[46]

Alison's own plan for Glasgow and vicinity was based on the organization of metropolitan police in Middlesex. The Peelite model had general appeal to Glasgow's civic leadership, "to the extent," writes Irene Maver, "that during the 1840s there were serious proposals to transfer ultimate responsibility for criminal law enforcement to the Government."[47] Alison wanted to keep local control. He proposed a police

42. Alison to the Duke of Hamilton, 6 March 1840, ibid.

43. "Gorbals, Calton, and Anderston had each a little police establishment of its own; while a considerable part called Bridgeton, with 15,000 inhabitants, for the most part in the very lowest grade of society, had no police whatever." Alison, *Some Account*, 1: 420.

44. Maver, "Guardianship of the Community," 252.

45. Alison, *Some Account*, 1: 420–1.

46. Carson and Idzikowska, "Social Production of Scottish Policing," 286.

47. Maver, "Guardianship of the Community," 254.

force centred in Glasgow which would cover all outlying districts within a fifteen- or twenty-mile radius and protect "the whole manufacturing districts of the west of Scotland." The costs would be covered by a "general tax," varied according to the degree of protection needed locally. He sent circulars describing his plan to magistrates and justices of the peace in several counties as well as to "the whole noblemen, gentlemen, merchants, bankers, and many other citizens in the district." In response, he received "numerous addresses ... signed by householders and shopkeepers in the populous villages round Glasgow, which at present had no protection," asking that government adopt the plan. Russell's Whig government approved of the plan but insisted on leaving it to local interested parties to implement. To Alison, this meant the plan was doomed, as he could not see local worthies submitting to a centralized assessment tax "without any prospect of gain to themselves."[48] Lanarkshire landowners, true to his prediction, subsequently refused to support a bill for county assessment for a rural police.

Not everyone shared Alison's sense of despair about the lack of a police force and about the civic virtues of local notables. The Liberal *Glasgow Chronicle* was opposed to establishing a rural police force as it considered that police officers were already "acting too harshly and arbitrarily" and that in any case there would not be enough officers to do a decent job. The paper approved the Lanarkshire gentry's "wise" resistance to the setting up of rural police.[49] Carson and Idzikowska believe the refusal of Lanarkshire voluntarily to set up a rural police force arose from a combination of local and regional developments. An inequitable mode of assessment, in which Rogue money was taxed as "an assessment on the *valued rent of land* rather than on property as such," was resented as "a burden to be borne by proprietors rather than tenants." Also, industrial development tended to be concentrated in the lower and middle wards of the county. Those landed proprietors in the largely rural upper ward resented the idea of paying tax to supply the wants of the more industrial areas.[50] Alison's account of the eventual imposition of a county police force on Lanarkshire in 1857 notes that once the recalcitrant landowners such as the Duke of Hamilton and Lord Belhaven "had become the greatest owners of coal and iron mines in the

48. Alison, *Some Account*, 1: 422–4.
49. *Glasgow Chronicle*, 14 February 1842.
50. Carson and Idzikowska, "Social Production of Scottish Policing," 296. Alison reported landowners' objections in his autobiography: *Some Account*, 1: 433.

country ... and ... began to see what it was to have several thousand colliers and iron-miners out on strike ... without any civil force to coerce
them," they no longer resisted the idea of a police.[51] This assessment
parallels Philips's account of resistance to policing in the Black Country;
there, opposition, mainly on the grounds of expense, was reluctantly
overcome only after the threat of disorder – especially from a miners'
strike of 1842 in Staffordshire – seemed to outweigh the inconvenience
of adding to the rate burden.[52]

Frustrated in his attempts to have a rural police established, Alison
had to soldier on with the forces he had. Chartism in Scotland might, if
we believe Alexander Wilson, have been in decline after 1840,[53] but
men in authority such as Alison went on talking about possible "insur-
rections" until at least 1848. Economic conditions began to deteriorate
again from 1839. Alison believed that this was caused by the "monetary
crisis, brought on by the great importation of foreign grain in the years
1838 and 1839."[54] By 1842, distress had reached the iron and coal
trades, "always the last to be affected by a similar calamity, and the last to
recover." Wilson notes that in Paisley destitution amongst the unemployed mounted from 4200 to 5600 during October 1841, to 10,670 in
November, and to 14,650 in January 1842.[55] Alison described discontent among the mining population, "which was soon turned into absolute fury by emissaries from the Chartists in England, who were
preparing the general insurrection in the central counties of its manufacturing districts, that soon after broke out." He claimed a "universal
strike accordingly was organised in the mining districts of the west of

51. Alison, *Some Account*, 2: 419.

52. Philips, *Crime and Authority*, 57. Steedman also reports resistance to policing based
on the parsimony of rate payers. She notes the belief, which may well have been operative
in many other rural areas, that as it was the towns and boroughs that were "nurseries of
crime," the urban areas, rather than the counties, were far more in need of a policing system: *Policing the Victorian Community*, 29.

53. Wilson, *Chartist Movement in Scotland*. This conclusion, and Wilson's general assessment that the Scots were not "ardent Chartists," is challenged by Young (*Rousing of the Scottish Working Class*), who points to specifically Scottish circumstances inhibiting Chartist
organization. But Clarke ("Early Chartism in Scotland"), in analysing the Conference of
Scottish Chartist Delegates held in Glasgow in 1839, suggests that "the Scottish movement
was much closer to the mainstream of the movement in Britain than is typically acknowledged"; that is, it was as much concerned with the feasibility and timing of measures of
"physical force" as it was with their legitimacy as such.

54. Alison, *Some Account*, 1: 486.

55. Wilson, *Chartist Movement in Scotland*, 188.

Scotland."[56] Here Alison seemed to be making a version of his claim, first set out in the mid-1820s in his text on criminal law: namely, that it was interference from England which caused discontent in Scotland to flare into class conflict and possible political insurrection. Wilson, however, doubts that the Chartists played a very important role among the unemployed and strikers. Most workers seemed mainly interested in "wages and local grievances." Moreover, most of the Chartist leaders "seemed to be alarmed at the dangerous nature of the situation, and endeavoured to prevent any outbreaks of violence. Few, if any, appeared to favour the use of strike action as a means of carrying the Charter, and strike action in existing conditions was generally deprecated."[57]

Nevertheless, in his later recollections Alison could see only conspiracy, depredation, and potential insurrection:

So resolute were the leaders of the strike, and so confident in the support of the multitudes who obeyed their mandates, that they openly announced that they were not going to starve when the country was full of food; and depredations in the fields immediately commenced in the night ... About 20,000 working men, involving with their families at least 70,000 souls, were engaged in this formidable conspiracy against property.

This was all the more serious because

there was no police whatever in Lanarkshire, and the regiment of cavalry which usually lay at Glasgow happened at that very time to have been sent to Perthshire, to escort the Queen in going from Dundee to Blair Atholl for her autumn residence. Five dismounted invalids alone were left at the cavalry barracks, to guard the two guns which were stationed in Glasgow, and the chief depot of ammunition for the west of Scotland.[58]

When the disturbances broke out in Airdrie in 1842, Alison went there with infantry and cavalry and asked the Duke of Hamilton to call out the yeomanry. Alison also issued a proclamation to the county landowners and magistrates, "calling on them to raise the *posse comitatus*, or constabulary force." However, once again, he found no response to such a call. Aside from a group of constables "armed with billhooks and

56. Alison, *Some Account*, 1: 486.
57. Wilson, *Chartist Movement in Scotland*, 190.
58. Alison, *Some Account*, 1: 487.

batons," organized from among the duke's tenants, "not one of the landed proprietors did anything, either for their own or the public defence."⁵⁹ The yeomanry, Alison was pleased to find, proved efficient; mainly from their knowledge of the area and their "moral influence" among the "insurgent population," many of whom knew them.⁶⁰

59. "On the contrary," he added sardonically, "they nearly all disappeared: it was surprising how many wives and daughters were suddenly found to require sea-bathing at Ardrossan, the waters of Harrogate, or the prescriptions of Dr Jephson at Leamington": ibid., 1: 488.

60. Ibid., 1: 489. Alison referred favourably a number of times to the yeomanry, or voluntary cavalry, an élite force organized under the lieutenancy (itself an importation from England). It is clear that for him they met the older civic humanist requirement of the martial spirit of the middling ranks – "gentlemen actuated by their feelings." Whetstone (*Scottish County Government*, 113) notes that from 1815 to the 1830s, the yeomanry was the favoured means of putting down small riots and tumults, for it possessed characteristics which made it an ideal force for dealing with civil disorder. It was cheap. Since it was purely local, it was always available. It could be more quickly raised and dispatched than could the disembodied militia. It was a more intimidating force than a few men on foot. And because it was composed only of wealthier landholders and substantial tenants, it contained no "untrustworthy" elements. Use of the yeomanry declined "as the efficiency of the police increased and the belief in the effectiveness of riots as a sign of discontent diminished. They lingered longest in the counties near the big towns. Here they were called out occasionally in the 1830s and 1840s. In Lanarkshire, they were called out as late as 1856, but 1856 was the last time they were used to put down a civil disturbance."

Dunkley, however, in discussing the English experience (*Crisis of the Old Poor Law*, 18–19), suggests ways in which the yeomanry might not have been so effective. Contrary to Whetstone, he suggests such a force was expensive to maintain, especially during protracted disturbances. Further, those groups from which the yeomanry came were often unreliable; for instance, farmers refused to form themselves into a corps during the Swing riots until their landlords promised to reduce rents and tithes. "An even more important deterrent to the use of yeomanry to quell unrest," he notes, referring to Mather's work, "was growing fears that it exacerbated discord by inflaming the passions of the populace, the members of the yeomanry themselves often being parties to the conflict and the forces having generally an unsavory reputation for brute repression." "In short," Dunkley concludes, "the yeomanry shared all the defects that were evident in ill-trained, *ad hoc* local bodies constituted to supplement an inadequately organized regular police force."

Radzinowicz offers a similar assessment (see above 70n21). The discrepancy between the assessments of Dunkley and Radzinowicz and those of Whetstone and Alison may be explained by differing definitions of the yeomanry – Whetstone sees it as composed of "wealthy landholders and substantial tenants" (a definition which Alison would accept), while Dunkley appears to lump together the yeomanry and special constables and therefore to include elements from lower down the social scale. This might reflect actual differences between the Scottish and English situations.

What is interesting about Alison's account of these events and his own role in them is not so much the obvious ideological stance, but his evident relish the more the conflict took on the nature of a military campaign. Here we can observe an overlapping of Alison's youthful fascination with the battles and battlefields of the Napoleonic wars; his later immersion in the accounts of those military campaigns and revolutionary skirmishes for his *History* which, it must be remembered, he was constantly writing and revising while carrying out his official duties;[61] and the actual campaigns against working-class "insurgents." This conflation of roles is clear in his account of skirmishes around Airdrie:

Airdrie and Coatbridge, where the military were stationed, were surrounded night and day by a chain of vedettes on the part of the insurgents, by whom every movement of the troops, and every step taken by the authorities, was carefully watched, and instantly communicated. If we went out with the military at night in one direction ... everything was perfectly quiet ... Meanwhile the whole mining population had spread over the country, in the direction which the military had *not* taken, in bands of from 50 to 100 each [who attacked and robbed farmhouses and fields] ... soon all the farmyards and potato-fields in the district were guarded all night by bands of armed men, as in France during the days of the Jacquerie ... I was at first extremely perplexed how to deal with this formidable Vendean warfare ...

Soon his roles of strategist and counterinsurgent leader were combined:

I issued a proclamation, recommending the persons whose houses or fields were attacked not to resist ... but to ... observe where [the attackers] went with their spoil, and send me information next morning where it was deposited, or where the bands went to. Having received this information, I set out at midnight on the following night with a body of dragoons or yeomanry; and proceeding at a rapid trot, so as to outstrip the scouts who were always on the watch, surrounded the village to which the insurgents had retired, and, myself entering, searched every house ... on some occasions I came back to Hamilton or Airdrie with eight or ten prisoners, who were next day summarily tried and punished, so far as the powers of the sheriff without a jury would allow.

Alison had indeed become a hero in his own romantic drama:

61. Indeed, his account of the 1842 disturbances is followed immediately in his memoirs by the story of a dispute over his account of Wellington's lack of preparedness before Waterloo: Alison, *Some Account*, 1: 499.

I took great pleasure in these night marches, in which I was most faithfully seconded by the Lanarkshire Yeomanry ... I still look back with unmingled satisfaction to many an expedition with the yeomanry by moonlight, with Sir Norman Lockhart, their colonel, riding by my side, and the long line of the Clyde, marked by a white mist along its course, visible in the distance.[62]

The year 1848 saw a surge of revolutionary movements all over Europe. John Saville "locates British domestic politics within the triangle of revolutionary Paris, insurgent Ireland, and a revitalised native Chartist movement in London and the industrial North."[63] Archibald Alison also made connections, between the "French Revolution," which "threw Europe into a state of combustion," and the Chartist leaders who immediately "saw that their time had at length come, ... issued from their dens, [and] inflamed the minds of the suffering multitude."[64]

The most serious period of disturbances and democratic political organization in Scotland in 1848 occurred between March and June. The evidence points to massive unemployment and despair among working people which frequently boiled over into hunger riots, a relatively high level of Chartist organization although mainly of moral force advocates, much alarm amongst the propertied classes that insurrection was a serious possibility, and a contest between the Chartists and radicals and the authorities for the allegiance of the middle class.

Local landowners frequently let the authorities know of their fears about working-class violence. For instance, the Earl of Mar wrote in an agitated state to the home secretary, Earl Grey, convinced that revolution was nigh. He had heard that pikes were being made in at least two villages, "with a view seemingly to an insurrection in favour of Chartism,

62. Ibid., 1: 494. It is worth commenting here on the connections between the military and the "New Police." Steedman, albeit referring mainly to the period after the 1856 County and Borough Police Act in England, notes (*Policing the Victorian Community*, 2–7) that many of the models and theories of control and order that shaped county police management in the mid-nineteenth century were military. Further, one of the chief justifications for a local police was "its ability to face local insurrection, and put it down." Steedman sees behind this "an earlier image of the army as a way of ordering life, of men and masters united in defence of property and social order." There was generally no perceived difference between use of the army and militias and use of the police; they were seen as part of the same system of control. Philips notes (*Crime and Authority*, 76) that the Staffordshire police force "seems to have been based, at least partially, on a paramilitary model, with the emphasis placed on the suppression of riots and disorders."

63. Saville, *1848*, 1.

64. Alison, *Some Account*, 1: 572.

or else to rob and murder the rich – Scotchmen seldom lay out money without hoping to recuperate it; & it seems likely that the pikes are made with the view to upsetting the present Government; or else robbing & murdering the rich: – or more probably these three objects are combined."[65]

Generally, however, reports to the Home Office from local government officials emphasized that Chartist strength was not overwhelming and that disturbances could be handled given sufficient force. In the aftermath of the Glasgow riots of 6 and 7 March, Alison reported to Grey that the disturbances on the night of the seventh at least had "passed off quietly owing to the strong civil and military force stationed in different parts of [Glasgow]." Alison was confident that the authorities were winning the battle for the hearts and minds of the people: "The disposition of the whole middle classes throughout these occurrences has been most excellent [as has that of] the most respectable part of the working people." Chartist agitation, which Alison was convinced was to blame, was proving unsuccessful. The loyalty of the "middle classes" made it possible to "raise a Voluntary Infantry Regiment 800 strong, and a troop of Yeomanry 80 strong, entirely equipped and mounted at their own expense."[66]

Despite the use of military force, the authorities were relatively diligent about collecting sufficient evidence on which to arrest Chartist leaders. On 11 March Alison reported to the lord advocate that the yeomanry, the "71st Co.," and a "large body of special Constables" had been present to deal with a meeting and demonstration by colliers at Airdrie. Alison had "got a Chartist agitator named Crossan who spoke the most violent seditions ... arrested ... last night and he is now undergoing examination." A warrant was also out "against another Chartist named Taylor ... the cases vs them all are quite clear." An itinerant orator named "Dr. McDoual ... can be got at any time, but as his language though dangerous seems to have been guarded I think it no [*sic*] advisable to execute the warrant vs him." The authorities, Alison reported, were doing all they could to collect additional evidence against him. Alison's report concluded that all the leaders of the riots were in custody on the clearest evidence.[67] By 25 March, things had quietened down and Alison was exuding confidence. He reported to Grey that a Chartist meeting held

---

65. Mar to Grey, 10 April 1848, PRO, HO 45/2410E/AH 881–883.
66. Alison to Grey, 8 March 1848, ibid., HO 45/2410E/AG 820.
67. Alison to lord advocate, 11 March 1848, ibid., HO 45/2410E/AG 803.

the previous night concluded without any disturbance. There were "about 3,500 persons present, which I should think is the utmost strength the Chartists as a Political Body independent of the unemployed can muster here." He understood that the speeches "were on a more subdued tone than at a similar meeting held here before the recent riots."[68]

From April to July, the reports of the Scottish authorities to the Home Office tended to assess Chartist activity as having peaked. Robert Stewart, the acting chief magistrate of Glasgow, reporting to Grey that a public demonstration "by the Chartists and Repealers" had included from 5000 to 7000 people, nonetheless concluded that there was no need to use the military. Chartist political aims were generally ignored. For instance Sheriff Handysides of Stirlingshire sent Grey notes of the Chartist proclamation for a meeting on 22 April on Bannockburn Green. He listed the Chartist principles "Universal suffrage, Voting by Ballot, Annual Parliaments, no property qualification, equal Electoral Districts, and payment of members" – but made no comment on them. His only concern was the meeting's potential threat to order. Handysides's report of the meeting was reassuring: the procession was orderly; the meeting itself was far less numerously attended, he reckoned, than its organizers probably expected. He thought they hoped for 10,000, but probably got about 2000, "& a large proportion was young people." The chairman was "a respectable Tradesman in Stirling keeping a Shoe Shop." A printer named Harrower (earlier arrested by Alison) was on bail for sedition. His speeches had been "of a violent character," but overall, "the meeting was orderly conducted and dispersed quietly."[69]

While meetings did occasionally turn violent – for instance, in Greenock in May police and special constables dispersed an attempt by several hundred men to "process ... not without some hard blows being received on both sides"[70] – Scottish Chartists by and large seemed reluctant to resort to "ulterior measures," perhaps until they were better prepared. However, by 1848, the possibility of massive Chartist resort to physical force seemed to have passed. By a combination of miltary and police suppression of disturbance, and legal pressure on the Chartist

68. Alison to Grey, 25 March 1848, ibid., HO 45/2410E/AG.
69. Handysides to Grey, 22 April 1848, ibid., HO 45/2410E/AH.
70. 6 May 1848, SRO, AD 58/71.

organizations,[71] authorities seemed to have little difficulty in keeping control. Negotiation and compromise often replaced coercion; probably far more often than Alison's bravado accounts would suggest. The provost of Dundee reported that when asked by Chartists if he would call a meeting to "petition for the extension of the suffrage to the mass of the people," he had refused to agree that it could be held in the open air but instead allowed it in a public hall. The Chartist deputation pledged that any "tendency to violence or disturbance" would be "repressed." "Nothing" he wrote, "has occurred to shake my confidence in the good feeling and peaceable disposition of the greater body of the inhabitants, although I deem it my duty to adopt measures of precaution."[72]

Government spies and agents regularly infiltrated meetings and attended demonstrations.[73] One George Salmon reported to the lord advocate in June that a Glasgow meeting of Chartists and Repealers "turned out to be a complete failure – about 4 to 500 of those who have been in use to attend such meetings were observed ... a great crowd of lookers on were about the place – but everything went off quietly."[74] His information was combined that from other sources in a report by Acting Chief Magistrate Stewart to Grey. The meeting on the green observed by Salmon had followed a city hall meeting which was also deemed a failure, only about 1500 attending. Stewart put the numbers at the green at no more than 7000 – many of them "respectable persons, drawn there from curiosity." Stewart's report went on to say: "The resolutions, I am informed, were of a harmless description, but one of the speakers, John Adams, stated that he had joined a society where they practiced firing at a target, for amusement, and he advised them all to do the same, and to

71. Two Whitehall lawyers, John Jervis and John Romilly, replying to a query about the legality of Chartist organizations, gave their opinion that the "National Charter Association as organised on the proposed plan is an unlawful combination and conspiracy": 5 June 1848, ibid. Campbell describes (*Lanarkshire Miners*, 218) how in Coatbridge, with "regard to the development of trade unionism ... the police and law courts served to bolster the authority of the coal and ironmasters."

72. Provost of Dundee to Grey, 13 June 1848, SRO, AD 58/71.

73. On government use of spies, see Roach, "Alexander Richmond."

74. George Salmon to lord advocate, 10 June 1848, PRO, HO 45/2410E/AG. Salmon said he was writing lest the chance of "hearing from the brown agent" might be frustrated. Salmon could well have been a veteran spy by this time: a "George Salmond" appears in the lord advocate's papers as early as 1823 and 1824, giving information to the then sheriff of Lanarkshire and to the crown agent. Whatley, "Labour in the Industrialising City," 400nn165–7.

purchase muskets at the wholesale price." In light of this, Stewart said, the magistrates had taken every precaution: the whole police force as well as part of the cavalry and the infantry were in readiness.[75]

Alison's account in his memoirs of the events of the first half of 1848 was predictably full of self-congratulation and exaggeration, in marked contrast to his cool and efficient communications with his political superiors at the time. Nonetheless his descriptions convey some of the flavour of the conflict as well as reiterating his attitudes towards the task of law enforcement. On 6 March, alarmed by reports that a mob of over "10,000 persons" assembled on Glasgow Green was intending to pillage the entire city, Alison and Stewart placed themselves at the head of a cavalry squadron and "set off at a canter across the Green in the direction which the mob had taken." They entered the main street of Bridgeton, "where the principal body of the insurgents was placed," and joined up with a group of armed pensioners. Shots were fired, killing two in the crowd. As the crowd was yelling for retaliation, Alison

went to the edge of the mob, and, standing up in my stirrups, addressed to them a few words; telling them that they must see they were overmatched, and their only chance was to disperse and go home; that an inquiry should be made into the circumstances of the melancholy event which had just occurred, and if the soldiers were in fault they should be punished, as most assuredly if they were in fault they should be punished themselves. The mob gave three cheers, and immediately began to disperse.[76]

Alison noted the support of "the better class of citizens," over 2000 of whom enrolled as special constables. Those among them who were merchants or shopkeepers were willing only to defend their own premises, however. The rest, young men from the Western Club (the chief club of Glasgow), "were gentlemen, and actuated by their feelings: timidity and selfishness are the great characteristics of the burgher class."[77]

75. Stewart to Grey, 10 June 1848, PRO, HO 45/2410E/AG.

76. Alison, *Some Account*, 1: 575–6. Alison's comments were characteristic of his military-style bravado: "They were the first persons I had ever seen killed in actual strife, but I regarded it at the time as a mere matter of course, looking on the bloody corpses without any sort of emotion. I had no longer any difficulty in understanding the *insouciance* of soldiers in actual warfare." Alison does not mention whether soldiers were ever charged with the killings.

77. Ibid., 1: 576.

The *Glasgow Saturday Post* account of the events of 6 March matched Alison's later description fairly closely, even his address to the crowd and its favourable reception. It was, however, of a decidedly different opinion as to the relative effectiveness of special constables and of the police. The former, "selected from amongst the respectable citizens" was clearly the best kind of force "for the suppression of popular tumult." Workmen were as ready to be sworn in as their masters. The *Post* was very concerned to show that the mass of respectable workers had the utmost respect for property and chastised the "gentlemen and magistrates" of Glasgow for not alleviating the poverty of the unemployed and homeless. It was very critical of the police who, it was claimed, were nowhere to be seen when the crowd had control of the city for about two hours. As few as twenty men could have controlled them. The large police force "disciplined under a chief from the Irish constabulary – that picked stalwart regiment ... was nowhere to be seen in the riot, and the only account we have been able to obtain of the corps is, that it barricaded itself for safety in its barracks!" As for the magistrates (including Alison), they may have galloped gallantly from garrison to garrison for the military but apparently failed to consider looking for assistance in the centre of the city where the disturbance actually was. "In such an emergency," chided the *Post*, they "should have considered the police useless and unsafe, till they had first cleared the streets for them with the military." The newspaper, recalling Alison's pledge to the crowd, charged that nothing had been done; that in fact the lord provost was preventing official investigation into the shooting at Bridgeton (nothing like which had happened since 1736).[78]

After breaking up, with the aid of 1500 troops and about 200 constables, an attempted demonstration on the green by 15,000 colliers and miners in March – Alison wrote that the demonstrators "were frustrated by Mr Stewart and myself riding at them with a squadron of dragoons" – Alison pursued the leaders in the following days. Informants told him of the workers' whereabouts, "and before a week was over, above thirty of the principal rioters were lodged in jail, and brought to trial at the next Circuit, where they received sentences of varying degrees of severity, from twenty years' transportation to six months' imprisonment. By these prompt and decisive measures the spirit of disaffection was entirely bro-

78. The *Post* did note that while the riot was "almost purely a destruction of property," cries were heard for " 'Bread or Revolution', 'Vive la Republique' etc." *Glasgow Saturday Post*, 11 March 1848.

ken in the west of Scotland." In his autobiography, Alison was in no doubt as to the seriousness of the potential "insurrection." He claimed that had the conflict lasted another day, or the workers "succeeded in their design of plundering the city, the whole urban population in the west of Scotland would have risen."[79] This was sheer hyperbole and self-justification. Indeed, it was contradicted by his own testimony as to the relative ease with which the "insurgents" were defeated.

This account of Sheriff Alison's responses to working-class protest and Chartist organization confirms three points made in recent work by W.G. Carson on policing in Scotland. First, it illustrates the resistance to the idea of rural policing in Lanarkshire, a resistance which was anomalous in the wider context of rural Scotland. Second, the actions of Alison (and other authorities) show that the relationship between policing and the military was a complex one. Alison prized the military virtues and frequently relied upon "the power of law by military display." However, he was also wary of too readily sending in troops and thus fairly consistently argued that a rural police force would be more efficient and legitimating. Third, the operation of policing was perceived by authorities to be more effective the more the police were seen to be "impartial." As Carson and Idzikowska suggest, "the police in Scotland, as elsewhere, played a crucial ideological role by the apparent fact of their dissociation from overt class domination and its cruder coercive manifestations."[80] Constitutional authority could be separated from social and economic dominance. Alison's repeated calls for the establishment of a professional police force and his conviction that it was unwise to use civilians to help keep other civilians in check shows that he was well aware of the ideological implications of policing for social control.

The relationship between working-class political strength and state power is also of interest here. One of the main arguments of John Saville's *1848* concerns the thesis, put forward most notably by Gareth Stedman Jones, that ruling-class attitudes in the 1840s became less harsh, more flexible, and were characterized by a " 'high moral tone.' " Saville suggests this thesis fails to recognize "that coercion is the other side of the government coin marked conciliation." Consent without violence, Saville agrees, was always the state's preference, but the state's coercive apparatus had nonetheless been honed over a period of fifty years, and the events of the 1840s called forth a response notable for its

79. Alison, *Some Account*, 1: 578–9.
80. Carson and Idzikowska, "Social Production of Scottish Policing," 268.

"cool, ruthless calculation with not much evidence of high moral tone."
Saville concludes that "the physical force content of what unrest and
turbulence there was remained manageable and it was contained without much difficulty by the combined strength of the regular police and
the special constables, with only a relatively limited intervention by the
military."[81]

Saville does not discuss Scotland, except to note that it was *relatively*
undisturbed in 1848.[82] This chapter's survey of the reactions of some
Scottish authorities to economic and political unrest during the period
1834–48 do nevertheless tend to support Saville's argument about the
confident use of coercion by the state.[83] First, authorities generally
ignored political demands or programmes put forward by workers and
Chartists and concentrated their efforts entirely on breaches of the
criminal law, from rioting and mobbing to sedition. Second, certainly by
1848, but probably even by the early 1840s, the majority of the middling
ranks supported the authorities – either actively in joining up as special
constables or passively out of abhorrence for social disorder. Third,
physical coercion by state agents was complemented by a fairly careful
attention to the use of the law, evident in the efforts to obtain as accurate information as possible about the language used by demonstrators.
Government did not wish to chance embarrassing acquittals. Fourth,
there was often a considerable gap between authorities' *expectations* of
disorder, even of insurrection, and the relative ease with which they handled disturbances. The main issue was obtaining sufficient reserves.

81. Saville, *1848*, 220, 222.

82. Ibid., 120. A comparison with Wales is interesting. While the general trajectory of
working-class and Chartist protest and action was similar to that in Scotland, it is possible
to see a more combustible tradition of class conflict in Wales. From the early years of the
nineteenth century Wales experienced even more drastic and disruptive social and economic change than Scotland, a stronger element of nationalism based on language, and a
split between popular Nonconformism and élite Anglicanism. Religion and culture reinforced class. Even if the focus is only on the more visible expressions of class conflict, between the end of the Napoleonic wars and 1850 Wales experienced a remarkable series of
popular upheavals. The "Scotch Cattle" underground movement (active from 1816 to the
late 1840s), the Merthyr Rising of 1831, the Rebecca riots of 1839 and 1842, and the Newport Rising of 1839 (displaying a degree of organization which Jones describes as a mass
movement) gave radicalism and class conflict in Wales a profile quite different from that of
Scotland. Archibald Alison would, of course, have regarded all this as of a conspiratorial
piece. On Wales, see Evans, *History of Wales*, 129–54; Jones, *Newport Insurrection*, and *Rebecca's Children*; Williams, *Merthyr Rising*; Wilks, *South Wales and the Rising of 1839*.

83. For a critique of Saville's assessment of Chartist decline, see Dorothy Thompson's
review of Saville, in *History Workshop Journal* (1989): 165.

Finally, Alison placed more faith in use of the military and was much more sceptical about the value of volunteer constables than Saville suggests was the norm for state authorities in this period. Still, for Alison, the ultimate safeguard for property and order remained a professional police force.

Archibald Alison's world-view was shaped by his Enlightenment upbringing. The values of disinterested public service and virtue – balancing, in the words of his father, the "contemplative" and the "active principles of our constitution" – could be found only among "gentlemen" and professionals. The "burgher class," while valuable for their commercial energy, were nonetheless selfish and parochial. (Alison himself saw no reason why Scots should be parochial. Scottish experience and Scottish traditions in fact provided a model for coping with rapid change. He could borrow from a metropolitan innovation – the London policing system – because this fitted so well the established framework of professionalism in Scottish local government.) The working class needed careful stewardship if it was to emulate the values of prudence, frugality, and foresight – a stewardship which included intervention by the state to provide poor relief. Lack of attention to these obligations of class and rank, in Alison's eyes, encouraged calls for excessive political reform which could so easily turn into revolution.

4

"A Little Aristocracy of Freeholders"

Archibald Alison's two-volume *Principles of Population and Their Connection with Human Happiness* was published in 1840. It was a contribution to the Malthus debate and the Scottish Poor Law debate as well as to the debates over land reform and crime and punishment. It was also an attempt to argue for the continuation and viability of an eighteenth-century agrarian commercial model of society.

The work was begun between 1810 and 1812, substantially added to around 1829, but withheld from publication for another eleven years. Alison claimed that he avoided publishing at the end of the 1820s because of the predominance of political economy and of political solutions to social unrest. He may simply not have wished to tackle the political economists head on. Alison considered his work "social economy." It aimed to suggest schemes for social amelioration which would render drastic political solutions unnecessary.

Alison attributed his critique of Malthus to his father who, in arguing that "by a fundamental law of nature the labour of one man's hands is more than adequate for his own support," provided the younger man with the core of his subsequent work. One of Alison's motivations for tackling Malthus arose from concern over the narrow scope of political economy[1] and consequently, he thought, its inability to solve the nation's problems: "the object of the work is to bring Political Philoso-

1. Fetter ("Economic Articles in *Blackwood's*," 90) points to this narrow focus of political economy: "in the decades between Waterloo and mid-century 'economist' was not a term to include all who were concerned with analysing economic relations or in formulating economic policy, but only those who felt that the market mechanism was the best guide to economic development, and who accepted the social and political changes that would follow as desirable."

phy *back* to the principles of Religion, Humanity, National Interest and Common Sense."[2] Of more practical concern were the current debates on the Poor Laws in Scotland, and particularly the recent contribution made by his brother, Dr. William Pulteney Alison to that discussion. In his memoirs, Archibald declared that the success of William's pamphlet, *Observations on the Management of the Poor in Scotland* (1840), showed him that the public were receptive to the subject "and the numerous though unsuccessful attempts to refute the Malthusian theory which had issued from the press, seemed to indicate that the general mind revolted at a system which ascribed the greater part of the misery of mankind to the fixed and unchangeable laws of nature."[3]

Alison's eclectic approach owed much to the eighteenth-century traditions of commercial humanism and natural jurisprudence as well as to the emerging nineteenth-century disciplines of statistics and social science. The kind of society he hoped to conserve was based primarily on the "middling ranks" of small farmers, yeomen, professionals, and civil servants. It would allow for a degree of social mobility while remaining firmly hierarchical; include industry but recognize the priority of agriculture; and promote values of revealed religion, civic virtue, prudence, and frugality, and a balance between the passions and reason.

This meant that Alison's work was indebted most fundamentally to Adam Smith's ethic of improvement. Smith favoured a predominantly agricultural society of gentleman farmers and wrote of the dangers it faced from the too rapid spread of commercial values. Alison made use of Smith's views, which Smith shared with Hume, of government and liberty. Another prominent influence on Alison, underlining particularly the civic humanist strain, was Adam Ferguson, especially his concern for the corrupting effects of wealth and luxury. Perhaps an obvious influence might be Dugald Stewart, his father's friend, who introduced the work of Smith, as well as of William Robertson and Thomas Reid, to the nineteenth century. Alison, however, was suspicious of Stewart's political economy because of the latter's support for Malthus.[4] Alison most likely found Stewart's moral philosophy more palatable, based as it was on Reid's refutation of the dangerous implications of Hume's and Smith's theory of ideas for human knowledge and for the role of Divine

2. Alison to Blackwood, 24 March 1840, NLS, Blackwood mss, 4050.

3. Alison, *Some Account*, 1: 462–3.

4. Stewart wrote in his *Lectures on Political Economy* (1: 205): "Mr. Malthus had shown, and I think with demonstrative evidence ... that in every period of the progress to the time when the whole earth should be cultivated like a garden, the distress for want of food would

Providence. John Millar was one other possible influence on Alison, but Alison seems to have ignored him completely. This is odd, considering that Millar's theory of history was essentially the same as Smith's; his "scientific whiggism" taken over from Smith and Hume.[5] However, it is possible that Alison took against Millar because of his reputation as a liberal and reformer who took a favourable view of the French Revolution.

Alison's work on population can be considered by tracing two main themes: the model of an agrarian commercial society, and the development of artificial wants as the way to counteract the social problems arising from poverty. Alison used the Enlightenment's four-stage (stadial) theory of history and a Smithian perspective on the superiority of agricultural society to situate his ideas on population increase and his specific criticisms of Malthus. As a response to what he saw as the fundamental issue of poverty and the "moral decay" of the cities, he developed a number of solutions based on the need to counter the predominance of the passions in human nature. He argued for state provision of poor relief, landownership by the poor, and closer attention to crime and punishment (including the importance of transportation and colonization).

Alison surveyed the operation of the principle of population through successive stages of history: savage, pastoral, agricultural, and civilized. Here he was employing a version of the common eighteenth-century stadial theory of history, developed particularly by Scots writers to help explain the evolution of society from its rude to its present civilized stage. The stadial theory of history had been given various emphases: for instance, the evolution of law (Kames), changes in property ownership (Smith), or changes in manners (Ferguson). Whatever the emphasis, the theory was very popular amongst Enlightenment literati and can be found in the works of Dalrymple, Kames, Robertson, Ferguson, Steuart, Smith, and Millar in Scotland as well as in the writings of Mandeville in England and Mirabeau, Turgot, Rousseau, and Montesquieu in France.[6] Smith developed this evolutionary explanation most fully in his *Lectures on Juris-*

---

be constantly pressing on all mankind, supposing them all on a footing of equality. Though the produce of the earth might be increasing every year, the population would advance much faster, and the redundance must be reduced by the return of periodical disease, or the constant action of misery."

5. Haakonssen, "John Millar"; Lehmann, *John Millar.*

6. See Hamowy, *Theory of Spontaneous Order,* 14–15, 44n; Smith, *Wealth of Nations,* 2: 689n; Meek, "Smith, Turgot,"; Hopfl, "From Savage to Scotsman."

prudence, where he described the stages as: "the Age of Hunters; ... the Age of Shepherds; ... the Age of Agriculture; ... the Age of Commerce."[7]

There is no direct indication that Alison knew of these lectures, but we know that he read *Wealth of Nations*, where briefer but similar discussions of historical stages occur in books 3 and 5. Also, Alison had read William Robertson and Adam Ferguson and would have been familiar with Lord Kames, at least through his father's work on Tytler (Kames's biographer). Alison seems to have employed a combination of Smith's and Ferguson's approaches, concerned as he was both with changes in the mode of production accompanying shifts in population – his second and third stages are labelled pastoral and agricultural – and with changes in manners – he uses the terms savage and civilized for the first and fourth stages. Alison had recourse to Ferguson especially when he wanted to stress the dangers to society posed by commercialism and luxury.[8] In the savage state only the unlimited increase of population could overcome the severity of the environment. Nomadic people were motivated only by instant gratification and by the excitement of the chase or of war.[9] Alison argued that human beings in such a state were happy on their own terms; savage life offered its own "ease, independence and casual excitements."[10] Eventually the pressure of numbers provided the impetus for change from nomadic or savage society to the pastoral or shepherd stage. This stage of history saw the beginning of the diversification of mental and physical qualities among peoples.[11]

In order for the strong tendency inherent in the agricultural stage to remain in one spot over successive generations to be overcome, two of "the most powerful agents" in human history had to come into play: "the spirit of commerce, and the ambition of democracy."[12] Commerce

7. Smith, *Lectures on Jurisprudence*, 14.

8. On the relationship between Ferguson, and Hume and Smith, see Kettler ("History and Theory," 453): "In the last analysis Ferguson differs politically from Hume and Smith because he believes that political life is primarily about power and the assertion of will, and only secondarily about property and the satisfaction of interest."

9. Alison, *Population*, 1: 12. Alison repeated the common eighteenth-century assumption that "man in the savage state is indolent and improvident in the extreme." See Hume, "Of Commerce," in *Essays*, 266.

10. Alison, *Population*, 1: 15.

11. Ibid., 1: 17, 18. See Smith, *Lectures on Jurisprudence*, 202–3, where the hunting stage, which is communal and "democraticall," gives way to the shepherd stage when "certain individuals" appropriate property in animals. "The distinctions of rich and poor," Smith notes, "then arise."

12. Alison, *Population*, 1: 28.

caused the civilized "races" to disperse geographically in pursuit of "artificial wants" and the wealth necessary to obtain them. Urbanization was a key consequence of this dispersion and in turn fostered democracy which Alison defined as "the desire of exercising the government of the state." Alison's conservatism did not mean that he condemned democracy out of hand. Rather, he appropriated it as one key element in the social balance. Combined with passions – "the love of power, the desire of distinction, the passion for wealth; envy of superiors – jealousy of equals – contempt for inferiors" – democracy drove individuals "ardent for the equality of rights, and the regeneration of society, into distant lands." From this combination came "the marvellous effects of colonization."[13]

As society progressed towards a civilized stage, the potential for rapid increase of population became a reality. It was the supposed impossibility of subsistence ever to keep up with this population increase which had animated Malthus. Alison's own overall argument was that by a law of nature (Providence) human society and the principle of population which operated within it were adapted to each historical stage. Population increase, necessarily rapid in the early stages, was eventually slowed by the growth of artificial wants in the more "complicated" stage of society. These limitations were in turn constrained by social decay and corruption. Only good government and religious instruction could keep the latter tendencies at bay. Alison sought to show that Malthus's expectation that population increase was constantly and ever more tightly pressing upon food supply was erroneous, that in reality the reverse was the case. Alison sought to demonstrate that society's capacity for the production not merely of subsistence, but of an ever increasing surplus, far outstripped a much slower increase of population, which in any case was constrained by "moral" factors. As one man could produce much more than was necessary to maintain himself, this meant on the level of society that "the produce of the soil derived from human labour had afforded a vast surplus over and above the food required by the cultivators in its production."[14] Further, the proportion of those employed in agriculture to those in manufacturing was diminishing, but as the case of Britain demonstrated, their capacity to feed the whole of society was increasing.

Alison argued that certain factors caused individuals in a civilized state to limit the size of their families voluntarily. These factors he gener-

13. Ibid., 1: 30–1.
14. Ibid., 1: 35.

ally labelled "moral causes." Moral causes in the later stages of society drew large numbers into commerce and manufacturing and caused people to limit the numbers of children they had. Alison seemed to use the term "moral" to refer to any process or phenomenon that was not "natural" ("physical") or divine in origin: in other words, including "artificial" processes affecting (although not necessarily under the control of) individuals in an advanced stage of society. This usage was similar to that of Hume, for whom moral causes were circumstances that affected the mind in the form of motives or reasons and which issued in specific political and social arrangements.[15] Alison thought moral causes stemmed from the propensity of human beings in the civilized stage of society to cultivate artificial needs, comfort, and luxury; needs which caused them to voluntarily limit their numbers, "if not counteracted by moral corruption or oppressive government."[16] All but one of the causes Alison discussed were benevolent consequences of social progress and advancing civilization: reason (and education); artificial wants; the desire to accumulate property and to better one's condition; the incentive to rise in the world provided by the "distinction of ranks"; and "the diminished fecundity of marriage in mature life." The other cause was, in Malthus's terminology, a positive check: the mortality of the great cities.

A key part of Alison's argument against Malthus turned upon the superiority of agriculture. Here Alison relied on Smith's powerful arguments in the *Wealth of Nations*. Smith regarded the main factor in the development of opulence to be the desire of individuals to better their condition. But Smith hoped this would operate within a social context which would guarantee social stability as well as "independency." "Smith's ethics," notes John Dwyer, "was distinctly capitalistic" and "assumed ... the kind of interpersonal negotiation which obtained in a market oriented society." However, this market society was based firmly on property in land and, furthermore, land regarded not "as a crude commodity but a part of nature which sustained the entire nation and which rewarded the attentive and prudent cultivator far beyond the capacity of strictly human institutions and contrivances."[17]

15. Hume (explaining the genesis of national character) thought physical causes came from the effect of "the air and climate" on "the temper": *Essays*, 202–3.

16. Alison, *Population*, 1: 55–6. Smith tended to refer to moral causes in a negative way, focusing on the desire for luxury which accompanied the commercial state of society and led to excessive lending and borrowing: *Wealth of Nations*, 2: 908–10.

17. Dwyer, "Property and Propriety."

Alison linked key concepts from Smith – the division of labour, the individual desire for betterment, the growth of artificial wants, and the desire for emulation – to his analysis of the principle of population. As the impulse for population increase was so naturally powerful, any limitations to it must come from equally powerful and universal propensities. Alison saw these as "the *artificial wants* and *habits of foresight*, which the progress of society developes [sic]."[18] Referring to Dugald Stewart's *Elements of the Philosophy of the Human Mind*, Alison noted that human beings distinguished themselves from animals by developing their intellectual faculties, thereby being able to plan their lives and not be slaves to gratification and impulse.[19]

The only way that an instinctive, pre-reasoning desire such as the principle of population could be restrained, suggested Alison, was by "the growth of desires *inconsistent* with its early gratification."[20] Such desires, which were not needed in the early stages of society, were called into play precisely when population began to increase rapidly in advanced societies. Alison pointed out that it was the division of labour which began the historical process of developing artificial wants. The labourer was able to amass a small surplus, exchange this for commodities, and in the process develop new wants. This of course had an impact on population. Indeed, Alison claimed "the indulgence of artificial wants was incompatible with a rapid increase of the human species."[21] He thought the best illustration of this principle was that the numbers in both the "higher" and "middling" classes were dwindling; both required continual additions.[22]

18. Alison, *Population*, 1: 87.

19. Ibid., 1: 92. Stewart was criticizing Reid's philosophy, which he claimed did not sufficiently stress the organic unity of the mind's intellectual and active powers. Haakonssen believes this is an erroneous interpretation of Reid: "Science of a Legislator in James Mackintosh's Moral Philosophy," 247.

20. While Alison had access to a rich eighteenth-century discourse on the subject of passions, it is worth noting its emergence in seventeenth-century France. Keohane describes (*Philosophy and the State in France*, 151–5) the realization that besides the disciplining of the passions by reason, possible only for superior men, ordinary men incapable of self-control could nonetheless have their dangerous passions channelled into beneficent activity. Alison did not use the term "interests" so much as he talked about countervailing passions or material "desires." It was a commercial language rather than a civic humanist one. See Hirschman, *Passions and Interests*, 14–20.

21. Alison, *Population*, 1: 109.

22. Ibid., 1: 111–12.

Alison believed complaints against the increase of luxury in society were unfounded because the "dangerous qualities" (tendencies to profligacy and vice) which could accompany luxurious living tended to disappear as luxury was diffused more generously. Luxury could never descend far in society in any case, but the beneficial effects of wealth could. In a passage very similar to Smith's argument in *Theory of Moral Sentiments*, Alison claimed: "the more that the rich advance in the refinements of luxury, the more do the poor advance in habits of comfort ... the extension of comfort among the poor is eminently beneficial to their moral character. The severe and incessant toil which is indispensable to the welfare of the labouring poor in civilized society, can be sustained only by the prospect of enjoyment from its fruits."[23]

It had been observed by Smith, Alison noted, "that the desire of *bettering one's condition* is so strongly imprinted in the human breast, that with a tolerable administration of justice and the ordinary security of property, it is quite sufficient to ensure the prosperity of mankind."[24] Here Alison was also explicitly following Smith's linking of the ethic of improvement to political justice. Alison considered "a tolerable administration of justice" to be sufficient, thus distancing himself, as had Smith and Hume, from doctrinaire vulgar Whiggism, so prone to lapse into "love of system." Education fostered habits of prudence and self-denial, but it also, through diffusion of knowledge and information, provided examples of successfully rising, "by however small an increment, above one's station." Alison was mainly concerned with the situation of the "lower orders," as he thought the general well-being of society depended upon their becoming imbued with habits of frugality and thrift.

Alison, like Smith, favoured a social structure which would ensure stability and order, with each in their proper station, and yet allow for a fair degree of social mobility; an infusion of "energy" from the lower ranks to the higher. Luxury confined to the rich only corrupted them, Alison was convinced, without assisting the poor, and also exacerbated class envy. Instead,

23. Ibid., 1: 116–17. Compare Smith (*Theory of Moral Sentiments*, 184): "The capacity of [the landlord's] stomach bears no proportion to the immensity of his desires, and will receive no more than that of the meanest peasant. The rest he is obliged to distribute among those ... [who] thus derive from his luxury and caprice, that share of the necessaries of life, which they would in vain have expected from his humanity or his justice."

24. Alison, *Population*, 1: 129.

it is the establishment of a numerous and wealthy *middle class*, approaching on the one side to the splendour of the great, and bordering on the other upon the indigence of the poor, which preserves unbroken the chain of society, and renders the progress of wealth, fatal to the prosperity of despotic states, instrumental only in increasing the industry, and improving the habits of those which are free.[25]

The desire for accumulating capital and property was another moral cause restraining the growth of population as well as contributing to order and prosperity. The accumulation of wealth, especially, generated the powerful disposition to transmit such wealth to an heir: a disposition which "lays the foundation of all the changes which ensue in the progress of society." These processes in turn helped limit the increase of population by guarding against disregard for the future and against imprudence. Each social stratum was thereby able to acquire habits which gave some of its members the opportunity to rise on the social scale: industrialists into the "great families"; frugal artisans into the "opulent middling class"; hard-working agricultural labourers into the "numerous and wealthy body of yeomanry." Alison's conclusion, which was to be the basis for his critique of the French Revolution, was that the "magnitude and wealth of the middling class of society constitute the great distinction between England and the other states of Europe." The existence of an "opulent aristocracy" acted as a magnet and an example to the rest of society.[26]

It was vital then, Alison argued, that the gradations of society be numerous; the more rungs the ladder could be seen to have, and the farther down in society they extended, the more people would be encouraged to climb it. It was the struggle "to commence [the ascent] which leads to the limitation of population among the labouring classes." One of the main failings of the Reform Act of 1832 in Alison's eyes was that it severed political power from the possession of property "by the fatal £10 *tenant* suffrage, which in all great towns had vested a preponderance of votes in persons worth little or nothing." Alison's alternative was an article of High Tory faith:

25. Ibid., 1: 119. He quoted from Sheridan's speeches: "no sullen line of demarcation separates the higher and the lower ranks, but all is one blended whole."
26. Ibid., 1: 124, 129.

The establishment of a *little aristocracy* of freeholders, each enjoying political power, as the fruit of industry and prudence in himself or his ancestors, is one of the most important elements, not only in the political, but social institutions of society, and indispensable to the development in this particular of the intended limitation on the principle of increase.[27]

Alison here echoed Smith's paean to the "small proprietor ... who knows every part of his little territory, who views it with all the affection which property, especially small property, naturally inspires, ... who upon that account takes pleasure not only in cultivating but in adorning it," and who "is generally of all improvers the most industrious, the most intelligent, and the most successful."[28] Contemporary political economists, according to Alison, ignored the social and moral context of economic processes. He preferred, for instance, Smith's emphasis on the "customary" determination of necessities or, as he himself put it, the "tastes and habits of the people" rather than relying solely on impersonal market processes.

The argument that the productive powers of nature could easily outstrip the increase of population was, Alison thought, a powerful rebuttal of Malthus. But he argued that an even more important issue for social growth was "getting at" those productive powers.[29] In other words, the issue was the demand for labour. The crucial relationship was between the surplus and the ratio of "cultivators" to other sectors of society. The progressive division of land and of labour in society had turned attention to the way in which every individual and community could "obtain a share of the fruits of subsistence." This was what would provide proper encouragement to population growth. Alison liked Smith's observation that the "real want" experienced in society was for "additional hands," because the question was not so much the capacities of the soil "as the amount of wages which can be obtained for employment."[30]

Alison then needed to reassure his readers that there were also checks to the demand for labour, so that a redundant population would not become too great and perhaps prove Malthus right after all. Checks on

27. Ibid., 1: 130, 134.
28. Smith, *Wealth of Nations*, 1: 423.
29. This phrase seems close to Smith's argument in *Lectures on Jurisprudence*, 343: "That state is opulent where the necessaries and conveniencies of life are easily come at, whatever otherwise be its condition, and nothing else can deserve the name of opulence but this comeattibleness."
30. Alison, *Population*, 1: 38.

the demand for labour, as with checks on population increase, occurred only in an advanced society. The two most important were the different employments of capital and the use of machinery.

Alison based his discussion of the different employments of capital squarely on that of Smith (although he was also concerned to show the effects on the increase of population), particularly in ranking these employments in terms of the "quantity of productive labour" put into motion in each of them and in stressing the clear superiority of agriculture. Capital invested in agriculture, argued Alison, not only furnished a return to the farmer, but it also enriched the soil in such a way as to maintain many more people for an extended length of time (perhaps "for ever"). Capital employed in manufacturing, on the other hand, "*only* yields a return for the capital employed: there is *no* permanent addition *besides this* made to the wealth of the state, which may afford the means of maintaining an increased number of individuals."[31]

Alison considered the activity of government crucial in either aiding or hindering this whole process. Both the "religious despotisms" of the east and the absolute monarchies of Europe were "subversive of the systems of nature" – of, in Smith's words, "natural liberty." Alison concluded that only a free state, as Smith explained in the *Wealth of Nations*, would know not to interfere with "the progress of opulence" and thus with regulation of the increase in population.[32] This last point may seem curious in the light of Alison's Tory protectionist beliefs. However, Smith and Alison can be seen to meet on a "sceptical whiggish" common ground: government should not interfere with "the progress of opulence," that is, in Smithian terms, with "perfect competition"; but government had plenty to do in a political sense in order to provide the requisite framework for the "progress of opulence" to continue.[33] The role of government was important for Alison, especially with respect to fostering artificial wants (which in turn encouraged the habits of industry, foresight, and "the increased control over the physical passions")

31. Smith, *Wealth of Nations*, 1: 360–3; ibid., 1: 148.

32. Alison, *Population*, 1: 161.

33. Government did have an economic function: promoting the growth of artificial wants. Alison never tired of arguing that the law of nature by which natural passions gradually became subdued by "acquired propensities" should be helped in its work, especially in remote and "barbarous" areas; "artificial encouragement to foster the beginning of manufacturing establishments is often indispensable." For instance, in the Irish provinces, "tailors and miliners [*sic*] would do more in the end to improve the habits of the lower orders, than all the efforts of the benevolent." Ibid., 2: 129.

and refraining from hindering economic improvement as well as ensuring freedom from oppression. Alison wished to emphasize the role of
good government so as to remove the responsibility from Providence
for the existence of misery in the world. He agreed with Malthus that
schemes for the perfectibility of society through politics or science were
utopian and indeed harmful; that human society was and always would
be in a state of "probation"; and that adversity was clearly necessary, in a
moral and material sense, in order to inspire individuals to acts of piety,
industry, and frugality.

However, he took issue with Malthus's argument that "'the misery
produced by Government is slight and superficial, compared with those
deep-rooted seeds of evil which have their origin in the principles of
human nature.'" Alison seemed to be in some confusion on this point,
as he himself often pointed to the corruption of human nature. He
wanted to read Malthus as not allowing for any change in the secondary
characteristics of human nature; that is, those which could adapt to
changed material circumstances. (In fact, Malthus would not necessarily
have had a problem with this.) The actual condition of the people was,
as far as Alison was concerned, the "only sure indication of the healthful
state of the political body." If all classes

exhibit the signs of prosperity and comfort; if the labouring ranks are at once industrious and opulent: if the higher are active and intelligent: if wealth accumulates without degrading the poor, and population advances without reducing
the wages of labour, – it may safely be concluded that the public institutions are
in practice beneficial, and the operation of the principle of population in uni-
son with the welfare of mankind.[34]

This was an obvious reference to Smith: especially the concern with the
"labouring ranks" being "industrious and opulent" and with the wages
of labour remaining high or at least steady. Alison did not mention profits, which may indicate agreement with Smith's contention that profits
in a healthy economy should be low.

More broadly, Alison went back to the older civic humanist tradition
of Francis Hutcheson and Adam Ferguson in order to attack Malthusian
political economy. Alison declared the need to "*re-establish the ancient connection between virtue, freedom, and happiness*" and to counter the opinions
of those whose theories favoured "the encroachments of despotic power

34. Ibid., 1: 229, 236–7.

on the part of the ruling powers, and the illusions of self-love in individ-uals," theories which suggested that the "sufferings of mankind are owing rather to the laws of nature, than to the prejudicial tendency of oppressive government, or the dissolving effects of human corrup-tion."[35] It is not clear why Alison regarded "human corruption" as not being part of the laws of nature. Perhaps it was the only way someone with a strong belief in the workings of Providence could see to allow for free will and avoid a thoroughgoing determinism.

When he compared countries with regard to the relationship between oppressive government and the degree of comfort and opulence, Alison thought it to be a reliable rule of thumb that when a people were numerous and comfortable, "government is practically beneficial, what-ever may be its form." Adam Smith thought the absolute government of eighteenth-century France, for instance, was not necessarily an obstacle to the diffusion of wealth and comfort.[36] Any evaluation of the impact of economic policies and developments thus hinged, for Alison, on how those policies affected the demand for labour and the numbers of wage labourers, especially in urban areas. The wisest policies in his view were those which acted to reduce the numbers in the "labouring classes" so that the remaining labourers could enjoy a "comfortable" existence. This desirable end could also be brought about by the division of labour and the increased use of machinery. While the role of the division of labour in depopulating the countryside was not a salutary one, it did also act to reduce the numbers of urban workers. Here Alison used Smith's famous example of pin production to show the reduction made in the quantity of labour by the simple division of labour without any machinery. Cru-cially for Alison, the division of labour in agriculture had raised the amount of food which a given number of labourers could produce.[37]

The division of labour had a negative side, however, as both Smith and Ferguson had recognized. It

is too frequently the melancholy effect of the division of labour, which takes place in the progress of opulence, to degrade the individual character among the poor; to reduce men to mere machines; and prevent the developement [*sic*]

35. Ibid., 1: 238. The question of whether Alison misread Malthus (especially around the issue of attribution of human suffering) is taken up at pp. 103 and 125–7.

36. With regard to Smith's opinion of liberty in France, Dwyer notes ("Property and Propriety," 27n9) that Smith's concept of freedom has less to do with abstract rights than with "freedom of manoeuvre."

37. Alison, *Population*, 1: 185.

of those powers and faculties which, in earlier times, are called forth by the difficulties and dangers with which men are then compelled to struggle.[38]

The resulting "habits of the manufacturing classes" and the "degradation of the human character" – large numbers of people in close confinement, "promiscuous intercourse of the sexes at an early period of life," and "the debasement of intellect which arises from uniformity of occupation" – produced the most "deplorable" effect of the progress of civilization.[39]

One limitation on the demand for labour that was a direct outcome of the division of labour, Alison noted, was "the invention and improvement of machinery." The pressure of taxes and the high price of labour sparked efforts to find a substitute for labour in order to meet foreign competition. It was Alison's opinion that there was no limit to the possible improvement of machinery: the "steam-engine, the cotton machinery of Sir R. Arkwright, the steam-power looms, have totally altered the relative situation of the British and foreign manufacturers; and enabled the former, notwithstanding the heavy burdens with which they had to contend, to undersell a great part of foreign artists, even in the supply of their own markets."[40]

The extension of exports as a result of the use of machinery did not however raise wages; but it did reduce the number of labourers. This in turn produced unrest among the working classes and arguments against the use of machines. This opposition, according to Alison, was mistaken. Far from allowing the operatives to receive the full benefit of their labours, the *elimination* of machinery would in fact prevent British manufacturers from competing and cost even the jobs of those who were employed. Therefore the numbers of manufacturing operatives would not increase in coming years, and might even decrease. This was a blessing for society, but also for the working classes, as their smaller numbers would enjoy a higher standard of living.

---

38. Ibid., 2: 8. Compare Smith (*Wealth of Nations*, 2: 781–2): "In the progress of the division of labour ... [the] man whose whole life is spent in performing a few simple operations ... has no occasion to to exert his understanding, or to exercise his invention in finding out expedients for removing difficulties which never occur. He naturally loses, therefore, the habit of such exertion, and generally becomes as stupid and ignorant as it is possible for a human creature to become."

39. Alison, *Population*, 1: 190.

40. Ibid., 1: 187.

The substitution of machinery for labour, then, was highly desirable in Alison's view, not only to counter the effect of depreciation in the value of money, and the rise in the wages of labour, but also to reduce the ranks of the manufacturing classes and prevent the dangerous consequences which multiplication of their numbers would undoubtedly bring. It is no surprise to find Alison regarding the use and improvement of machinery as a law of nature, "destined to restrain the demand for labour in the advanced stages of society." As he saw it: "The substitution, ... of steam-power looms for manual labour, of mechanical contrivance for human multiplication, is a most fortunate change in the progress of society, and more particularly to be desired in a country such as Britain, whose political greatness is intimately connected with its manufacturing superiority."[41]

Alison's praise of the beneficial effects of machinery may seem surprising for a High Tory. Maxine Berg, for one, has simply assumed that Alison, whom she has categorized as a Country Tory, would share that group's anti-machinery sentiment as part of a broader anti-industrial attitude.[42] As we have seen, however, Alison's response was more complicated (revealing, incidentally, the difficulty of labelling in a period of such ideological flux). Alison was able to be so optimistic about the beneficial effects of machinery because of his basic assumption of the general superiority of agriculture and its necessarily dominant position in the national economy. Agriculture of course, and here Alison followed Smith, did not admit of the wholesale introduction of machinery and had to depend on "the industry of mankind," particularly intensive schemes of husbandry.

Alison was insistent that political and moral factors played a vital role in social change, as against those like Malthus who, he mistakenly claimed, emphasized a universal, unchanging human nature. A key factor was the ability of societies with a virtuous "middle rank" to control corruption in the higher ranks. Just as the energies of the pastoral "barbarians" were infused into the agricultural-commercial states, so the "independent spirit" of modern states came from the comparatively uncorrupted middling and lower orders. Sounding very much like James Mill, although clearly taking his inspiration from Hume, Alison argued that the middle classes were the natural guardians of "public tranquillity and general freedom." This was particularly evident in

41. Ibid., 1: 192.
42. Berg, *Machinery Question*, 254.

"England," where prosperity was based upon "habits of freedom, and general information ... and the salutary control which public opinion exercises over the higher classes of society."[43]

Alison's analysis of economic policy was always carried on within a broad theological framework of the providential progress of mankind. As had many eighteenth-century philosophical historians and theologians, he attempted to balance an account of human progress which stressed the inexorable changing of circumstances with allowance for an element of control that human beings could exercise over their circumstances. As one of the animating principles of his work, Alison had recourse to a force very similar to Adam Smith's "invisible hand": the operation of "a mysterious agency, which in the end brings good out of evil; which compels the vices and passions and disorders of men to work out the purposes of Divine administration."[44] Even if that invisible hand played less of a role in Smith's system than previously thought,[45] it is easy to see how it would appeal to the more religiously minded Alison. It was in the increase of population particularly that the "mysterious agency" had been at work, constantly adapting human beings to their circumstances. However, individuals and societies could, through their own actions, affect their interests and control the increase of population for their welfare by attention to just government ("tempered freedom") and religious instruction.

Belief in the law of nature which governed the rise and fall of civilizations placed limits on Alison's notion of progress. He had no doubt, for instance, that the British empire would decline and fall in its turn: "It is neither possible nor desirable for the interests of humanity, even in this country, that such a perpetual tenure of greatness should be assigned to any single state."[46] Even though population increase became limited once societies had inculcated countervailing desires in their members, these in their turn were checked by human wickedness and oppression

43. Alison, *Population*, 1: 292.

44. Ibid., 1: 4.

45. Recent work on Smith has emphasized that his references to an invisible hand were few, and not necessarily in accord with one another. The reference in *Theory of Moral Sentiments* assigned a positive role to selfishness, suggesting that it generated demand; "the invisible hand of *The Wealth of Nations*, on the other hand, causes selfishness to optimize production, a matter of supply." A third reference, in the "History of Astronomy" essay, saw the invisible hand as preserver and enforcer of the natural order. Ahmad, "Smith's Invisible Hands," 140. See also Davis, "Smith on the Providential Reconciliation of Interests."

46. Ibid., 1: 216.

by ruling classes. History therefore needed, Alison argued, checks to human depravity, and these nature provided in the inevitable decay of "national virtue," caused particularly in pre-modern times by war. Here Alison returned to the broad themes of his opening chapter, and it is not surprising that his references were to eighteenth-century historians and moral philosophers who had been preoccupied with the principles of change in history and their moral consequences. Alison's governing motif for this discussion came from Edward Gibbon: "the history of the world contains one perpetual round: valour, greatness, discord, degeneracy, and decline." This was backed up by a lengthy quotation from Adam Ferguson, whose main point was that "'the progress of societies, to what we call the heights of national greatness, is not more natural than their return to weakness and obscurity.'"[47]

Alison, as late as 1840, envisaged Britain becoming a nation of predominantly small farms, cultivated by intense small-scale husbandry, a state of affairs which would support a very large population in a great degree of comfort. He mentioned favourably the arrival of a "stationary condition of society" in terms remarkably similar to those used by John Stuart Mill. This development was not necessarily a nineteenth-century preoccupation; Smith had considered the possibility of most societies reaching a stationary stage and then declining. Although his discussion in *Wealth of Nations* was mainly concerned with the effect on profits and on the wages and the condition of the labouring poor,[48] Smith, from Alison's point of view, did question the effect of optimal opulence on general happiness. In the nineteenth century Malthusians of course viewed the arrival of a stationary economic state as both inevitable and calamitous. Mill, writing eight years after Alison's work was published, was very conscious of going against established opinion when he praised a stationary state. The latter would occur after the general level of production and comfort in the country reached a peak and, according to Mill, would afford society the opportunity to forsake the incessant and soul-

47. Alison did not give the citation, but the passage was from Ferguson's *Essay on the History of Civil Society*, 208–9.

48. "It ... is in the progressive state, while society is advancing to the further acquisition, rather than when it has acquired its full compliment [*sic*] of riches, that the condition of the labouring poor, of the great body of the people, seems to be the happiest and the most comfortable. It is hard in the stationary, and miserable in the declining state." *Wealth of Nations*, 1: 99. See Chisick, "The Wealth of Nations and the Poverty of the People," for a discussion of the extent to which Smith's outlook for the labourers was more pessimistic than generally supposed.

destroying pursuit of material gain and to cultivate the higher plea-
sures.[49] Alison saw no reason why such a state should not enjoy "a high
degree of public felicity, if general virtue remains among the people,
and a tolerable administration of justice is preserved by the government." He noted statistics from contemporary writers such as Adolphe
Quetelet and James Cleland which showed the decreasing rate of mortality and increased life expectancy, a process surely conducive to increased human happiness.[50]

For many writers in the latter part of the eighteenth and the early
nineteenth centuries, the condition and progress of the United States
was of consuming interest. As a society starting off without the encum-
brances of a feudal system, the new nation occasioned great curiosity as
to the degree of liberty and opulence it would be able to achieve – it was
for many a glimpse into the future. It is interesting, then, to examine
Alison's view of that country, a view which brought together his opinions
regarding population, property, and liberty, in much the same way as it
did for Smith. Smith saw the "American farmer as the ideal type of a cultivator who had chosen farming over manufacturing because of the
independence which it brings."[51] Indeed, Smith generally regarded the
"American colonies" as the best advertisement for the superiority of
agriculture.[52]

Alison concurred with this, although his reliance on the work of more
recent writers, especially of Alexis de Tocqueville, gave his picture of the
United States a more pessimistic cast. His imagination was caught by
what he saw as an astonishingly rapid increase of population, which he
attributed to the "vigour" of the "Anglo-Saxon race." Further, this
increase had been accompanied by a very high level of "comfort," the
cause of which was to be found in the peculiar economic and political
system. The United States was a country of small proprietors, a condition which Alison also suggested as the best long-term solution for the
poor in Europe.

However, the distribution of landed property among the American
working class was accompanied by a less admirable characteristic, one
which Alison thought "had been neglected by political philosophers."
Historically, the acquisition of landed property had carried with it an

49. Mill, *Principles of Political Economy*, 111–17.
50. Alison, *Population*, 1: 221.
51. Dwyer, "Property and Propriety," 31n56.
52. Smith, *Wealth of Nations*, 1: 366.

extremely strong emotional attachment to the soil. However, "in America, for the first time in the history of mankind, this strong and universal feeling seems to be entirely obliterated." Farmers were happy not only to sell and divide property at the death of a family head, but during a lifetime "immigration from one spot to another is so frequent that it may be considered as the grand characteristic of the American people."

The accumulation of capital was the all-engrossing occupation, claimed Alison; he coined the label "NOMAD AGRICULTURAL STATE" to describe the present condition of the country. He explained this unique characteristic as the combination of "the industrial [*sic*] character which the Americans have inherited from their English ancestors" and the "effect of democratic institutions on the human mind when society is in a state of universal and rapid progress." In the United States, wealth was seen as the universal passport to influence, self-elevation, and happiness. Who knew to what extent this state of mind might eventually degrade the national character, but at present it seemed to provide a generally high standard of living.[53]

Alison cautioned that the United States was still in a transitional stage; there remained ample room for expansion. However, some signs of conflict were appearing: as Tocqueville pointed out, many complained of the tyranny of wealth. Eventually, Alison expected, separate interests would become powerful; "democratic passion, which already chafes against all the restraints of law or justice, will find it more profitable to plunder than to create property." The "furious popular passions," for now channelled into occasional random violence, "will gradually but certainly induce the curse of civil warfare." Echoing Tocqueville, he claimed the irreconcilable difference between blacks and whites would involve the Southern states "in the horrors of a servile war."[54] In short, once the safety-valve of the West was closed, the nation would experience the very same conflicts and troubles which rent all societies. Democracy, concluded Alison, was not the end for society, but a means. It provided an infusion of energy into modern nations, just as the barbarians had done for the ancient world.

53. Alison, *Population*, 1: 542, 550–1, 552.
54. See Tocqueville (*Democracy in America*, 639): "If there ever are great revolutions [in America] they will be caused by the presence of the blacks upon American soil. That is to say, it will not be the equality of social conditions but rather their inequality which may give rise thereto."

Probably Britain's most visible and pressing social problem in Alison's view, the existence of which frequently forced him beyond the more comfortable intellectual and moral framework of the Scottish Enlightenment, was the "moral decay of the great cities." One of the most deplorable conclusions of Malthus's theory was that it denied the need for state-provided poor relief. Alison proposed a threefold solution. Legal provision of poor relief and the ownership of land by the poor would complement each other. The other solution – more vigilant attention to crime and punishment (especially transportation, which, operated in tandem with colonization, would soak up the redundant population) – has been discussed in the context of Alison's law career (see pp. 55–60).

Alison's explanation of the causes of urban misery comprised four main themes. The "enormous accumulation of wealth in a few hands" had the effect of creating "a vast and indigent population who live upon its expenditure, and are dependent upon its support" and who crowded into the towns and cities. Alison, echoing his father and Adam Smith, reminded his readers that " 'God made the country but man made the town'," and it was in the latter that the overwhelming preponderance of corruption and "wickedness" was to be found. The extremely rapid growth of manufacturing, while the basis of Britain's economic power in the world, had at the same time created "a diseased and dangerous population." The effect was "to coin gold for the master manufacturer, and multiply children in his cotton-mills."[55]

The factory system itself played a role in urban misery. Employing children as operatives ruined the health, moral character, and "habits of increase" of the nation. The factory system had as its "appendage," trade unions and strikes. Alison was opposed to strikes (although not to trade unions as such) because of their detrimental effect on both the economy – "the immense loss which they entail upon the manufacturing community" – and the operatives themselves – tyrannized by strike committees in the vain hope of raising wages during an economic downturn, which added to their already well-developed feeling of insecurity and lack of concern for the future.[56]

Compounding the effects of the accumulation of wealth, the growth of manufacturing, and the factory system was the "total want of poor's rates, or any legal provision whatever for the indigent in [a] great part

---

55. Alison, *Population*, 1: 518.
56. Ibid., 1: 530, 532–3, 520.

of Scotland, and the miserably parsimonious spirit in which they have been administered." Landowners had been permitted, he warned, "to shake themselves loose altogether of the great Christian duty of succouring the unfortunate, and in consequence throw them in overwhelming multitudes on the great towns; where that duty is, however, imperfectly performed."[57] Alison traced the path of an hypothetical family arriving in the city and eventually succumbing to the alienation of wage labour, drunkenness, crime, and prostitution. In comparison with the prevalence of face-to-face relationships in the country, in the city such a family was totally alone, dependent only on wages. Unemployment, illness, or death meant the workhouse, with their places being speedily filled. No compassion or help was to be expected from creditors, "cruel landlords," or neighbours.[58]

What is striking about this and similar discussions in *Population*, and indeed in most of Alison's writings, is that aside from a concern with poverty and indigence, Alison's work offers little discussion of legislative solutions to social problems. The factory system is a case in point. The first major Factory Act was passed in 1833. Yet not only did Alison not refer to the movement for factory reform (a movement which included Tories such as Richard Oastler, Michael Sadler, and Lord Ashley), he also spent almost no time discussing factory conditions. This may be partly explained – in the case of *Population* – by the fact that most of the sections on the condition of the poor were written during 1828. A concerted factory reform movement did not get under way until 1831. Moreover, Alison did not move to the heavily industrialized Glasgow area until 1834. Still, one searches his later articles published in *Blackwood's* in vain for any discussion of this issue.[59] It seems Alison thought factory conditions would be improved as a matter of course – he may have regarded the 1833 act as a major advance – and that his more general prescriptions for reducing the urban labouring population through the use of machinery and emigration would obviate the problem.

57. Ibid., 1: 535, 536n.

58. There is an echo here of his father's sermon on the moral danger of great cities; see above, pp. 21–2. On the subject of landlords, Alison told the Poor Law Commission in 1844 that "the landlord watches, and gets [paupers'] money out of their hands the moment they get it out of the parish": *Poor Law Inquiry Scotland*, 20: 470.

59. An 1841 article, "Social and Moral Condition of the Manufacturing Districts in Scotland," found Alison marvelling that "manufacturing and commercial industry have

Alison believed that the most effective immediate solution to the problem of poverty was state-provided poor relief. His criticisms, and those of his brother William, of the Scottish Poor Laws, were fairly well grounded. Indeed, the Alisons' suggestion of a commission of inquiry into the Scottish Poor Laws was accepted by Peel's government.[60] Sheriff Alison was one of the key witnesses at the inquiry.[61] The role of the industrial revolution in causing poverty was not considered seriously by most Scottish observers in the early years of the nineteenth century. Few writers defined the causes of indigence in economic terms. Poverty was largely taken to be the result of personal behaviour and "moral degrada-

---

received the most astonishing development in Lanarkshire generally, and in Glasgow in particular." There followed a detailed examination of the "wretched condition to which a large proportion of the working classes is reduced under the present manufacturing system, in the great marts of that species of industry," and this "under its most favourable and splendid auspices." When he turned to solutions, Alison was quite firm that it was completely unwise to "make any attempt to restrict the manufacturing industry of the country ... to check the growth of those huge limbs of the community into which so large a portion of the life blood of the state has come to be poured." Yet this analysis was not set out as a reason to support the repeal of the Corn Laws, a change which would elevate manufacturing at the expense of the agricultural interest. Adam Smith was correct, said Alison, that industry was best supported by leaving it alone. However, it was with regard to the consequences of industrial growth – poverty and misery – that the central state should intervene. Neither individual initiative nor local self-government (tried in Lanarkshire for the past forty years) was sufficient. This was what Alison meant by "a very material change in our social organization." This was essentially the same message as that in *Population*, although one might expect more specific measures to be outlined in a journal piece.

60. See Hilton, *Age of Atonement*, 63.

61. An example of Alison's testimony (*Poor Law Inquiry Scotland*, 20: 472–3): "Have you considered the bearing of poor laws on population either as giving a stimulus to its increase, or the contrary? – ... The absence of poor laws is most fatal in its influence on the increase of population. Pauperism, when accompanied with the possibility of getting a livelihood, is a prolific source of the greatest and worst increases of population. A christian country like this is not exempt from the operation of such a cause; and the result[s] flowing from insufficient parochial relief are these – no artificial wants, no habits of foresight among the poorest classes of labourers; and parties marry invariably at the earliest possible period. Would you propose to give work to able-bodied persons out of employment? – If provision were made that the act of Parliament relating to that class should be carried out, the best way would be to give them work. But in the altered state of society [he means the economic disruptions], it would be difficult to get work. And when people apply for work and cannot get it, it would be best to combine with the plan a system of immigration. If we were to say, 'we will give you a free passage to Canada – to the back settlements,' – I am sure they would agree to such an offer."

tion."[62] It was not until after the Napoleonic wars that attention began to be paid to the consequences of industrialization. Even then the main concern with regard to the poor was to avoid giving the able-bodied unemployed a right to relief and to avoid institutionalizing legal assessment. A few Scottish doctors – foremost among them William Alison – made "the first, and indeed the only, massive attack upon the Scottish poor law system." "The physicians' arguments," notes R.A. Cage, "were clear and concise, strengthened by a wealth of data concerning the outbreak of epidemic fever. The equation of poverty with moral failure was a sterile starting point: instead, thought about a cure should begin with basic physiological needs."[63]

By 1819, four years after William Alison began to work in the Edinburgh New Town Dispensary, he had already made the connection between destitution and fever. William accepted the overall thrust of Malthus's theory,[64] much to the chagrin of brother Archibald, who nonetheless could console himself with the knowledge that William was opposed to Malthus's attack on the Poor Laws. Malthus's great error, stated William Alison,

lies in arguing as if there were no dependence but dependence on the law; and therefore *as if all who are kept off the poor-rate are independent.* Whenever any individual of our species is not provided for, either by his own labour, or the labour of his ancestors, or of his immediate relations, he is in a political sense *dependent,* and the moral and political dangers affecting his character, or the good of his country, which are to be apprehended from the loss of his independence, *are already incurred,* whether he is dependent on the law or on the bounty of individuals.

Therefore, Alison concluded, only state-provided poor relief would afford "*security* against destitution."[65]

William Alison was a strenuous opponent of Thomas Chalmers, who attempted to establish a parish system of poor relief based upon volun-

62. Cage, *Scottish Poor Law,* i. See also Paterson, "Poor Law in Nineteenth-Century Scotland"; Mitchison, "The Poor Law" and "North and South"; Crowther, "Poverty, Health and Welfare."

63. Cage, *Scottish Poor Law,* 126.

64. "The observation of Malthus I believe to be perfectly just, at least in relation to continued fever, that it is always to be apprehended in an epidemic form when the population considerably exceeds the demand for labour, and the means of comfortable subsistence derived from labour": William Alison, *Management of the Poor,* 23.

65. William Alison, *Observations on the Famine,* 36.

tary contributions. In 1840 Alison debated Chalmers at the Glasgow meeting of the British Association for the Advancement of Science. Alison's main indictment of the old Scottish Poor Law had appeared in his 1840 pamphlet, *Observations on the Management of the Poor in Scotland, and Its Effects on the Health of the Great Towns*. Into this "devastating"[66] attack, Alison incorporated his criticisms of Malthus. The Scottish Poor Law was the most inefficient system of relief in Europe. It relied too much on voluntary charity, and by limiting relief to disabled individuals of "sound moral character," it doomed innocent victims of environmental conditions to a cycle of despair. The only way to break this cycle, Alison argued – as did his brother Archibald – was to provide every individual in poverty with a regular, uniform, and sufficient subsistence. This entailed, and again both Alisons were in accord, reforming the old Poor Law to more closely approximate the 1834 English Poor Law Amendment Act.[67]

The English act was a response to the Poor Law Report and was designed specifically on the assumption that the old Poor Law was the cause of poverty. The report had recommended making application for relief by able-bodied males a much less attractive proposition than before. Perhaps the main formal difference between the Scottish and English systems had been that the latter had required aid be given to the able-bodied unemployed (although in practice the Scots had of necessity supplied outdoor relief to the able-bodied). Separate workhouses would be created for the aged and infirm, for children, for able-bodied females, and for able-bodied males. The act of 1834, more politically cautious than the report, dropped the recommendation that relief for the able-bodied would cease.[68] While a considerable step forward in its realization of the effects of environmental conditions on individuals, this approach was still limited by being tied to the workhouse concept.

66. Brown, *Thomas Chalmers*, 290. William Alison's critique of Chalmers and of the poor law system generally are treated in varying degrees of detail in: Brown, 289–93; Cage, *Scottish Poor Law*, 126–30; Checkland, "Chalmers and William Pulteney Alison."

67. This was somewhat ironic, as the aim of many in England before 1834 who wished to reform that country's system was to model it more closely on the traditional Scottish system, which they saw as cheaper because more closely based on voluntary payments, and to jettison the "allowances" system of Speenhamland.

68. Evans, *Forging of the Modern State*, 221–2. For a fuller comparison of the two systems, see Cage, *Scottish Poor Law*, chap. 5. For recent analyses of the old and new English Poor Laws, see: Poynter, *Society and Pauperism*; Himmelfarb, *Idea of Poverty*; Brundage, *Making of the New Poor Law*; and Dunkley, *Crisis of the Old Poor Law* and "Whigs and Paupers." For the view that the Poor Law was engineered by Liberal Tories, see Mandler, "Tories and Paupers."

Archibald Alison hoped to give the Scottish Poor Law debate a broader context, one shaped by his critique of Malthus's theory but also providing a philosophical and "social" critique of political economy and an argument for what Alison still considered to be a viable agrarian commercial society.[69] Alison developed his critique of voluntary assessment and his argument for legal assessment around a broader critique of the abrogation of social responsibility by both landed proprietors and commercial groups. Voluntary charity and education were the most commonly suggested solutions. Alison rejected both as inadequate; they appealed only to the conscience and the reason without countering the passions or instincts. A very good example for Alison of the scale, and the inadequacy, of voluntary relief was Glasgow. In the previous fifty years the city had grown at a rate unparalleled in Europe, and the amount of charity had also been enormous. However, all the main charitable institutions were heavily in debt and many were attempting to obtain the aid of a public assessment.

The Alisons argued that a "complicated" state of society required government intervention on behalf of the poor. The poor, noted Archibald, had always been protected: in the "rude" stage of society it was by means of slavery, which, incidentally, he thought was still appropriate for such societies (including Ireland) in his own day. He argued that "at no period of ancient history was it found necessary to levy a tax on the higher classes for the support of the poor." This had occurred in modern times only with the growth of freedom: the emancipation of the peasantry and the suppression of the monasteries cut off the traditional sources of support for the poor. They became a burden on society.[70] A more complicated commercial stage of society brought into existence great inequality in the distribution of wealth, alienation of labourers from the wealth they created, and the rise of unemployment. Benevo-

69. That Alison's decision finally to publish *Population* in 1840 was related in large part to the crisis of the old Poor Law is reinforced by Mitchison's conclusion ("The Poor Law," 266): "The crisis created by the failure of the old Scottish Poor Law to sustain the unemployed did not arrive until the 1840s, by which time the general urban situation had deteriorated dangerously. It was entirely proper that it was unemployment in Paisley in 1841–2 which forced on reform of the Poor Law, since it had been the crisis there in 1819 that had enabled the lawyers to destroy the appeal system and to rewrite the scope of the law to exclude the unemployed. By so doing they had made certain that the Scottish Poor Law became an inadequate instrument for social welfare in an industrialising country."

70. A fact first reflected in "43 Elizabeth and the act of 1579" in Scotland: Alison, *Population*, 2: 174. Alison must mean the act of 1574; as Cage notes (*Scottish Poor Law*, 2, 9), this was the first act to provide public maintenance for the poor.

lent intentions to relieve distress were useless unless they addressed these material causes.

Leaving the poor to the voluntary support of the rich was entrusting them to "a class who neither can nor will maintain them" because the resources needed were so vast. A legal assessment was the only solution. Alison found that the information annexed to the 1834 report of the English poor law commissioners confirmed his argument that "legal establishments for the relief of the poor were universal in all parts of the continent where society exists in a complicated form, and the people were exposed to the destitutions of freedom." Dr. Johnson's saying was profoundly true, Alison thought: " 'a decent legal provision for the poor is the true test of civilisation'."

In arguing for compulsory assessment, Alison's attack on manufacturers and industrial capitalism and on the "opulent" generally became even harsher, and he returned to his moral argument for disinterested measures free from popular passions. Compulsory assessment equalized the burden of maintaining the poor between the "selfish" and the "humane." This was only just:

It is the selfish for the most part who bring the labouring classes into that crowded state where legal relief becomes indispensable. The extravagant expenditure of the opulent, – the competition of master manufacturers, – the encouragement of commercial enterprise, – afford the inducements which draw the poor into great cities, and leave them to starve after the purposes of their assembling have been served ... It had been said that the manufacturers create the poor, and leave it to the landholders to feed them. With more justice it may be asserted, that the opulent of every class assemble the poor, and leave it to persons of moderate income to relieve their distress.[71]

Not only were the rich ignorant of this distress, but even when they were aware of it, it was easy for them to avoid contributing in any real proportion to their wealth.

Assessment would prevent the humiliation and degradation of the poor which resulted from their having to solicit largely inadequate charity. Legal relief for the poor would prevent them "from sinking into that state of utter wretchedness which leads to immediate crime and ultimate dissolution of manners." The great advantage of assessment was its regularity; it could be "permanently relied on, because it alone was independent of

71. Alison, *Population*, 2: 177–82, 188.

the passions and fleeting emotions of the people."[72] Finally, the system of legal provision could be easily adapted to the circumstances of the poor; in other words, contracted in times of prosperity, enlarged in times of distress.

A key effect of the Poor Laws for Alison was their retarding influence on the increase of population. Here he was attempting to refute the assumption that poor laws, "by providing an asylum for the poor in sickness, distress, or old age," simply encouraged them to have more children. The truth, Alison claimed, was quite the opposite. Destitution alone would not prevent marriages being contracted. The reason was a law of human nature: "The passions of our nature are universal and inherent; the controlling principles partial and acquired; the former act most powerfully where the latter are unknown." That is, limitations on population growth were most effective in those social groups with the highest standard of living, as only they were able to develop countervailing material desires.[73] Indeed, the aristocracy, if placed in conditions of destitution, would themselves acquire those habits which led to a redundant population.

Four principles should govern distribution of the proceeds of a legal assessment: it should be administered to all who required it regardless of nationality[74]; it should be adapted to the circumstances of the individuals who required it (for instance, work should be provided for the able-bodied but unemployed); some portion of the funds should go "to providing the means of emigration to the young and the active of both sexes"; and, an equal means of assessment should be adopted, so that, for instance, manufacturers who contributed a great deal to the accumulation of the poor and benefited from their labour should not escape assessment.

Alison's criticisms of England's new Poor Law clearly show the limits of his social philosophy, and the extent to which he wished to change the Scottish system. His concerns were relatively minor, mainly focused on keeping families intact. He accepted the English act's fundamental belief in workhouses and in the discouragement of assistance to the able-

72. Ibid., 2: 117, 201.

73. Ibid., 2: 205, 207.

74. Natives of England, Ireland, and the Isle of Man could be legally removed to their own countries when they applied for relief in Scotland, but these removals were the subject of much controversy, particularly in the case of the Irish which was complicated by the possibility of racial and religious bias: Paterson, "Poor Law in Nineteenth-Century Scotland," 185–6.

bodied. This was in line with his general anti-urban bias: the numbers of urban labourers were to be kept as low as possible through the workings of the economy; those who fell into destitution were to be aided by the state, but confined and put to work. Any surplus should be reduced by assisted emigration and controlled by stricter attention to law and order. The criminal justice system, transportation, and colonization were to work together as a kind of mopping-up operation: removing the destitute and the criminal from their immediate environment, making them productive, and, if possible, reforming them into the bargain.

A common theme in Alison's arguments for proper administration of both the Poor Law and the criminal justice system was the importance of using professionals to manage both systems. Further, he regarded the "middling ranks" as the sector of society from whence came the necessary sense of social obligation which supported the professions and which was conspicuously lacking amongst the "opulent."

Amelioration of poverty through legal provision for the poor and prevention of crime as solutions to poverty and social misery were incomplete for Alison without a third measure. Until the poor themselves could own property, society would not find harmony. He believed landownership by the poor was a way to ensure the existence of an agrarian commercial society into the mid-nineteenth century. Alison thought the real socio-economic cause of destitution was the inequality of property that accompanied the progress of society and widened as society became more opulent. If men of property were diffused among the rural poor in the ratio, say, of a hundred thousand to a million, then voluntary charity might have sufficed. If the ratio was ten thousand to one million, however, then the condition of the poor was "utterly desperate, if not supported by public assessment." Justice therefore demanded that the class of proprietors shoulder the burden of poor relief. The prodigious profits of master manufacturers and merchants depended on the employment of the poor, but the operatives shared least in the wealth "which their industry had created." Therefore, "to relieve them so far as human aid can go, is the duty ... of a ... beneficent government." Alison was not arguing for a redistribution of property in any radical sense; rather for a more graduated social order. The implication was that if such an order existed, then charity might be enough.[75]

75. Alison, *Population*, 2: 182–6.

The "division and appropriation of land" had, Alison noted, rightly been seen as key steps in material progress from one historical stage to another. For instance, the key historical transition was from pastoral to agricultural society, and there the first step to improvement and to civilized society[76] arose from the acquisition of landed property. However, philosophers had not so easily recognized the effect of land ownership "on the character and habits of the people among whom it takes place." Central to his argument here was Hume's opinion that people in a primitive state of society were indolent. Only something which could create "new desires in the human breast" could overcome "the impressions of the present moment" and provide "a durable object in life." The division and acquisition of land accustomed men to connect labour, remuneration, and happiness, and thereby to develop foresight; it inculcated habits of "privation and self-control, as well as prudence and frugality." The distribution of landed property among the poor, combined with "religious and moral education," would provide an important remedy for the degradation of character caused by the division of labour.[77]

England offered a number of examples of the beneficial effects of giving land to the poor. Studies of the state of agriculture in several counties – Lincoln, Rutland, and Norfolk – where cottagers had been provided with an acre or two on which to keep a cow or several pigs revealed to Alison orderly and industrious habits. He cited cottage industry in Yorkshire, Lancashire, and Nottinghamshire as additional evidence for his argument: a happy marriage of agriculture and manufacturing producing well-behaved, industrious, and frugal freeholders and copyholders. Further:

The *statesmen* of Westmoreland have long been celebrated for their comfort and good conduct, not less than their independent spirit; no symptoms of a redundant population are to be found in their dwellings; and they exhibit ... the most

76. Consistent with his Scottish Enlightenment perspective was Alison's argument, familiar in the writings of the Moderate literati, that women could refine and civilize commercial society: see Dwyer, *Virtuous Discourse*, chap. 5; Rendall, "Virtue and Commerce." Alison suggested that while in "savage" societies, the situation of women was debased and their finest traits almost obliterated by hardship, "the acquisition of a home, ... of a permanent object" allowed the development "of those gentle qualities and domestic dispositions, for which they are peculiarly fitted by the wisdom of Nature." These dispositions in turn helped men acquire "habits of order" and "love of domestic happiness." Women's role "in the economy of Nature," then, was to impart gentleness and peaceable habits to future generations. Alison, *Population*, 2: 6.

77. Alison, *Population*, 2: 2, 3, 9.

interesting examples which the British dominions afford, of the combination of manufacturing industry, with the possession of small landed properties.[78]

Here, of course, were the perfect examples for Alison of his ideal economic system: manufacturing set in a framework of intensive agriculture. He thought this would avoid the most alienating consequences of capitalist industry: the extreme division of labour to be found in the great towns with its attendant poverty, vice, and redundant population. Social control was another positive outcome of such a scheme. Alison approvingly cited the author of an agricultural survey who argued that " 'the labourer who can keep a cow or a pig is always a faithful servant of his employer' " and " 'had a stake in the common interest of the country, and is never prompt to riot in times of sedition like the man who had nothing to lose, but, on the contrary, is a strong link in the chain of national security'."[79]

Distributing land to the poor connected the "higher and lower orders of society," broke down "the fatal barrier between the rich and the poor," and established "a gradation of rank among the poor themselves." All this completed "that beautiful chain in the social system which links together all the different classes of society." Alison was disturbed that the landed aristocracy was increasing in numbers at the expense of "the little proprietors." This not only distorted the social balance but set a dangerous sequence in motion. To the extent that the aristocracy was idle and unproductive and prevented land from going on the market, the wealth of the "middling and lower orders" flowed instead into the money markets, increasing the already huge burden of public and private debt.[80]

The issue of productivity was crucial. William Alison discussed agricultural improvement at length in a pamphlet of 1850. He argued that reclamation of waste lands and cultivation by croft husbandry could cause the labour of paupers and criminals, which prevailing wisdom considered should be unproductive, to be "an addition to the production of the nation."[81]

---

78. Ibid., 2: 31.

79. Ibid., 2: 26–7. Arthur Young, in his 1801 paper, told the landlords a man " 'will love his country the better even for a pig' ": Hammond, *Village Labourer*, 47.

80. Alison, *Population*, 2: 20; Alison, *Some Account*, 2: 64, 65.

81. W.P. Alison, *Observations on the Reclamation of Waste Lands*, 1–2, 16. Alison's further objection to John Stuart Mill's argument in favour of large farms was its assumption that the only object of political economy was the production of wealth, whereas "in all practical applications of that science, the main object is the *happiness* of the people." (p. 17)

Land reform was a contentious issue in Britain throughout the eighteenth and nineteenth centuries and is one area where Archibald Alison could not always appeal to Smith. Smith had attacked both entail and primogeniture for blocking the progress of improvement. Alison was extremely critical of entails. They allowed estates to remain in families, many of whom could not afford to make them productive. They shut out the investment of the middling ranks. And they contributed to the climate of opinion which prohibited the poor from acquiring landed property. Government needed to reform the law of entail. This indeed happened during Andrew Rutherfurd's second term as lord advocate. "Rutherfurd's Act of 1848," writes Michael Fry, "permitted heirs to disentail their estates and dispose of them at will. This let the less prosperous landowners get rid of the burden on their families and made for a freer flow of capital into efficient agriculture." This was an outcome Alison had hoped for. However, he could not have been so happy about the other consequence of the act: it guaranteed that the connection between landed property and hereditary aristocracy would be broken in the not-too-distant future. "As the new rich bought out the effete gentry," claims Fry, Liberalism was extended in the counties.[82]

Alison, while attacking entails, defended primogeniture. He claimed land gave the human mind a permanent object of attachment and that allowing the family acres to be dispersed (for a one-time profit) destroyed local and family ties. On the one hand, Alison seemed to believe primogeniture was necessary to ensure that families held on to their land. On the other, he also wished to see land circulate on the market and be apportioned more equitably down the social ladder, as long as such distribution did not threaten the aristocracy as a class.[83]

While some of Alison's language on this issue was quite populist – wanting to "preserve the free and independent race of peasantry," for instance, or demanding "a continual alienation of the land" – he clearly had no political affinity with the Whig and Radical land reformers. One possible explanation of his radical language was that the land question in Scotland was so much more acute, with much larger tracts of land owned by fewer landed proprietors and a rural labouring population (including increasing numbers of Irish) always close to vagrancy and pauperism, but with little or no means of relief. The other possibility is that Alison was prepared to countenance a fair degree of "social amelio-

82. Fry, *Patronage and Principle*, 60.
83. Alison, *Some Account*, 2: 58.

ration," including state intervention, in order to forestall potentially more dangerous "political innovation."

While Alison was pleased with the initial response to his work on population, he soon realized that it was not going to get the attention he felt it deserved. Comparing its reception with that later accorded his *History*, Alison thought that the latter became a bestseller because it appealed as much to the sentiments as to the reason, whereas *Population*, an entirely didactic work, was too difficult and dry to be popular.[84] The truth was that Alison had simply waited too long to publish it and thus his eighteenth-century agrarian bias no longer had any real political resonance. The Liberal Toryism of Peel was coming to dominate the Conservative Party by 1840. Also, to the extent that Alison's work had a fairly strong Scottish dimension and application, it perhaps had less relevance for an English public.

Some journals did pay attention to *Population: Blackwood's Magazine* (December 1840, in a review by William Henry Smith), the *Church of England Quarterly* (April 1841), and the *Spectator* (25 July 1840) reviewed it at reasonable length. Of the three, the Whig *Spectator* was the least impressed with Alison's refutation of Malthus (although it did like his stadial approach to the history of population). Overall, the reviewers tended to see the part of Alison's work that dealt with practical issues, such as the growth of artificial wants as a counter to population growth and the argument for poor relief, as the most effective. His attempt to refute Malthus's "laws" was greeted enthusiastically only by the *Church of England Quarterly* reviewer ("Mr. Alison ... completely and finally extinguishes the rival theory.")

Ironically, Alison's work received some favourable notice from a quarter for which he had absolutely no sympathy. Frederick Engels, in his *Outlines of a Critique of Political Economy*, turned to Alison for evidence that "the productive power at the disposal of mankind is immeasurable."[85]

---

84. Ibid., 1: 465–6. In his autobiography, Alison claimed that newspapers as well as literary journals received *Population* with favour, the consensus being that "Mr Malthus' doctrines had at last met with a decisive refutation." This assessment was somewhat inflated: some of the journals Alison mentioned in his autobiography or in letters to his publisher either did not publish a review or were more guarded in their reception than he suggested. Alison had twice expected a review in the *Quarterly*, the High Tory journal, and had made a number of suggestions as to a reviewer. In the event, his manoeuvring was to no avail for the *Quarterly* never did publish a review. He also mentioned reviews in *Fraser's Magazine*, the *British Critic and Quarterly Theological Review*, and the Whig *Examiner*, but a search of the relevant issues failed to find them. One must assume either that Alison's memory was faulty or that he was aware only of a promise to review which did not eventuate.

85. Meek, *Marx and Engels on the Population Bomb*, 57.

Engels also used Alison's work, as well as William Alison's pamphlet on poverty and disease in the cities, in *The Condition of the Working Class in England.* Dr. Alison, Engels said, "proves that a period of privation, a commercial crisis or a bad harvest, had each time produced the typhus epidemic in Ireland as in Scotland, and that the fury of the plague had fallen almost exclusively on the working-class."[86] Writers and observers such as the Alisons and J.C. Symons were useful to Engels because their conservatism gave them at least a paternalist compassion for the poor and a determination that the state had an obligation to intervene in social matters. Also their professional concern for statistics seemed to give their work a solid foundation. They were more reliable, from a socialist point of view, than liberal writers, because in accepting the class system as natural and inevitable, they described it more accurately.[87] "Sheriff Alison," Engels allowed, "is humane enough to admit [the exploitation of labour as the cause of poverty]; he is no thoroughbred Liberal manufacturer, but only a half-developed Tory bourgeois, and he has, therefore, an open eye, now and then, where the full-fledged bourgeois is still stone blind."[88]

Many of Malthus's critics, Alison included, became fixated on the "laws," the apparent focus on vice and misery as the only effective checks, the stark prognosis, and specifically the attack not just on the existing Poor Laws but on the need for poor laws at all. The successive changes Malthus made in the second and subsequent editions of his *Essay* were ignored or obscured. In particular, his awareness that the productive capacity of British agriculture was greater than he had thought and that, as the first census in 1801 showed, the population of Britain was far greater than he thought led Malthus to place more emphasis on moral restraint and prudence as the most important checks as well as suggesting that the Poor Laws should be phased out in a "very

86. Engels, *Condition of the Working Class,* 130–1.

87. For instance: "Dr. Alison [here Engels confused his Alisons; he should have named Archibald] explains to property-holding readers, with the greatest exactness, what the consequences of social oppression must be for the working-class." Ibid., 145; Alison, *Population,* 2: 197–8.

88. Engels, *Condition of the Working Class,* 150; Engels followed with a long quotation from *Population* (2: 76ff) describing the crime and destitution of large cities. Here Alison argued that the "higher orders," for reasons of profit, were to blame for the misery of the poor, the latter having no control over their situation. But Engels had no further need of this witness: "Enough! The half-bourgeois Alison betrays to us, however narrow his manner of expressing himself, the evil effect of the great cities upon the moral development of the workers." Engels, *Condition of the Working Class,* 150–1.

gradual" fashion. Malthus's approach was essentially moderate, and like Alison, he placed a good deal of reliance on the regulating actions of good government.[89]

How well did Alison understand Malthus?[90] He seems to have mistakenly charged Malthus with attributing human suffering to the laws of nature, or at least to "unchanging" laws of nature. He did not dwell on the ratios, or subject them to the same intense mathematical scrutiny as did, for instance, William Hazlitt, "Piercy Ravenstone," and David Booth.[91] Alison contented himself with arguing that as subsistence increased so much faster than population, the ratios were back to front. He did, however, marshall a great deal of evidence to attack Malthus's "American example": the latter's use of the rapid rise of population in the United States as proof of his theory. Alison, as did several other critics, argued that immigration accounted for a good deal of that population increase. Two of Alison's other arguments had also been made by earlier participants in the debate: that the limits to population growth came partly from good government and lack of superstition (meaning religious beliefs other than Protestantism); and that the lower orders could learn to emulate their social superiors. Of course, these arguments were perfectly acceptable to Malthus as well.

Alison's two main arguments against Malthus had more validity. First, although he ignored the fact that in this later editions of his work Malthus came to rely almost entirely on moral restraint and prudence as checks to population increase, Alison did, in his expectation that the growth of "artificial wants" would establish habits of prudence, foresight, and frugality, provide a more solid base for an explanation of "embourgeoisement" (to use Donald Winch's term[92]) than Malthus's rather vague prescription. Second, Malthus clearly did not want to remove all support for the poor at a stroke, especially during periods of economic downturn. However, he only very grudgingly conceded by the

89. See James, "Introduction" to her edition of Malthus's *Essay*; Winch, *Malthus*.
90. Alison was clearly aware of the subsequent editions of Malthus's *Essay*. The very title of the former's work is a clue: its subtitle "Connection with Human Happiness" is close to that of Malthus's second edition ("A view of its past and present effects on human happiness"). More specifically, although Alison dealt with Malthus's theory directly in only one chapter of his work, and actually quoted him only six times, two of these references were to the second edition (1803) and two to the fifth edition (1817) of his *Essay*.
91. Smith, *Malthusian Controversy*.
92. Winch, *Malthus*, 53.

1820s that in the absence of general understanding of what was wrong with the Poor Laws, the best that could be hoped for in the medium term was "an improved administration of our actual laws, together with a more general system of education and moral superintendance [*sic*]."[93] Alison seems to have been more realistic (if more paternalistic) about the permanent need for state-provided assistance.

What is perhaps most interesting about comparing Malthus and Alison is how similar their overall perspectives actually were. Both showed a marked "agrarian bias" in favouring an agrarian commercial society based on the industrious middling ranks, both relied a great deal on Hume and Smith (but departed from Smith in their support for protection and for the Corn Laws), both were at odds with the political economists in their basically eighteenth-century conviction that (in Malthus's words) "the science of political economy bears a nearer resemblance to the science of morals and politics than to that of mathematics,"[94] and both had a fundamental faith in human progress. In religion, too, they were not so far apart. Both accepted the workings of a divine plan which nevertheless provided some space for human will.[95]

However, broadly speaking, Alison's view of Divine Providence and free will, and his distaste for laissez-faire political economy with regard to social problems, put him at odds with those theologians who have been labelled Christian political economists: Malthus, William Paley, John Bird Sumner, Edward Copleston, Richard Whately, and Thomas Chalmers. As A.M.C. Waterman points out, these men saw a fundamental congruence between the tenets of Christianity and those of political economy (in its basic sense of self-interested behaviour regulated by an impersonal market mechanism).[96] Alison could not have accepted their assumption that, in Waterman's words, "scarcity, competition and inequality produced by population pressures were optimal for intellectual, moral and spiritual development."[97]

93. Quoted in James, *Population Malthus*, 450.
94. Quoted in Winch, *Malthus*, 76.
95. See Santurri, "Theodicy and Social Policy in Malthus' Thought." Santurri is criticizing in particular Bowler, "Malthus, Darwin, and the Concept of Struggle." See also: Hilton, *Age of Atonement*; Pullen, "Malthus' Theological Ideas"; LeMahieu, "Malthus and the Theology of Scarcity."
96. Waterman, "Ideological Alliance." On Christian political economy, see also Hilton, *Age of Atonement*, and Mandler, "Tories and Paupers."
97. Waterman, "Ideological Alliance," 241.

Malthus was not willing, as Alison was, to use government to induce "social amelioration." Malthus preferred, in the last analysis, the discipline of the market. While Malthus's Whiggism was of an eighteenth-century "country" stripe, which in the nineteenth century could lend itself to liberal or conservative purposes,[98] he was nevertheless a Whig, and the political differences between Malthus and Alison were clear. Aside from his desire to end the poor law system (albeit with extreme caution), Malthus supported the Reform Bill and Catholic Emancipation. The next chapter examines Alison's position as a High Tory prepared to use state intervention and contrasts it to those Liberal Tories who, while they held an essentially static view of society, nevertheless saw the market as more efficient than the state in ordering that society.

It is difficult to say whether Alison deliberately ignored aspects of Malthus's later position that were not so different from his own. It does seem as if Alison's rather unbalanced critique of Malthus was a means to distance himself from Whig political economy and Whig politics in general, and a starting point for his attempt to build an argument for agrarian capitalism in a rather unpropitious nineteenth-century context. If he had been less politically partisan, Alison might have found an unexpected ally in Population Malthus.

How plausible was Alison's argument for an agrarian capitalist society in 1840? Aside from the examples Alison gave in his book, he could have drawn supporting evidence from a number of facets of life in Scotland at this time. As R.H. Campbell and T.M. Devine note: the "assumptions, attitudes and experiences of a rural society still permeated much of Scotland in 1830. The sights and sounds of the countryside were not far removed from the urban and industrial areas, many of whose inhabitants had known rural life at first-hand." Large proprietors still dominated the pattern of landownership and continued to acquire more land throughout the nineteenth century. In 1878 about 68 proprietors owned nearly half the land of Scotland, and some 580 owned three-quarters of it. Nonetheless, a new rural middle class had acquired and held land, thanks to the feu system and the land market,[99] a class sizeable enough perhaps for Alison to think what was possible if entails could be ended. Alison may have been aware of the large number of planned villages created in

98. See Winch, *Malthus*, chaps. 5 and 6, for Malthus's differences with Ricardo and the *Edinburgh Review* Whigs.

99. Checkland, *Industry and Ethos*, 56; Campbell and Devine, "The Rural Experience," 46.

Scotland between 1745 and 1845, many of which combined agriculture with rural manufactories. "Though many of these planned villages failed to meet the expectations of their founders," notes Bruce Lenman, "it is clear that landlords continued to think of them as a worthwhile enterprise up to about 1850."[100] Economic growth was uneven; Alison's own county, containing some of the heaviest concentration of industry, was still one-third rural.[101] Raphael Samuel argues that even in England the onset of industrialism in the sense of a full-blown factory system was slower to become the norm than was formerly supposed and that the industrial revolution "rested on a broad handicraft basis, which was at once a condition of its development and a restraint on its further growth."[102] In England also, land reformers kept promoting schemes for a wider distribution of property, perhaps for a nation of property owners, home owners, and peasant proprietors, long after Alison's death. Leasehold enfranchisement and the allotments and smallholdings movements enjoyed some popularity, although no success, in the last two decades of the century.[103]

Yet the reality was that the rapid industrialization of lowland Scotland[104] and the commercialization of agriculture[105] were moving the country in the opposite direction from the hopes of Alison and like-minded critics. There was to be no turning back. Lenman's judgement of the ideas of William Alison is applicable to his brother Archibald as well:

100. Lenman, *Economic History of Scotland*, 162. See also Smout, "The Landowner and the Planned Village."

101. Carson and Idzikowska, "Social Production of Scottish Policing," 296–7.

102. Samuel, "Workshop of the World," 8, 60. See also Berg, Hudson, and Sonenscher, eds., *Manufacture in Town and Country*, esp. chap. 1.

103. Perkin, "Land Reform," 190–1.

104. Dickson (*Scottish Capitalism*, 181, 183) notes that "industrialization in Scotland was in comparison with some regions in England relatively late but at the same time extremely rapid." Economic development benefited from being complementary to developments in England and from the worldwide British market. "After 1830 the Scottish economy became increasingly geared to the manufacture of a highly specialized and intricately related mix of heavy industry products, having complex backward and forward linkages involving many other economic activities."

105. "By 1830 all parts of Scotland, even the more remote, had experienced the effects of the commercialisation of agriculture." Campbell and Devine go on to discuss ("The Rural Experience," 48) three forces which operated to bring about a profound transformation in rural society thereafter: the "decline of older forms of industrial activity in the countryside, which contributed to rural depopulation and reduced the labour available for seasonal and part-time employment in agriculture"; "the advent of new scientific and mechanical ways of agricultural production"; and "the expansion of the market."

In a deep sense, critics like W.P. Alison were out of time with the society they lived in. Victorian Scotland rose to industrial greatness on market economics; a hierarchical social structure, albeit a fluid and flexible one; and a great deal of sheer ruthlessness on the part of its ruling elites. Their achievement was to keep control of a society continually experiencing traumatic economic and social change. They were ruthless with any section of the current elite which refused to accept the often brutal rules of the game of survival.[106]

Politically, Archibald Alison was also "out of time" in his own Conservative Party, the dominant element of which from the 1830s was the Liberal Conservatism of Peel. In the final chapter, we see Alison in the context of nineteenth-century Conservative politics, grappling with the issues of reform, free trade and protectionism, currency, and the church. But first, we consider his other major intellectual project, the *History of Europe*, which was designed to show his contemporaries how easily political reform could usher in revolution.

106. Lenman, *Economic History of Scotland*, 164–5.

5

"Mr. Wordy's History"

Archibald Alison believed that his most important intellectual task was to warn his age of "the consequences of democratic ascendancy upon the civil condition."[1] Alison's analysis of the French Revolution, and his comparison of it with the development of liberty in Britain, provided him with the political framework within which all his subsequent accounts of contemporary politics were set. The ten volumes of the *History of Europe from the Commencement of the French Revolution in 1789 to the Restoration of the Bourbons in 1815* appeared between 1833 and 1842, and this chapter examines the work's genesis, method and influences, and argument. In general, Alison's popular work was informed by the eighteenth-century tradition of philosophical history, although it also showed the marks of the transitional stage of historical scholarship in the early Victorian period.

The first books the young Archibald bought were by historians: David Hume's *History of England*, William Robertson's studies, and the works of Thucydides and Gibbon. In 1818 he began a "course of historical reading." He tells us "Gibbon, Hume, and Robertson's 'Charles V' were read with care for the third time." He preferred Henry Hallam's work on the Middle Ages to the dull "load of antiquarian details" in that writer's constitutional history. In good civic humanist fashion, he read Sismondi's *Italian Republics* and Machiavelli's *Discourses*. Livy, Xenophon, and Herodotus were valued for "the magic of their language" while the most historically instructive passages came from Sallust, Tacitus, and Thucydides. Already the eighteenth-century notion of balance – between reason and passion, entertainment and instruction, antiquari-

1. Alison, *History of Europe*, 1: iii.

anism and philosophical reflection – was present in Alison's approach. It remained a key theme in all his major works.

In 1819 and 1820 Alison's reading concentrated on the Napoleonic wars and the life of Napoleon. He devoured volumes of mainly French accounts of the various campaigns, from which he claimed to have "learned to think for myself on military subjects, and to disregard the supposed limitation of the power of understanding them to military men."[2] It was not until about seven years later that his interest in this period shifted to a more political perspective. Alison claimed that during the serious illness of his brother, which caused him to reflect on providential warnings about one's purpose in life, he happened to read "Clery and Hue's account of the last days of Louis XVI, in the Temple." He was so moved by "these simple and pathetic narratives," and by the contrast of the royal family's "resignation, piety, and charity" with "the malevolence, the infidelity, the cruelty of their persecutors," and so struck by the king's testament as "one of the most perfect commentaries on the Gospel" that:

I resolved to devote myself to the elucidation of the unbounded wickedness, the disastrous results of the French Revolution, and of the angelic virtues displayed by its principal martyrs. This was the first time I had thought of writing the domestic history of that convulsion; my former visions, originating in the great review at Paris in 1814, had related to the military annals of the period.[3]

This decision, couched in terms of a religious conversion – "from the tower of the Temple a light had appeared" – confirmed Alison's ideological stance towards his own time and not incidentally gave him the means by which to become a bestselling author.

The *History* thus had an overt political purpose, which Alison claimed was sharpened at the beginning of the 1830s by his perception of the political and economic state of Britain at the time. He thought "a revolution was approaching in Great Britain," fuelled by what he saw as mistaken expectations of the benefits of rapid social change and by the postwar distress and commercial crisis. A study of the disastrous revolutionary experiment in France might help stem the tide and cause some to reflect on the consequences of hasty "projects of alteration in institutions."

2. Alison, *Some Account*, 1: 178, 181.
3. Ibid., 1: 244–5.

Also, he was anticipating that the 1830 revolution in France would eventually degenerate into violent excess as that of 1789 had done. Beginning in January 1831, *Blackwood's* featured a series of twelve articles by Alison, based on his research for the *History*, drawing parallels between the French revolutions of 1789 and 1830 and the demands for reform in Britain. His original interest in the period, his fascination with battles and military glory, nonetheless persisted: the ten volumes of his *History* primarily comprise accounts of the military campaigns. Alison tried to write popular military history that would not only be "esteemed by military men and admired by the lovers of animated warlike narrative" (as, according to Alison, Napier's *History of the Peninsular War* had been) but would also be found "in the cottage or by the fireside."[4]

Once Alison began to immerse himself in the literature of the revolutionary period, he also started to collect such material; for instance, "the great collection of revolutionary memoirs, published in Paris in sixty-four volumes, which I fell in with and immediately purchased."[5] Yet not only was the number of works on the revolution already immense, many were extremely rare, while others were prohibitively costly: "No small labour and attention, frequent journeys to London and Paris, an ample command of money, and the continued effort of ten or twelve years in reading and buying, seemed requisite to make such a collection." Alison found, as have countless students before and since, that using the public libraries was unsatisfactory, either because the books he wanted were not there or because he could not keep them long enough to use for reference as he wrote. It was a daunting task to ensure the availability of material: "How this was to be accomplished by a professional man, chained to the oar by incessant and laborious avocations, unable to leave home for more than a few weeks in autumn, possessed of no fortune but what he could make at the Bar, and with a rising family, which had entailed heavy life insurances upon him, was not apparent."

Unlike most students, Alison eventually solved his problem by buying his sources. His urge for completeness was, in part, fuelled by insecurity: he feared that "one of the race of critics" would discover an obscure book, pronounce it indispensable, and charge him with neglecting it. By the time he wrote his memoirs, Alison could report with proprietary satisfaction that he was "surrounded ... by a noble library, containing all

4. Ibid., 1: 270. There are echoes here of Gibbon's claim that his *Decline and Fall* "was on every table, and almost on every toilette." : Porter, *Gibbon*, 2.

5. Alison, *Some Account*, 1: 246.

the works of value or interest relating to the revolution and its wars, acquired at a cost of above £4000." As each of the original ten volumes and subsequent editions of the *History* was published, Alison had invested some of the profits in his library.[6]

Alison always expressed a great deal of confidence in his own capacity as an observer of his era and in his assessment of his audience. In November 1830 he sent Blackwood three chapters of his *History* "with a view to future publication." Blackwood was the obvious recipient, "both from former friendship & connection & because the prevailing views in the work are the same as those supported in your magazine." Alison's main purpose in sending the chapters was to suggest a contemporary critique: comparing the French Revolution of 1789 with that of 1830. Besides the *History*, Blackwood's published Alison's criminal law texts, his *Population*, a collection of *Miscellaneous Essays*, his later *History* (post-1815), and a two-volume life of Marlborough. In addition, between 1831 and 1852, *Blackwood's Magazine* (or "Maga," as it was more generally called by its readers) featured 171 articles written by Alison, on topics ranging from contemporary politics and foreign policy to literary criticism. Alison often worked simultaneously on two or even three of these projects.

Alison's long correspondence with his publisher is replete with examples of his very close stewardship of all his works through the process of revisions, corrections, publication, and sales, and includes constant discussion of the arrangement and negotiation of his profits. The Alison-Blackwood correspondence shows in particular Alison's almost obsessive concern with correcting, revising, and reacting to criticisms of his published work; and with the details of optimal publication dates, sales, and financial arrangements. Alison wrote Blackwood several letters in which he proposed a fairly precise timetable for the appearance of the first two volumes of the *History*. He thought the "opening of the first session of the Reformed Parliament" to be politically opportune. Specifically, "I think the work should come out on the 5th March [1833] and be reviewed if you feel inclined in the Magazine of March 1st. This would catch the spring vacation of Edinburgh; and make the work somewhat known before the Easter Holidays of London."[7] Two years later, he thought Christmas or New Year publication was optimal, as it caught

6. Ibid., 1: 261.

7. Alison to Blackwood, 9 November 1832, NLS, Blackwood mss, 4032. Later that month Alison proposed terms for publication: Blackwood was "to be the Proprietor ... for

"the Christmas vacation" in Edinburgh, "when the lawyers are all in town and ... at leisure." Just as importantly, this gave "the London & Provincial Papers a month to have the work" before Parliament sat. Alison even gave his publisher a detailed timetable for the printers:

[September] would be fully late enough to begin to print, if we are to get 1200 pages through hands and cast off by Christmas – To accomplish the object it would be necessary to have arrangements previously made for printing at the Rate of a sheet a day in Each Volume; and both Volumes going on together – In 600 pages there are nearly forty sheets, which would nearly do the two volumes supposing them to go on together in seven weeks, but making allowances for unavoidable delays, the drunkenness of Printers, the time required for throwing off etc it is impossible to calculate on its being done even at that rate in ... three months, which would bring us to the 25 December, just in time to be put in the Binder's hands for the new year.[8]

Alison wrote regularly to Blackwood during the course of the next five years, expressing pleasure at the number of sales – as early as 1835, the second edition was "in hand" which Blackwood intended increasing to 1500 copies – at favourable reviews, especially one by the novelist Frederick Marryat, and at French and German translations. There is some indication in Alison's letters that Blackwood was not entirely happy about the ever increasing size of the work; Alison had to plead that 750 pages was the minimum length of volumes, but that in subsequent editions he could reduce this to 600 pages by making the entire work 10 or 12 volumes.[9] The sheer size of the work, as well as Alison's somewhat plodding style, became a frequent object of amusement in literary circles. The most well-known instance is in Disraeli's 1844 novel, *Coningsby,* which contains a minor character modelled on Alison, named "Mr. Wordy."

---

an Edition of 2000 copies of the first volumes of my History of France."
The terms were:
"1. A Bill for £200 @ 12 months after pubn.
 2. One for £150 @ the same time when 150 are sold off.
 3. One for £150 at the same time when the whole Edition is disposed of."
Later this was changed to a first edition of 1000 copies and a second of 1000: Alison to Blackwood, 30 November 1832, NLS, Blackwood mss, 4032.
  8. Alison to Blackwood, 18 August 1834, NLS, Blackwood mss, 4038. For the growth of the book trade, particularly technological innovation and organization, during the industrial revolution, see Feather, *History of British Publishing,* esp. chaps. 10, 11, 12.
  9. Alison to Blackwood, 30 July 1838, NLS, Blackwood mss, 4046.

Mr. Rigby (modelled on John Wilson Croker) urges Coningsby to read "Mr. Wordy's History of the Late War, in twenty volumes, a capital work, which proves that Providence was on the side of the Tories."[10]

While slogging through his project, Alison was of course also carrying out his duties as sheriff, complaining occasionally of having to dictate a chapter in the evenings "after the fatigues of ten hours Registration on each day," or of being "so much interrupted of late by the combinations here"[11] (in this case the cotton spinners' trial). As well, he was also writing articles for "Maga," trying to keep to his promise of sending one each month.

The spring and summer of 1842 saw Alison pushing to complete his massive work, begrudging time spent in London giving evidence before the Poor Law Commission of the House of Commons as well as official duties in Glasgow. But on the seventh of June he triumphantly wrote to Blackwood that he had "concluded the work altogether this morning at Six; having sat up writing all night."[12] Two days later he described the last hours, in a passage interesting for the view it gives us of his endurance, not to mention his intellectual pretension:

[The] concluding passages were written in [the Sheriff's] office one forenoon, including the whole parallel of Napoleon & Wellington & his Internment at Paris, while I was taking as commissions a long Proof under a Permit from the Court of Session, and when my Pen was stopped every five minutes to decide a disputed point of Evidence, or dictate a contested passage – The last forty-eight pages … to the internment of St. Helena was written at a stretch in Eighteen hours without stopping, and finished at six o'clock on Tuesday morning the 7th June.[13]

How did Alison conceive of his project in terms of both historical method and political perspective? He decided to order the mass of events into distinct categories, as well-defined epochs in the general narrative, rather than chronologically. The anticipated advantage of this method was not only a clearer narrative but also a far higher degree of interest for his audience:

10. Disraeli, *Coningsby*, 110.
11. Alison to Blackwood, 3 July 1838 and 1 November 1838, NLS, Blackwood mss, 4046.
12. Alison to Blackwood, 7 June 1842, ibid., 4058.
13. Alison to Blackwood, 9 June 1842, ibid., 4058.

The great thing complained of by ordinary readers of history is, that it is so dull; ... By classifying the events of the French Revolution in this manner, I early saw that I would gain one inestimable advantage – variety. The record of the civil dissensions would bring into view the great questions which have divided society; and that of the warlike transactions a most astonishing aggregate of naval and military efforts and virtues.[14]

With regard to balancing didacticism and readability or "variety," Alison had "observed how carefully Sir Walter Scott and all great novelists studied the introduction of variety into their compositions; and in Gibbon's Rome had long admired the happiest application of it to the complicated thread of historical narrative." One obvious model for the combination of chronological narration and thematic discussion was Hume's *History of England*. Another model for this procedure which must have been familiar to him was described in his father's memoir of the historian Alexander Tytler. Tytler's system was an amalgam of the narrative and "Didactic" approaches. Tytler, the Reverend Mr. Alison commented, "saw a principle of natural arrangement was afforded him, which might give to his course a sufficient degree of unity and order; and which, while it preserved to the student the interest of historical narration, gave to the teacher the opportunity of exhibiting those general views of the progress of the human race, which form the most important instruction one can derive from its history."[15] Young Archibald Alison, wishing to combine chronology with some degree of didactic arrangement, could well have been influenced by Tytler's system.

The examples of Herodotus, Tacitus, and Gibbon gave Alison the idea of adding a geographical dimension to the historical narrative. History and geography "had been so long and unhappily divorced":

I saw no reason why advantage should not be taken of the revolutionary war to bring under the reader's eye almost all the countries of the world, and enliven the narrative by a description of the most remarkable of them, – stored with part at least of the more accurate statistical information which the laborious researches of later times have accumulated ... My old love of drawing and passion for travelling returned.[16]

14. Alison, *Some Account*, 1: 264–5.
15. The Rev. Archibald Alison, "Memoir of Tytler," 531–2. It should be noted that Tytler thought this method sufficed only for ancient history; for modern history, study of the student's own nation should be the central organizing principle.
16. Alison, *Some Account*, 1: 265–6.

As Alison was writing a book which he hoped would be a bestseller, he needed to enliven the story with colour and drama as well as more "scientific" data. He turned for a rhetorical strategy to Charles James Fox, who had "classed the arts of composition thus: 1, Poetry; 2, History; 3, Oratory." Alison found this appealing and thought that "history, combining as it might the thoughts of the philosopher, the eloquence of the orator, and the descriptions of the poet, was fitted to take a very different place in the arts of composition from that usually assigned to it." Fiction produced by great masters was so fascinating precisely because "it described, with sufficient graphic power, an imaginary scene of existence. Why should not the real portrait equal the interest of the imaginary picture?" There was one important difference between the writing of history in antiquity and in modern times: the former dealt with a greatly simplified subject and could take on the nature of biography, thus "enabl[ing] the historian to clothe his simple and succinct narrative with the colours, as we say, of romance, but in truth fully painted nature." Historical writing could combine "the minuteness of biography and the colours of poetry."[17]

This "artistic" principle could be followed in modern histories by combining the most faithful description of scenes and events with the most vivid language. For example, in describing the activities of the great military commanders Alison tried "to study carefully and minutely the account of them as contained in the best narratives, if possible of eyewitnesses, and having done so, to form a conception of what at certain stages of their progress their appearance must have been, and then describe in as vivid language as I could that conception." Similarly with scenes, "I was careful to adopt, on every occasion where it could possibly be obtained, the images, the incidents, even the sounds and colours which had been seen and described by eyewitnesses of the events." His own travels and visits to the battlefields of Napoleon's victories and the theatre of his campaigns in Italy, France, and Germany made it "easy to clothe well-remembered scenes with the animation and tumult of battle."[18] This aspect of the work certainly impressed Henry Cockburn: "the columns are seen actually moving, and the sound of the guns is heard, and the smell of the powder is felt, in his battles."[19]

17. Ibid., 1: 268.
18. Ibid., 1: 271.
19. Cockburn, *Journal,* 2: 233.

In an article on the historical romance published in *Blackwood's* after
he had completed the *History,* Alison elaborated on this principle. Criticizing the modern tendency towards "naturalism," especially in overly
detailed portrayals of the middle and lower classes (Dickens being the
chief offender in Alison's view), he extolled the historical romance:

[It] unites the learning of the historian with the fancy of the poet; ... discards
from human annals their years of tedium, and brings prominently forward their
eras of interest; ... teaches morality by example, and conveys information by giving pleasure; and ... [by] combining the charms of imagination with the treasures
of research, founds the ideal upon its only solid and durable basis – the real.[20]

In a recent essay on Macaulay and Scott, Mark Phillips suggests that
Macaulay, in many respects a practitioner of the eighteenth-century "exemplar" theory of historical writing which stressed truth and instruction
above all,[21] nonetheless felt a tension and a loss in historical writing that
was otherwise philosophically sound. What was lacking was "vividness."
A "perfect historian," Macaulay claimed: "must possess an imagination
sufficiently powerful to make his narrative affecting and picturesque. Yet
he must control it so absolutely as to content himself with the materials
which he finds." Phillips argues that terms such as "imagination," "affecting," and "picturesque" "are not part of the classical lexicon of the
exemplar theory": "Rather they belong to the literary criticism of the
late eighteenth century, in which a revolution in literary theory had put
feeling and imagination at the centre of art."[22]

Macaulay hoped that the historian could unite accurate representation and vivid instruction. He was uneasy, even fearful of the success of
Scott's historical novels and of the possibility that "fiction had captured

20. Alison, "The Historical Romance," 346.
21. As theorized by, for instance, Hugh Blair, in his *Lectures on Rhetoric*: "As it is the office
of an Orator to persuade, it is that of an Historian to record truth for the instruction of
mankind." This did not necessarily mean an obsession with facts; antiquarians (and Alison
himself makes this point) could trivialize history: "At the same time, it is not every record
of facts, however true, that is entitled to the name of History; but such a record as enables
us to apply the transactions of former ages for our own instruction." Phillips, "Literary Challenge to Historiography," 120.
22. Phillips, "Literary Challenge to Historiography," 121. It may seem to students of
Scottish Enlightenment culture that Phillips is obscuring the extent to which feeling and
imagination were central to Scottish moral philosophy. I think Phillips does tend to draw
too definite a line between the eighteenth-century rhetorical tradition and Romantic liter-

a large part of the historian's traditional territory."[23] Indeed, Scott was praised by his contemporaries for grounding the novel in "actual existences," and Alison's article on the historical romance was full of praise for Scott's achievement.

Alison admired the philosophical historians of the eighteenth century: Hume, Gibbon, Robertson, and Tytler. He was responding to their examples – especially in such discussions about the need to appeal to interest, to give pleasure, to apply the charms of the imagination – as much as he was to the early-nineteenth-century Romantic influence. "The advantages found in history," wrote Hume, "seem to be of three kinds, as it amuses the fancy, as it improves the understanding, as it strengthens virtue."[24] Duncan Forbes describes Hume as a "philosophical" historian:

The scientific or "philosophical" historian relates the behaviour of rulers and statesmen to the nature of the constitution and the laws, or to the absence or imperfection of these restraints. Therefore he must have a knowledge of the progress of civilization and of the degree of knowledge and improvement of the particular epoch or society whose politics he is studying.[25]

Alison himself described the kind of history he favoured as "philosophic" history which drew "from particular facts, the conclusions applicable to all ages." In a review of Horace Walpole's memoirs of George III's reign, Alison lamented that no historian of the eighteenth century had appeared to take up "the mantle of Hume." Such a historian would have a "philosophic mind, to appreciate the effects of the

---

ary theory and practice, restricting the appeal to imagination to the latter. As I suggested in chapter one, the connection between morals and aesthetics was crucial for the Scottish moralists, as was the role of the imagination in directing the active powers of the mind. In Phillips's defence, it is true that the Scottish moralists and the Romantics saw the role of the imagination differently. Engell (*Creative Imagination*, 161) characterizes this as the difference between imagination as "a perceptive and connecting activity" and as "a strictly creative power turning to the arts." The "associationists," including the Reverend Archibald Alison, were in the middle of this transition.

23. Phillips, "Literary Challenge to Historiography," 128.

24. Hume, "On the Study of History," *Essays*, 560.

25. Forbes, *Hume's Philosophical Politics*, 285–6. "Philosophical history" and "conjectural history" were terms employed extensively by eighteenth-century writers. They are sometimes taken to be more or less the same. However, Sher (*Church and University*, 366) makes a distinction between "'conjectural' or 'theoretical' history" and "its less glamorous cousins, antiquarian, controversial, and narrative/philosophical history." Hume and to some extent Robertson practised the latter kind of history.

great convulsions of the preceding century, and an impartial judgement, to discern the causes which were preparing the still more terrible catastrophe of the nineteenth." While Alison wished readers to be able to draw philosophical truths from their reading of history, he thought the two disciplines had separate tasks: "philosophy, though a corollary from history, is not its primary object. That is, and ever must be, the narrative of human events."[26]

Still, Alison envied the way in which the Romantic novelist was not "fettered" by "the prodigious number of details" which "encumbered" the historian. "Selecting for the objects of his piece the most striking characters and moving incidents," the historical novelist "can throw full light upon them and paint the details with that minuteness of finishing which is essential to conjuring up a vivid image in the reader's mind." Alison thought one of the most important requirements of historical fiction was that "its principal interest must be sought in human passion and feeling," and that "description of manners, scenery, dresses, buildings, processions ... and customs" should be digressions only.[27]

Alison, for his part, aimed for an impartial work by presenting characters as neither wholly good nor wholly bad and by basing his work mainly on revolutionary sources: "I had a distrust of party writers on the royalist side, and early perceived that enough was to be found in the undisputed facts of the struggle to condemn the Revolution." Alison was careful "to state no fact for which I could not find authority on the side opposite to that which my own impressions, whether political or national, inclined." He hoped this would prevent the work being dismissed as "a mere rhapsody on the aristocratic side." He was "too old a lawyer not to know the strength of a case depending chiefly on an opponent's testimony."[28] In fact, the Tory *Quarterly Review*, which regularly sniped at the *History*, complained that he did not use original authorities on the royalist side. Alison was pleased with his impartial method:

No one can read [the *History*] without perceiving that its main design is to illustrate the danger of revolutions; and yet I have the satisfaction of thinking that, though it has frequently been censured for being unduly favourable to the popular leaders and not sufficiently minute in its details of the horrors of the Revo-

26. Alison, "British History," 360; Alison, "Tocqueville," 527.
27. Alison, "The Historical Romance," 346, 354.
28. Alison, *Some Account*, 1: 271–2, 258.

lution, it has never yet been stigmatised by the popular party as containing an unfair or exaggerated representation of their principles or actions.[29]

Alison clearly felt that he had established an objective context within which he could feel free to express his own opinions; "those who do not go along with these conclusions, will find in the context the materials for correcting them." He believed that as military and political science, no less than mathematical science, was "progressive" – that is, each age attained a better understanding than the one before it – truth and impartiality could only be achieved if the historian, especially of contemporary events, was fearless in presenting the flaws as well as the achievements of public figures. Historians must be sensitive, Alison warned, to the forces constraining individuals' consciences and actions, especially in times of great turbulence. Relentless criticism of "false principles" must be accompanied by leniency and consideration when judging individual actors.[30] Along with Hume, lesser known eighteenth-century historians such as John Hill and Robert Heron combined an insistence that history improve morality with a concern that the historian be an impartial judge. "Disinterest, but not uninterest" notes David Allan, "was the disposition of the narrator."[31] Colin Kidd suggests that Hume and other eighteenth-century Scottish historians were attempting to correct the English Whig partiality for myth making and to detach "a scientific knowledge of historical processes ... from partisanship and wild libertarian rhetoric."[32]

One of the few historical controversies into which Alison was drawn had to do with his assessment of Wellington. He had suggested that Wellington may have been caught unaware at the outset of the Waterloo campaign. The subsequent complaint from a crusty old soldier that he was belittling "the Illustrious Hero whose exploits it is one main object of my work to commemorate," led Alison into a Humean defence of his historical method:

if I have spoken freely of [Wellington's] Errors as I have done of his Greatness it is because I feel that *Fearlessness* is the first quality of an historian as it is of a General; because I am not the Panegyrist of any Nation or Man but the annalist of

29. Ibid., 1: 259.
30. Alison, *History*, 1: xxi, xxiii.
31. Allan, *Virtue, Learning and the Scottish Enlightenment*, 182n114, 183n116.
32. Kidd, *Subverting Scotland's Past*, 211.

an Epoch in which great & general principles were brought into collision; because I am an independent man working for posterity not the Eulogist of any Party or Individual.[33]

"Mr. Wordy" *was* sure that Providence was on the side of the Tories, but he did not wish to be considered a vulgar propagandist.

Alison's account of the causes of the French Revolution was centred around the development of "freedom." He traced the connection between freedom and the distinction of ranks based on property. On the one hand, England, which was fortunate to develop "middling ranks," was able to pass from barbarism to civilized society gradually and with minimal violence. France, on the other hand, developed no conduit between monarchy and people; consequently, progressive reform was delayed, and when it did come, the "spirit of innovation" could not be kept within civilized bounds. The progress of freedom in the world arose from "the refinements of ancient taste" being "engrafted ... on the energy of barbarian vigour."[34] Both the regulated liberty of England and the democratic excesses of the French Revolution were the result of a long struggle between "high and low, throne and people."[35]

The revolution starkly posed the alternative paths which the spirit of freedom could take: the path of "regulated liberty," as in England, or the path of "democratic oppression," as in France. As catastrophic as the French Revolution was, it did provide a salutary lesson about the weakness of despotism in the face of freedom. Surveying the development of freedom, Alison saw "the efforts of laborious industry to emancipate itself from the yoke of aristocratic power." However, the pendulum had swung too far in the other direction. Modern sympathies were all with "the oppressed" as a reaction against slavery, but the French Revolution revealed how tyrannical the oppressed could be in their democratic frenzy.[36]

As did many contemporary commentators, Alison set out to explain the causes of the French Revolution by making a comparison with England. But while most compared the French Revolution with

33. Alison to James Hall, 25 September 1842, NLS, Blackwood mss, 4058.

34. Alison, *History*, 1: 2.

35. Alison's analysis of the relationship of revolution and liberty occupies a relatively small part of his massive *History*: the first three chapters in the ten-volume 1842 edition, for example. My concern here in this chapter is with this analysis – and not with his descriptions of the military campaigns.

36. Alison, *History*, 1: 41, 42.

England's Glorious Revolution of 1688 because the latter event established England's "matchless constitution," Alison instead drew a comparison with the English revolution of 1642 because he wished to show how England experienced an upheaval similar in several respects to that of France but was able to preserve its liberty.[37] The key factors were the different social structures of the two countries (a consequence of different national trajectories) and their relationship to property.

In the English Civil War the higher classes were represented on both sides, and while the popular party contained a preponderance of those farther down the social scale, the "ranks of Cromwell's bands" were filled with "the sons of the yeomanry." This war, as a consequence, provoked "no massacres or proscriptions ... none of the odious features of a servile war." The French Revolution, in contrast, was not a contest in which members of the natural governing class were found on both sides, "but a universal insurrection of the lower orders against the higher." The storming of the Bastille was the signal for the "bands of authority" to be dissolved and for a "universal invasion of private property." In contrast England's civil war was characterized by moderation on both sides, as the higher orders "guided" the contest. Paradoxically in France, where the government offered no resistance to the revolutionaries, the successes of the democrats "were stained by a degree of cruelty unknown in history."[38]

By comparing the outcomes of the two revolutions, Alison claimed to show the crucial importance of property as a stabilizing influence. In England, even though the rights for which the opponents of the crown had fought were established, "the great features of the constitution remained unchanged." In France, however, the victory of the republicans was followed by "an immediate change of institutions, private rights, and laws." Ominously, the "descent of property" was shifted into a different channel by the abolition of the rights of primogeniture. "The great estates of England," Alison noted, "were little affected; nobles, landowners and yeomanry alike retained their possessions, and under the new form of government [the Commonwealth] the influence of

37. Nicholes does point out, however ("Revolutions Compared," 261–2), that the Romantics tended to favour the Civil War analogy rather than that of 1688: the "English Civil War became a framework of reference throughout the Romantic period for contemporary political events on the Continent and at home." Comparisons were made between the execution of Louis XVI and that of Charles I, and between the "tyrants" Cromwell and Robespierre (later replaced by Napoleon).

38. Alison, *History*, 1: 45–6.

property remained unchanged." In France, all the landed property of the church and of "the greater part of the nobility" was confiscated, a state of affairs whose continuance the Bourbons were compelled to guarantee when restored to the throne in 1815. Alison pointed to a consequence of this: the number of landed proprietors in France was almost equal to the rest of the population and many of them lived in poverty and made no contribution to feeding others. Meanwhile in England, the one-tenth of the population with land fed the rest. This argument surfaced again in Alison's attack on Malthus, *Principles of Population*, as evidence for the capacity of agriculture to sustain a large population.[39]

Politically, the two revolutions bequeathed different class conflicts: in Britain, a manageable conflict between "patricians and plebeians"; in France, a more dangerous cleavage between the crown and the people. This was "a natural consequence of the maintenance of aristocracy in one country and its destruction in another." "Political weight, in the end," Alison concluded in the vein of the utopian writer, James Harrington, "always centres where the greater part of the national property is to be found."[40]

Alison argued that the source of the different revolutionary outcomes lay in the earlier history of the two countries. His explanation of the rise of liberty in Britain centred around the growth of the "middling ranks" and the early development of liberty under the Saxons. The separation of nobles and "plebeians," which Alison claimed led to the destruction of freedom in Europe, was "softened" in England: "The different ranks of society were blended together, by a link descending from the higher, and ultimately resting on the lower orders."

The crucial contest, for Alison, was that between the nobles and the crown. The Wars of the Roses were a watershed: a juncture when the power of the feudal aristocracy "received its final blow" and the "fabric of Gothic power" was destroyed. The consequent Tudor despotism was a "critical period for English liberty." Liberty was saved by the "enthusiasm" of the Reformation, and particularly by the "universal phrenzy" of the Puritans during the reigns of James I and Charles I. Here Alison's analysis was based firmly on that of Hume, for whom, in Nicholas Phillipson's words, the "Matchless Mixed Constitution ... was not the invention of Saxon legislators; it was the work of a party of Puritan zealots whose minds

39. Ibid., 1: 46–7. See above, p. 97.
40. Ibid., 1: 48.

had been shaped by the peculiar political circumstances of the age, and who had little understanding of what they were about."[41] Still, for Alison, the effect of those "ancient liberties and institutions" that he had traced was to ensure that that "universal phrenzy" did not predominate in England. The constitution remained in balance, whereas in Scotland, which had not developed a sturdy middling rank, the "spirit of freedom was wasted in visionary and impracticable schemes," leading invariably to "servitude" and worse (and a forewarning of what was to ensue in France), "the horrors of popular licentiousness."[42]

Thus, the main problem in France was the absence of a viable middling rank which could have counteracted the steadily growing influence of the crown and the nobility. Alison thought the preservation of high aristocratic power perhaps the most important cause of the revolution. The democratic spirit did develop in France, but its occurrence, not being guided in any way by the nobility, issued in "licentiousness" and violence, in events such as the Jacquerie peasant revolt of 1358. The militarization of the nation, which bolstered monarchical absolutism, also revived the military spirit of the common people rather than of the nobility.[43]

Alison's explanation of the causes of the French Revolution, then, focused primarily on the pride of the aristocracy, "based on centuries of exclusive power, and galling in an age of ascending ambition." The "extraordinary character" of the revolution

arose, not from any peculiarities in the disposition of the people, or any faults exclusively owing to the government, but the weight of despotism which had preceded, and the magnitude of the changes which were to follow it. It was distinguished by violence and stained with blood, because it originated chiefly with the labouring classes, and partook of the savage features of a servile revolt; it totally subverted the institutions of the country, because it condensed within a few years the changes which should have taken place in as many centuries; it speedily fell under the direction of the most depraved of the people, because its guidance was early abandoned by the higher to the lower orders; it led to a general spoliation of property, because it was founded on a universal insurrection of the poor against the rich.[44]

41. Phillipson, *Hume*, 90–1.

42. Alison, *History*, 1: 66–9, 72. "Visionary" and "impracticable" were Alison's code words for the effects of Presbyterian enthusiasm. He was to describe Thomas Chalmers in precisely these terms.

43. Ibid., 1: 80–1.

44. Ibid., 1: 98–9.

Alison's explanation combined sociological determinism – certain social structural changes did not occur in France – and psychological reaction – a failure of will and a natural propensity for irrational behaviour in certain circumstances. He was by no means denying that profound changes were needed in French society (whereas Burke believed that the constitutional arrangements of the Ancien Régime were only in need of repair[45]). Anyone observing the condition of the lower orders in France before the revolution would not have been surprised that the upheaval occurred. A revolution never occurs, he noted, "unless grievances affect the great body of the citizens." Once the revolution broke out, "subsequent innovations" were the result of a combination of "expanded wants" and social-psychological reactions such as "restlessness following high excitation," distress caused by suspended credit, and "audacity" arising from the perception of "unpunished crime."

Alison listed sixteen causes of the revolution which can be loosely grouped into socio-economic, political, and moral categories. The socio-economic causes included: the destruction of the power of the nobles and the consolidation of control by the monarchy, with the concomitant "silent" accumulation of wealth by the lower orders; maintenance of the privileges of the nobles; taxation (the exclusion of the privileged orders from the *taille* and the unequal distribution of taxes); the indigent state of the labouring poor; the number of non-resident proprietors (with the result that "no kindly feelings, no common interests, united the landlord and his tenantry" and no "improvement in agriculture" occurred); oppressive feudal services and rights; and the "embarrassment of finances," which Alison thought was "the immediate cause of the Revolution."

Political causes included: abuses in the administration of justice; abuse of the royal prerogative (no consultation with the citizens on any crucial issues); corruption at court ("everything was deranged in the public feeling and manners"); and the "imprudent" involvement in the American War of Independence. Moral causes were: the military spirit of the French people; the freedom of thought and "spirit of investigation" of the Enlightenment, which the monarchy foolishly did not curb; the irrational nature of some of the Catholic Church's tenets, which gave the philosophes carte blanche to attack religion as such; and, finally, what Alison regarded as the "immediate source of the convulsion" – the "spirit of innovation" which had spread "like a malady" over France.[46]

45. Burke, *Reflections*, 85.
46. Alison, *History*, 1: 119ff, 308.

The road to revolution passed the point of no return, in Alison's view, with the restoration of abuses such as the corvée and monopolies after the death of Louis XVI's minister of state, Maurepas, in 1781. The triumph of the Jacobins and the descent into terror, and the return to absolutism under Napoleon, were more or less inevitable, given the earlier refusal of the governing classes to correct the abuses combined with the propensity for irrationality and violence which Alison believed was always unleashed when innovation was attempted too suddenly.

Alison's analysis of the French Revolution was informed by a more general philosophical understanding of the development of liberty, gained especially from his reading of Hume and Smith. Alison closed his discussion of the general causes of the revolution, for instance, with an analysis of the "two great objects of popular ambition": "the love of freedom" and its contrary "the principle of democratic ambition." The former he defined as "immunity from personal restriction, oppression, or injury." Politically, "every concession which is calculated to increase this species of liberty, is comparatively safe in all ages and in all places." The latter, however, included "the desire of exercising the powers of sovereignty, of sharing in the government of the state." This was a dangerous principle because it meant "exercising power without control." The first principle sought to redress existing abuses, while the second aimed at "visionary improvement." In periods of political crisis, a true statesman would remove the "real causes of complaint" but resist giving in to democratic ambition. Jacques Necker's tragedy was that he did not resist.[47]

Alison's two principles recall the two kinds of liberty found in the political science of David Hume and Adam Smith. The true end of government was liberty: in Duncan Forbes's words, "the personal liberty and security of individuals guaranteed by law, equivalent to justice, peace, order, the protection of property, the sanctity of contracts." In Forbes's view, placing this kind of liberty at the centre of their view of government was what made Hume and Smith "sceptical" rather than "vulgar" Whigs. For the latter, "political liberty" referred to the form of government and led them to condemn as unjust and enslaved any state where there was no participation by the people in government. Absolute monarchy therefore was not regarded as a proper form of government.[48] Both Hume and Smith, however, thought that absolute

47. Ibid., 1: 367, 369.
48. Forbes, "Sceptical Whiggism," 184–5.

monarchies were "governments of laws, not men" and that personal liberty could very well exist under them.

Alison's "love of freedom" clearly meant the same as "personal liberty," and his "democratic ambition" came very close to the "political liberty" of the sceptical Whigs. Alison said that the distinction between the love of freedom and democratic ambition "coincides with that ... between *personal* and *political* freedom. It lies at the foundation of all rational discussion on this vital subject."[49] The desire to share in the enactment of laws, if indulged, opened the door to excessive innovation and to terror. In his own day, the Whigs may have been sincere in their benevolence, but their principles led inexorably to a connection between their politics and the politics of Radicals and Chartists.

Alison's brand of nineteenth-century Conservatism and eighteenth-century sceptical Whiggism were connected through the notion of personal liberty. Under the pressure of revolutionary events, Alison was extending the sceptical Whigs' concern about vulgar Whiggish doctrinaire conceptions of liberty into a warning of the consequences of "visionary" political schemes. One of the bulwarks of personal liberty for Alison was the existence of the "middling rank" in society. For Hume, too, this class was the main support of liberty. For instance, in the essay, "Of Refinement in the Arts," he noted that "where luxury nourishes commerce and industry, the peasants, by a proper cultivation of the land, become rich and independent: while the tradesmen and merchants acquire a share of the property, and draw authority and consideration to that middling rank of men, who are the best and firmest basis of public liberty."[50]

In the *Wealth of Nations* and particularly in the *Theory of Moral Sentiments* Smith too made it clear that freedom and stability in society depended on the "natural aristocracy" and on "men in the inferior and middling stations of life." As David McNally suggests, Smith "clearly believed that beneficial social effects were produced by the economic activity of lower- and middle-class people (amongst whom he included at least the bulk of the landed gentry) in commercial society." The presence and prosperity of this group ("by far the greatest part of mankind" said Smith) was conducive to social stability but not necessarily to political virtue or wisdom.[51]

49. Alison, *History* (New York: Harper's 1842), 1: 65n.
50. Hume, *Essays*, 284.
51. Smith, *Wealth of Nations*, 2: 74; McNally, *Political Economy*, 186–7.

Smith worried that the thrust of commercial prosperity might cause men to value their social system more for its utility as a system than for its propensity to promote happiness. In fact this admiration for political systems as such could lead to the mistaken yearning after political innovation for its own sake. The "man of system" became a danger especially in turbulent times. Smith discussed two different principles which could arise from the "love of our country" (principles which bore some resemblance to Alison's "love of freedom" and "democratic ambition"): "first, a certain respect and reverence for that constitution or form of government which is actually established; and secondly, an earnest desire to render the condition of our fellow-citizens as safe, respectable, and happy as we can." In tranquil times, these principles reinforced each other. However, "in times of public discontent, faction, and disorder [they] may draw different ways." Then, "it often requires ... the highest effort of political wisdom to determine when a real patriot ought to support and endeavour to re-establish the authority of the old system, and when he ought to give way to the more daring, but often dangerous spirit of innovation."[52]

That Alison owed at least some of his analysis of reform and revolution to Smith's speculations was illustrated in Alison's attempts to draw parallels between 1789 and 1830 in France, and reform in England, in a series of twelve articles he wrote for *Blackwood's* between January 1831 and January 1832. His main argument was a familiar one: revolutions typically go through stages; the two most important being the moderate stage, in which some needed reforms are achieved, and a more radical stage, in which the spirit of innovation takes command inevitably resulting in violence and terror. He warned that even though the 1830 revolution had so far been bloodless, so had the 1789 revolution for its first three years. The implications for Britain were obvious, but Alison hammered them home anyway. He began one article with a lengthy quotation from Smith on the "spirit of system." While this was Smith's most emphatic warning about the dangers of precipitate innovation, Alison made some passages even more emphatic:

52. Smith, *Theory of Moral Sentiments*, 231–2. The editors of the 1976 edition of this volume note (p. 231n) that Smith was probably referring to the French Revolution in this and succeeding paragraphs; perhaps particularly to the "constitution-makers of 1789, or perhaps to the rationalist philosopher Richard Price." Compare Alison (*History*, 1: 65), wondering who were worse, "the haughty aristocrats, or factious demagogues": the "true patriot is the reverse of both." When "liberty is endangered, he will side with the popular, in moments of agitation, support the monarchical party."

"The leaders of the discontented party *seldom fail to hold out some plausible plan of reformation* ... They often propose ... *to remodel the constitution*, and to *alter, in some of its most essential parts*, that system of government under which the subjects of a great empire have enjoyed ... peace, security, and even glory ... The great body of the people are commonly *intoxicated with the imaginary beauty of this ideal system, of which they have no experience.*"

"One would have imagined," remarked Alison, "that this illustrious philosopher was here portraying the history of the present Reform Bill, instead of calmly reflecting on the effects of public folly in former times."[53]

If Smith and Hume provided Alison with a broad philosophical approach to the development of liberty, Edmund Burke helped him understand the particular relevance of the French Revolution. Alison clearly borrowed freely from Burke's analysis of the development of liberty in England and its subversion in France. Alison, as did Burke, quoted the famous phrase from the Petition of Right, where parliament said to the king: "Your subjects have *inherited* this freedom"[54] and followed it by quoting Burke's eulogy on the British constitution. Alison shared Burke's assessment of the revolution as in large part a consequence of the predominance of men with no propertied stake in the country. So closely did Alison rely on Burke for this analysis that he plagiarized from Burke's account of the social composition of the Constituent Assembly. Burke noted the great number of lawyers; not "distinguished magistrates," but those who were "unlearned, mechanical, merely instrumental members of the profession." "From the moment I read the list," claimed Burke (and this was the one sentence Alison actually acknowledged), "I saw distinctly, and very nearly as it has happened, all that was to follow." As a lawyer, Alison must have felt acutely the way in which his profession could offer up so many cadres to the revolutionary cause. Such bush lawyers had "talent without property, and the desire for distinction without the principles which should regulate it."[55]

Alison was not self-consciously a theorist of revolution, in the way that, say, Tocqueville or Marx was. However, in his explanation of the causes, process, and outcome of the French Revolution, we can see elements of

53. Alison, "On Parliamentary Reform," 745.

54. Alison, *History*, 1: 40. Burke, *Reflections*, 82.

55. Alison, *History*, 1: 70. Burke's assessment of Jacobinism was "the revolt of the enterprising talents of the country against its property": *Reflections*, 95n1.

later sociological models of the causes and the patterns of revolution. A comparison of Alison's analysis with that of Tocqueville must be unkind to the former. Both men aimed to warn their contemporaries of the consequences of unbridled reform, both placed a good deal of the blame on the old French nobility (Alison for its despotism, Tocqueville for its abdication in the face of state centralization), and both noted the role of ideas and irrational moods. However, Tocqueville's analysis was a far more sophisticated *structural* explanation centred around the conflict between the state and its ruling class. It is true that Tocqueville's characterization of the revolution as an unintended consequence of naively benevolent policies could be said to have been foreshadowed by Alison. Also, Alison did suggest that once the revolution had broken out, it was fuelled by rising expectations and inflamed desires. However, this was not the same as Tocqueville's claim that the revolution was a consequence of the improving, reforming policies of the monarchy.[56]

The almost immediate popular success of Alison's *History* was gratifying. From then on, it was a matter of putting out as many printings as the response of the public would indicate were needed. In these reprintings Alison added material from more recent reading and responded to reviews and correspondence. He was quite willing to make changes suggested by reviewers and just plain readers: from Peel and the *Edinburgh Review*[57] to "an extraordinary number of correspondents." Most of the corrections were matters of fact, although even these could become contentious, as in the controversy over whether Alison was belittling the duke of Wellington. In 1844 Alison was forced to postpone a publication deadline because of the "vast additions." You would see, he told Blackwood, "how desirable it was to make such an Effort from the nibbling of [John] Croker in the last Quarterly – which by the bye apply only to the first Edition: the things he complains of as wanting being all supplied in the second & subsequent ones." Alison, in a long letter to Blackwood, detailed all the mistakes Croker had made and all the authorities Alison had used of which Croker "does not seem to have had the least Idea." Alison thought "it would be well to cut up that style of

56. See Tocqueville, *The Old Regime*, pt. 3, chap. 5.
57. Alison was "gratified by the Edinburgh Review of my History – I shall not fail to weigh it anxiously, and correct many things, which require amendment – I consider the Review in the highest degree fair and impartial, and deserving in every point of view of the most respectable consideration." Alison to Blackwood, 18 October 1842, NLS, Blackwood mss, 4058.

reviewing in your magazine; & I could furnish materials for crucifying him as completely as Macaulay did his edition of Johnson."[58]

Always acutely aware of his audience, Alison hoped that his work would appeal to "scholars and men of reflective habits, the chief class on whom in any form we must rely for our sales."[59] But he and Blackwood had their eyes on other classes as well. By 1852, the *History* appeared in a luxury library edition[60] and an octavo "Crown edition" aimed at middle-class readers. Further, why not use the work to help enlighten the working class, now that the Chartist threat was over? Alison wrote that he entirely agreed with Blackwood "that now is the time when the working classes are so comfortable to come out with a people's Edition." Ten thousand copies were printed of an edition "for the use of the working classes."[61] Several months later Alison noted that the sales of the two more expensive editions had "not been materially affected by the publication of the People's Edition." This showed, he claimed, "that the throwing open the one shilling Gallery has not lessened the Sales of the Tickets for the Boxes & Pit."[62]

As well as these attempts to reach all classes with the original *History*, Alison was by 1853 well into the third volume of a new one: *History of Europe from the Fall of Napoleon in 1815 to the Accession of Louis Napoleon in 1852*. This work spoke more directly to contemporary events: he told Blackwood that the third volume should be published "early in May [1854], both as the opening of the London season and as being the very time when to all appearance the Eastern war & the new Reform Bill the very points discussed in the volume will be occupying the public's attention."[63] Blackwood also published an "Epitome," or abridged version, of this eight-volume work "for the use of young persons and to be taught in schools," and an atlas, for which Alison selected the maps and plans from his own collection.[64]

Alison's original *History*, *Miscellaneous Essays* (1850), and *Marlborough* (1852) all sold well in North America. Alison wanted to take advantage

58. Alison to Blackwood, 8 April 1844, ibid., 4068.

59. Alison to Blackwood, 30 May 1846, ibid., 4077.

60. "I am agreeably surprized by the magnitude of the sales, especially of the Library Edition. 302 volumes of so Expensive a work is a most remarkable circumstance." Alison to Blackwood, 22 January 1853, ibid., 4101.

61. Alison to Blackwood, 7 February 1853, and 10 February 1853, ibid., 4101.

62. Alison to Blackwood, 11 July 1853, ibid., 4101.

63. Alison to Blackwood, 9 December 1853, ibid., 4101.

64. Alison, *Some Account*, 1: 553.

of opportunities to be published in the United States but had no control over the conditions of publication because of the lack of an Anglo-American copyright agreement. Blackwood's were understandably wary of involvement in the unregulated American market. Alison's *History* ("entirely published for four dollars") was one of the many cheap re-publications in America in the early 1840s, along with E.L. Bulwer's works, and Dickens' *Martin Chuzzlewit*. American publishers reprinted British works without any advance notice to either author or British publisher. This cavalier approach did not necessarily worry Alison. In February 1843 he reported to Blackwood: "I hear *two* Editions [of the *History of Europe*, probably of the first three volumes] are printed at New York: one by Greenfell at 17/8d. & another by the Harpers in 8vo. I have written to the latter for a copy – I hear also it is translated into German and much read at Dresden."[65] Alison's *History* continued to sell well in the United States. He received a letter confirming this fact in July 1848 from R. Skelton MacKenzie, an American residing in Britain who occasionally served as correspondent to American newspapers. MacKenzie relayed information given him by "a very intelligent American." This person had said that, "of the standard English works, your History has had the largest sale in the United States."[66]

Alison was involved in a brief tug of war with his publisher over copyright. In February 1846 he received notice that the American publishers, Carey and Hart, had sent him a parcel of American editions of his books. He had not yet seen these editions, and he found it was not that easy to do so. He complained to Blackwood that he could not get the books through the customs without "the person appearing as the Holder of the Copyright in the ... Schedule, giving his consent – As your firm appear as such in regard to the first and certainly in regard to the last will you have the kindness to send them on authority."[67]

This experience convinced Alison that he should take steps to secure his proprietorship over his work. He informed Blackwood he wanted a clause inserted in the new edition of the *History* to the effect that the edition was sold to Blackwood but that "the Copyright remains with myself" and that the register entry at Stationer's Hall showing Blackwood as holders of the copyright should be corrected. However, Black-

65. Alison to Blackwood, 13 February 1843, NLS, Blackwood mss, 4063.
66. Barnes, *Authors, Publishers and Politicians*, 275n10; MacKenzie to Alison, 6 July 1848, NLS, Blackwood mss, 4084.
67. Alison to Blackwood, 5 February 1846, NLS, Blackwood mss, 4077.

wood claimed that the exclusive right of publishing future editions had been transferred to them. Alison denied this and, while acknowledging a strong *moral* bond between himself and the publisher, argued that he wanted the copyright vested in him and his heirs and the right to publish successive editions made the subject of successive agreements "as has hitherto been done."[68]

Alison's assertion of proprietorship over the products of his intellectual labour is an illustration of the close connections existing between literary production and entrepreneurial activity. Alison was not a professional author in the sense that, say, Dickens and Trollope were; that is, selling his literary product was not his sole source of income. An older generation, the generation of Scott, looked askance at the notion of a professional writer.[69] Twenty-one years younger than Scott, and twenty years older than Dickens, Alison straddled the divide between the writer as aristocratic client and amateur and the writer as professional. His occupation and main source of income was the law and law enforcement; however, the practice of writing was vital to his being, and he believed it was his task to enlighten his contemporaries (and, Providence willing, posterity) about the problems besetting modern society. He also sincerely believed that belonging to and helping perpetuate the society of manners was a privilege and an obligation. However, this lifestyle was costly and so literary success paid off in another sense.

Contemporary critical opinion of Mr. Wordy's *History* tended to divide along political lines. John Stuart Mill, for instance, grudgingly allowed Alison's attempt to be impartial – "Though a Tory, ... he is most unaffectedly candid and charitable in his judgement." But Mill warned that Alison's was not "that highest impartiality which proceeds from philosophic insight, but abundance of that lower kind which flows from milkiness of disposition." Mill's overall judgement was that "a *more* useless book than this of Mr. Alison's, ... we believe we might go far to seek." It lacked power and "vivacity," dealt only in "general reflections," and was deficient in originality and use of research.[70] The Whig Henry Cockburn took a more balanced view: although "encumbered by tedious disquisitions on matters not pertinent to his proper subject, and on which his opinions are poor ... the narrative is in general spirited ... his char-

68. Alison to Blackwood, 12 February 1846, ibid., 4077.

69. Patten comments (*Charles Dickens and His Publishers*, 10, 11): "An ardent advocate of self-help, Dickens thought that society should reward the author for his labours just as it rewarded the factory hand or navvy for his."

70. Mill, *Collected Works*, 20: 115–16.

acters of individuals are always candid ... his knowledge of the subject is as accurate as historical knowledge derived almost entirely from books and records can ever be."[71] The conservative *Dublin University Magazine* thought Alison's work to be "instructive and interesting," a product of "great research, and a calm, investigating, and comprehensive mind," although one now and then flawed by overly dogmatic dissertations on finance and international law. The reviewer read Alison's main lesson to be a religious one: a warning about "the progress of those passions and propensities which are sure to manifest themselves in corrupt human nature when the restraints of religion are removed."[72]

A modern survey of historical writing on the French Revolution by Hedva Ben-Israel suggests that there was not much difference between Whig and Tory views. Both focused on the development of liberty and its connection to property, and both divided the revolution into two main phases – the early stages were moderate and admirable, the later stages violent and terrible. Both were critical of what they saw as the (mainly French) "fatalist" approach which viewed the revolution as more or less inevitable, prepared for by centuries of French history. English historical writing remained stoutly empirical. There were of course differences between Whigs and Tories. In the early nineteenth century the Whig approach in writing on the revolution stressed more general themes, exhibited some degree of self-contradiction around attitudes to liberty, social order, country, and constitution, and tended to scorn close attention to the gathering of facts. The Tories, as fiercer critics of the revolution, were more or less forced to base their opposition on a "more determined search for facts."[73] The Tories, however, often found the "fatalist" approach fairly convenient, especially between 1830 and 1832. Ben-Israel also suggests that Romanticism barely affected English historical writing, touching it mainly with regard to attention to specific details, the use of colour, immediacy and sympathy, and the attention given to heroes.

Alison's history fits into the general framework sketched above: in its view of liberty and property; in its analysis of the moderate and violent stages of the revolution; in its combination of empirical and "fatalist" approaches; and in its modest flirtation with Romanticism. I find it much more difficult, however, to see, as Ben-Israel does, Alison's history

71. Cockburn, *Journal*, 2: 233-4.
72. "Alison's French Revolution – Conclusion," 583-97.
73. Ben-Israel, *English Historians*, 35.

propounding a new middle-class theory of the revolutions of 1789 and 1830. Under this theory the ultimate achievement of 1789 was the advancement of the middle classes in France, although the revolution had gone off the rails because the middle classes were not strong enough to act on their own and direct it to a safer destination. The 1830 revolution was less threatening precisely because the middle classes were now stronger. Middle-class confidence was above all confidence in education and knowledge: "What could be a more relevant and effective education than that which combined in a history of the French Revolution an orderly view of divine and human affairs in religion and in history? Alison's success was largely due to the fact that he supplied this demand, and embodied in a full-sized history of the French Revolution prevailing middle-class opinions."[74] Alison was, in fact, deeply hostile to middle-class reform and expected the 1830 revolution to progress in much the same manner as its predecessor had done. His approach to historical writing was essentially drawn from the eighteenth century, an approach which traced the importance of the "middling ranks" for social stability and "tempered freedom," but which had no room for the middle class playing the leading role in society.

The fact that Alison was a Scot seems to have played little if any direct role in his historical work. Indeed, his main contrast was between the evolution of liberty in France and in England. One of his few direct references to Scotland was not flattering, as he drew attention to the military successes of the English yeomen, armed with the long bow, over the Scots. This is not to say that there were no Scottish influences in Alison's work. He was deeply influenced by the Enlightenment stadial theory of history. To this extent, Alison can be regarded as having the Anglo-British perspective described by Colin Kidd: "It was within the overall framework of Anglo-British progress established by the sociological whigs, generally accepted within most spheres of Scottish political and cultural life, that Scotland's 'romantic' historical revolution took place. The trend towards understanding the past on its own terms coexisted

74. Ibid., 150. Ben-Israel categorizes Alison, along with Croker, Smyth, and Macaulay, as a member of a group of historians motivated by the agitation over the Reform Bill, seeing it in the context of the two French revolutions of 1789 and 1830. Because they were constrained by this context, she argues that none of this group produced original thought on history. As the title of her book indicates, the fact that Alison was a Scot is of no consequence in her analysis. Yet, as we have seen, Alison's work was deeply influenced by Scottish Enlightenment historiography, if not by Scottish nationalist themes.

with an apparently contradictory stadial history."[75] This perhaps helps explain why Alison did not write a history of his own country. His subject was liberty, the greatest exemplar of which was England; Scotland shared in this glorious tradition by virtue of the Union.[76] However, Alison's relation to Scotland was more complicated than this; he does not fit so easily into an Anglo-British perspective. There were strong elements of Scottish nationalism in his outlook, even if they did not explicitly appear in his *History*. In the final chapter, we see how he participated in the Tory quasi-nationalist defence of traditional pre-Union Scottish institutions.

Alison's *History* seems to have been considered the standard version of the events it described, and he is said to have stolen a march on several other writers, particularly Croker and Mill, who had also been collecting materials for the first full account of the revolution in English.[77] Alison's work competed to some extent with Carlyle's, although they appealed to very different publics. Discussing Carlyle's *The French Revolution*, J.P. Kenyon notes that it is "doubtful if many people went to him for a factual account, and most of them would have already read their 'Alison'." Kenyon adds that Alison's history "apparently dominated" the market. In 1848, Cockburn was "assured by a person who certainly ought to know that including the current new edition, the author has already realised £20,000 ... There seems to be no satiating the public with it ... America devours it."[78]

Kenyon places Macaulay and the Catholic historian, John Lingard, in a transitional phase in historical scholarship: "their working careers spanned the period, roughly 1815 to 1850, during which government archives across Europe were progressively opened to scholars."[79] Alison must be included in this transitional group: he was aware of the importance of sources, although completely dependent on printed ones. The judgement of one modern commentator is that Alison "knew the

75. Kidd, *Subverting Scotland's Past*, 251.

76. "An important reason for the failure of a radical 'nationalism' to develop," argues Kidd (ibid., 250), "was the continued emphasis on the micropolitics of personal freedom to the exclusion of the independence of the national community."

77. Ben-Israel, *English Historians*, 58.

78. Cockburn, *Journal*, 2: 232–3. By 1848, there had already been seven "editions" of the *History*, with two more to come, in 1849 and 1853. The sixth edition (1844) had sold 100,000 copies in the United States by 1848. "I do not believe," Cockburn added, "that any Scotch author ever received so many 'Testimonials' in the form of pieces of plate."

79. Kenyon, *The History Men*, 100, 89.

sources but not how to use them." His real importance was that "he made the first scholarly attempt at a detailed, complete history of the Revolution, putting it in its European setting. He also mastered and surveyed Revolutionary literature." This, and his prodigious historical knowledge, explain the "weight and forcefulness" of his historical illustrations and detailed analogies.[80]

Alison's was the first history of the French Revolution in English. It was a bestseller, coming close to rivalling the popularity of Macaulay's work in Britain and the United States. Alison hoped it would instruct at the same time as it entertained. While not a critical success (although Alison's attempt to be impartial was given some credit), it found its way on to the bookshelves of Tories, military men, and the well-to-do, and perhaps even of some workers. It found its way to Earl Grey's fireside, as he read it aloud to his wife to pass the wintry evenings. It made Alison a well-known author and was to some degree a weapon in the rearguard action against reform.

80. Ben-Israel, *English Historians*, 153, 101.

6

"The Oldest of the Tories"

Alison's work and career, if considered as a whole, covered a wide spectrum of conservative attitudes. As no one has yet written on him at length, he has usually been given a convenient label, depending on the writer's particular preoccupation. Thus, he has been variously designated a "Scottish journalist," a traditional Country Party Tory, a "Tory and a historian with working-class sympathies," or simply a paternalist.[1]

1. Stewart, *Foundation of the Conservative Party*, 70; Berg, *Machinery Question*, 254. Maxine Berg, tracing reactions to the "machinery question," categorizes Alison as one of the *Blackwood's* Country Tories. Within this côterie, she argues, "*Blackwood's* gathered together what almost amounted to a school of anti-political economy: Sir Archibald Alison was its most prolific economic commentator, and Thomas De Quincey its most analytical economist ... Tory economic and social perspectives had ... an intense and ever present anti-industrial and anti-machinery sentiment. Behind all the divisions within Toryism in the period there was one common principle of unity over the machinery issue: none of the groups expressed enthusiasm over technical progress." As noted earlier, Berg is mistaken regarding Alison. While Alison clearly and consistently deplored the effects of manufacturing in general and the division of labour and activities of industrialists in particular, he also as clearly welcomed the improvement and use of machinery: Lenman, *Economic History of Scotland*, 159. Roberts ("Social Conscience of Tory Periodicals") groups together a number of contributors to several Tory magazines under the general label of "tory paternalists." Alison is described as "*Blackwood's* leading social theorist." Roberts's comments about the reviewers' acceptance in practice of political economy's laissez-faire principles, even though they abhorred its "cold and impersonal" character do not apply to Alison. Roberts uses three reviewers' writings to illustrate this point. He notes De Quincey's praise of Ricardo, and Croker's attacks on government intervention. The third witness is Alison, but Roberts's evidence for *his* adherence to laissez faire is skimpy indeed: "Alison, *Blackwood's* leading social theorist, avowed that in his youth 'I took with ... ardour to the study of political economy'." Alison may have taken to studying political economy with ardour in his first years at university, but it was in order to attack its main principles and to emphasize a "social economy" approach which insisted on government intervention for social problems, especially with regard to poor relief.

Although Alison's response to social issues sometimes appeared to be quite radical, this was consistent with a High Tory line on the political questions which dominated legislation and parliamentary debate. His opinions on these issues need to be read in the context established by the previous chapters, which show his conservatism issuing from an eighteenth-century Scottish tradition. The dominant practical theme in his writings was that agriculture was superior to manufacturing – which linked his opposition to "Peel's" currency bill of 1819 to the importance of an established church as well as to reform and protection.

Modern conservatism emerged with the ideological polarization produced by the French Revolution and the radical claims made by its supporters.[2] Before this, attitudes belonging to what James Sack calls the "Right"[3] could be found across a broad spectrum of groups and individuals. Eighteenth-century Whiggism, to the extent that it was ideologically dominant throughout at least the latter part of the century, could itself provide the soil out of which grew nineteenth-century Liberals, Liberal Tories, and High Tories. Often, ideological positions coalesced around political figures such as Pitt, Fox, and (to a lesser extent) Burke. Recent scholarship, especially the work of Sack and Jonathan Clark, has made strong claims for the importance of religion as the defining characteristic of the Right.[4]

Burke made the first systematic statement of reaction to what he saw as the universalizing abstract claims to rebuild society from first principles. Burke "moved eighteenth-century Lockean Whiggism in a Conservative direction,"[5] situating the liberal "free" enterprise system in a traditional, concrete, hierarchical, and Anglican social and political

2. Sack argues (*Jacobite to Conservative*, 255) that British "right-wing" thought did not arise as a response to the French Revolution but rather can be traced to indigenous debates around the consequences of 1688. This seems overstated. Certainly radical and reform support for the French Revolution, at least in its moderate stage, forced conservatives, whether Tory or Whig, to spell out their defence of the established order much more sharply.

3. Sack's decision to use the anachronistic term "Right" for conservatism in order to avoid the ideological quicksand of the late eighteenth and early nineteenth century is useful, but as he failed to define that term very clearly, it loses a good deal of its effectiveness.

4. Clark, *English Society*.

5. O'Gorman, *British Conservatism*, 18. See also: Eccleshall, "English Conservatism as Ideology," and *English Conservatism since the Restoration*; Greenleaf, *British Political Tradition*; Honderich, *Conservatism*; Nisbet, *Conservatism*; O'Sullivan, *Conservatism*; Quinton, *Politics of Imperfection*.

context.[6] While Burke's writings and speeches provided the most all-encompassing response to revolution, he was not alone in defending the British constitution. As Thomas Schofield demonstrates, a variety of conservative tracts appeared in the 1790s in response to radical claims. Their common starting point was to reject "the appeal to reason of the radicals," especially as it concerned the rights of man. Conservatives could produce their own versions of moral and political theories such as natural law and contract theories, also used by radicals, because they distinguished themselves from radicals not by adherence to a particular theory but by "their attitudes towards inequalities of property, rank and power in civil society."[7] Their main concern, in other words, was to deny radicals the use of arguments which gave each person the natural right to determine governance and each society the freedom to design itself anew. Both of these outcomes threatened the security of property and therefore the whole basis of civil society and indeed of civilization. Liberty was not defined as individual autonomy but as secure enjoyment of one's place in a naturally unequal society. Gregory Claeys sees loyalist arguments against the revolution as for the most part uniting Whigs and Tories. He suggests their most successful argument against Thomas Paine and his followers "was the accusation that the Painites sought to undermine the existing system of property."[8]

Nineteenth-century conservatives could not safely assume that the social order was basically sound. Their over-riding practical concern,

6. There are conflicting readings of Burke. An older view sees him championing a "Gothic" or feudal society, where commerce is to be restrained by the ideals of aristocratic chivalry. More recently, Pocock (for one) sees a more modern Burke, defending politeness and commerce: see the introduction to his edition of Burke's *Reflections*. Claeys nevertheless suggests ("French Revolution Debate," 80) that Pocock still "argues that Burke in many ways now feared the growing influence of the middle classes, and in some respects tried to displace the Scottish vindication of their social, economic and cultural position by arguing that both 'modern manners' and commerce owed much to feudal *mores*, and might indeed decay if the latter, their 'natural protecting principles', disappeared." Pocock's interpretation, according to Claeys, seems to support the view "that Burke was less 'liberal' than many loyalists in his emphasis upon the virtues of monarchy and aristocracy rather than the balance of the constitution, and upon Gothic manners rather than manners and commerce together."

7. Schofield, "Conservative Political Thought," 604, 615.

8. "The central and perhaps the most successful loyalist argument deployed against Paine did not concern the danger of extending political participation but the problem of reconciling republican ideals with unequal, and especially modern, commercial societies without destroying their opulence": Claeys, "French Revolution Debate," 75, 74.

therefore, was "deciding how much political and social reform could be accommodated within the mixed or balanced constitution in which Burke had found the key to the English reconciliation of order and liberty."[9] Cobbett, Coleridge, and Carlyle, for instance, advanced differing ways of doing this, utilizing strategies and mechanisms such as populism, the idea of the clerisy, and the cult of the hero, respectively. The various attempts to go beyond Burke resulted in a wide variety of attitudes, and some distinct Tory groups, differentiated by their responses to industrialization, urbanization, and political economy. For instance, for Country Tories, society should remain "aristocratic, community-spirited and religious," and rural.[10] Young Englanders and Tory Radicals were also opposed to the consequences of industrial capitalism, but they refused to follow the Country Tories in pining for rural eighteenth-century society. Both groups tried to work out a scheme whereby capitalists and workers could find a dignified and harmonious co-operation within a humane but deferential system. The Tory Radicals displayed stronger sympathies for labour, and in several respects they were close to Chartist attitudes.[11]

These broad philosophical and social attitudes formed the ideological context for specific issues confronting conservatives in the nineteenth century. In the early part of the century, when conservatism emerged as an identifiable affiliation on the level of practical party politics,[12] positions were taken around such issues as parliamentary reform, Catholic Emancipation, free trade and the Corn Laws, and currency. Here Tories divided into Liberal and Ultra or High camps, depending on how far

9. O'Sullivan, *Conservatism*, 83. Conservatism, as opposed to traditionalism, was self-conscious: "Conservatism is the representation of the gap between the traditional and the political; for conservatism as an ideology is self-conscious. It is a reflection of the fact that the meaning of tradition is no longer self-evident. Conservatism is the political recreation of the meaning of tradition and in doing so puts tradition to work in the struggle of political ideas." Aughey, Jones, and Riches, *Conservative Political Tradition*, 13.

10. Berg, *Machinery Question*, 255. Some commentators have also identified Romantic Toryism as a version of the Country position especially opposed to Enlightenment rationalism and to industrialism. Romantic Toryism proposed the "elevation of the spirit of man and nation set against an idealised version of the past." Its icons were the church, the Middle Ages, and the nobility. Romantic Toryism emphasized feeling over commercial calculation, intuition over reason and science, religion over atheism, and imagination over reality. However, Eastwood, in his recent re-evaluation of Robert Southey ("Robert Southey," 312), believes Romantic Toryism arose from "an intellectual partnership between High Tories and Radicals" around opposition to political economy and hostility to the social consequences of industrialization.

11. Berg, *Machinery Question*, 256.

they were prepared to accept the new political economy and its view of the "free" market. Liberal Toryism became the most important and influential conservative tendency at the level of government from the end of the war under the Liverpool administration until Peel split the party over repeal of the Corn Laws. Many Liberal Tories drifted into the Liberal Party, while the remaining High Tories, including Alison, renamed themselves the Protectionist Party. Hutchison notes that Liberal Toryism did not develop in Scotland, leaving a Scottish Tory Party almost completely opposed to the Reform Bill, and widely reviled as a consequence.[13]

By 1831 when Alison began writing articles on current affairs for *Blackwood's* on a regular basis,[14] the earlier nineteenth-century period of responding to issues by shifting governmental coalitions was coming to an end. The passing of the Reform Bill hardened party organization as well as ideological position. Alison took an unmistakably High Tory and protectionist position. The main consequence of this for his analysis of the political and economic issues of the first three or four decades of the century is that he had difficulty in distinguishing moderate or intermediate political positions. Whether he was writing about the financial policy of 1819 or 1826, or about free trade, Alison drew a hard and fast line between the Tories on one side and Whigs, Radicals, and "democrats" (or "revolutionists") on the other. Peel's "betrayal" on free trade therefore came as a tremendous shock.

Alison's opposition to reform, while extreme, had its roots in eighteenth-century sources – as did so many other facets of his life and thought. As we have noted, his analysis of liberty, which distinguished be-

12. "The word 'Conservative' was first used in the 1820s but its common use in a Tory context dates from 1830–1. Within a few years it had become common usage ... In terms of nomenclature ... the 'Conservative' as opposed to the 'Tory' party appears during the rearguard action against the Reform Act": O'Gorman, *British Conservatism*, 62n23.

13. Hutchison, *Political History of Scotland*, 1.

14. Between January 1831 and February 1855, Alison had 171 articles published in "Maga": Houghton, eds., *Wellesley Index*, vol. 5. Broken down by subject, this total included: British domestic political and social affairs – 67; foreign policy and other nations' affairs – 31; economic policy – 21; articles on literature and the arts, historical and biographical subjects – 39; church and religious affairs – 5; and Scottish society and politics – 3. Alison also had two articles published by the *Edinburgh Review* and one each by the *Dublin University Magazine* and the *Foreign Quarterly Review*. The breakdown of his articles by subject is interesting in light of Berg's characterization of Alison as "*Blackwood's* most prolific economic commentator": he wrote three times as many articles on politics as he did on economic or financial issues.

tween the "love of freedom" and "democratic ambition," was essentially the same as that sceptical Whiggism of Hume and Smith, which distinguished between "personal liberty" and "political liberty." The "love of freedom" and "personal liberty" placed emphasis on the security of individuals guaranteed by law, on order, and on the protection of property rather than on the form of government as such. Undue emphasis on the latter – on "political liberty" or "democratic ambition" – could easily lead to the "love of system" and the desire for wholesale political innovation. For Alison, the desire to share in the enactment of laws, if indulged, opened the door to excessive innovation and to terror. While the Whigs of his own day may have been sincere in their benevolence, he felt their principles led them inevitably to become political bedfellows with Radicals and Chartists.

Alison claimed that the basic principles of a balanced constitution and government were established in the seventeenth century and reinforced in the eighteenth and should not be tampered with. He shared Hume's condemnation of the corruption of Whig oligarchical politics. Applying the principle that "all power which is not systematically watched, will become corrupt," he saw the period of Whig rule as just such an unchecked wielding of power. Alison's version of what was by then a political commonplace – the balanced constitution – required that the "people" keep government honest: "The natural check in a free country upon this corrupt system, into which every constitutional monarchy has a tendency to run, is found in the vigorous opposition and incessant watchfulness of the people. It is this which has been so powerful a restraint upon the abuses of government during the last half century."[15]

During the Whig oligarchy, then, the "two powers, that of the government and the people, usually opposing each other, had come to draw in the same direction, and they raised between them a spring-tide of cor-

15. Alison, "British History," 364. Compare this passage from a sermon of his father (*Sermons*, I, sermon IV, 84): "the voice of the people forms the firmest support of its government; their passions determine the conduct of those who govern them; and it is their wisdom or folly which, in a great measure, marks the character of the international era." Also, Dugald Stewart's argument (*Lectures on Political Economy*, 2: 417) for balancing the power of a "natural aristocracy" by "a *popular assembly*, on the one hand ... and a *single magistrate*, on the other." The main difference between the latter two, as eighteenth-century Whigs, and the nineteenth-century Tory Archibald Alison is that the Alison senior and Stewart were both prepared to allow more of the "people" to "share ... in the enactment of laws" than was Sir Archibald.

ruption, which wellnigh submerged the state." Furthermore, Alison wished to insist that this state of affairs was the inevitable result "of successful revolution." He took this principle from Montesquieu: " 'the most degrading despotisms recorded in history have been those which have immediately followed a successful revolution.' " The rot was stopped and the polity saved by George III and his ministers, especially Lord Bute and Pitt. This, Alison claimed, "was the turning-point of English [*sic*] history":

It, for the first time since the Revolution [of 1688], restored the government to its proper position – it rested it, in its ultimate effects, on property, and put numbers in opposition. This is the only proper basis of good government – for without property ruling there can be no stability in administration; and without numbers watching there is no security against the multiplication of abuses.[16]

What had happened in France after about 1790, and again under Louis-Philippe, and what had been happening in Britain "during the ten years of Whig power which succeeded the downfall of the Tories in 1830" was precisely that the "popular party" – that is, numbers – ruled unchecked. Alison was at pains to point out that his was not a personalist theory of politics; structure determined how individuals would act:

It is not that the popular leaders are worse men, or by nature more inclined to evil, than their Conservative opponents, but that, when they are elevated to power by the result of a revolution or social convulsion, the controlling has become the ruling power; its leaders and followers alike profit by corruption and mal-administration; and therefore there is no longer any possible restraint on abuse. It is not that the Conservative leaders are by nature better men ... than their popular opponents; but that, as the basis of their government is property, which necessarily is vested in comparatively few hands, they are of course opposed and narrowly watched by numbers; and thus are deterred from doing evil, from the dread of its consequences recoiling upon themselves.[17]

One important consequence, from Alison's vantage point, of untrammelled popular power and its attendant corruption – a consequence moreover which Alison noted had been exposed by Burke – was that "the radical vice of parliamentary influence had almost banished talent

16. Alison, "British History," 365, 366.
17. Ibid., 366.

and ability from the public service." It was a large part of Burke's condemnation of the French Revolution that French society, in its financial, legal, and public spheres, had fallen into the hands of mere "enterprising talents." Both Alison and Burke, of course, felt vulnerable to the charge of being simply "enterprising talents." Disinterested public service could be carried out only by those with a propertied stake in the country; by those not dependent upon patronage. For such individuals public and private interest coincided: the "maintenance of tranquillity" together with the "desire to transmit their estates unimpaired to their descendants."[18]

These, then, were the principles which led Alison to warn of the dangers of the Reform Act. Even though "the Act's chief significance was its acknowledgement of urban, middle-class status ... it did not usher in a period of middle-class political ascendancy over, nor even parity with, the landed elite." Not only did the landed élite continue to dominate the House of Commons and the cabinet, the Conservatives, benefiting from superior electoral organization as well as from traditional deference, and in Scotland especially from Whig ineptitude, recovered sufficiently to win the 1841 election, although much less convincingly in Scotland than in England.[19]

Before the bill was passed, Alison had predicted revolutionary consequences for this reform. His immediate response to the act was a message to the Conservative Party to wake up and organize; prescient advice, as it turned out, from the party's "best propagandist."[20] As low as the franchise has been fixed, he argued, "in order to let in the meanest class of householders, in too many places to overwhelm the suffrages of men of education and property, we feel convinced, that almost every

18. Ibid., 366, 367.

19. Hutchison, *Political History of Scotland*, 1–3, 15; Stewart, *Party and Politics*, 22–3; Fry, *Patronage and Principle*, 33. For divergent views on the Reform Act, see: Moore, "The Other Face of Reform," and "Concession or Cure"; Cannon, *Parliamentary Reform*; Gash, *Politics in the Age of Peel*, chap. 1. Mandler (*Aristocratic Government*, 1) argues that instead of a steady progression towards liberalism following the passing of the Reform Act, "England witnessed a reassertion of *aristocratic* power in the 1830s and 1840s." This was partly due to the resistance put up by popular forces to traditional forms of liberalism. A recent article by Phillips and Wetherell ("Great Reform Act of 1832") argues that the act was a "watershed"; that it "quickly destroyed the political system that had prevailed during the long reign of George III and replaced it with an essentially modern electoral system based on rigid partisanship and clearly articulated political principle." This assessment has been challenged, in regard to Cornwall at least, by Jaggard: "Political Behaviour in England's Small Boroughs."

20. Fry, *Patronage and Principle*, 36.

where, except in the large and manufacturing towns, the Conservative party could by proper exertions, still at the next election secure the return."[21] The main target should be "the trading classes" who "think that the reform they have got is to save them from all calamities." But having "cast down the barrier of the aristocracy ... the middling classes will speedily find" their commercial interests were at risk from the revolutionary tempest which the passing of the bill had surely set in motion. Conservatives therefore should sign and publish a declaration to support "only a member of Conservative principles." As well, economic sanctions should be put into effect: the Conservative Party should withdraw their business "from all tradesmen whom they employ who do not support the Conservative candidate."[22]

Alison's call for action was indeed answered, not with an immediate electoral victory, but soon enough. Tory interests, which had been in decline in Scotland since the resignation of Melville over Catholic Emancipation spelled the end of the highly successful "Dundas despotism,"[23] certainly suffered from the Reform Act and indeed remained eclipsed in the burghs. However, if Ferguson is correct, the Scottish Whigs, notably Henry Cockburn, the solicitor-general and Francis Jeffrey, the lord advocate, who boasted that they had obliterated the old system, miscalculated terribly. The Scottish Reform Act, which quantitatively seemed thoroughgoing – the Scottish electorate was increased from 4,239 to 65,000 – is described by Ferguson as "the worst drafted of all the acts which deal with the representation of Scotland." Traditional feudal law retained its importance after 1832, and the possibilities for manipulation of the property qualifications allowed the landed interests, mainly Conservative (but also Liberals such as Gladstone), to perpetuate their power in the counties until the third Reform Act in 1884 made faggot votes illegal.[24]

The importance of Scottish developments for Alison's attitudes and perspective is examined in greater detail below. Here, let us consider Alison's evaluation, made four years after the event, of the effects of the

21. Alison, "Duties of the Conservative Party," 140.

22. Ibid., 140–3. O'Gorman (*British Conservatism*, 131) notes that the suggestions in Alison's article "bore a distinct resemblance to some of the items in [Peel's] Tamworth Manifesto" of 1834.

23. The most recent assessment of the Melvilles, which presents the "Dundas despotism" as producing real political benefits for Scotland, is Fry, *Dundas Despotism*. On Dundas, see also Dwyer and Murdoch, "Paradigms and Politics."

24. Ferguson, "Reform Act (Scotland)," 106, 108ff.

first Reform Act. Democracy in theory, claimed Alison, was a fine-sounding thing. Only when it was put into practice was it discovered that "the popular party are mere men; just as selfish, corrupt, and tyrannically disposed as their aristocratic or monarchical predecessors; [and] government in their hands, even more than in that of their antagonists, requires to be upheld by patronage and influence."[25] This *Blackwood's* article was one of the most polemical and mean-spirited pieces of Alison's political journalism. While never disguising that all his writing (including the *History*) aimed to further the conservative cause, Alison generally tried to maintain a distance from direct political partisanship, striving for a more scholarly, professional disinterestedness (and, no doubt, increased sales). However, this 1836 article betrayed a bitterness and sense of defeat. It also perhaps revealed frustration that the passing of the Reform Act had not brought the revolutionary consequences of which he had been warning and which his understanding of the "laws of nature" told him were inevitable. Still, he thought the consequences deplorable enough and "instances of a law of nature as universal, as irresistible, as that which retains the planets in their course."

His main targets were "the rapacity of the Popish priesthood, and the cupidity of the liberal swarm."[26] The latter accompanied the displacement of legislative talent and wisdom in Parliament, and the proliferation of offices (especially from innumerable commissions, "the vehicle of jobs or party spleen.")[27] Every bill the Whigs introduced for domestic government "swarm[ed] with offices." Municipal and corporate reform seemed most alarming. Too many boroughs had "fallen under the curse of the Penny Rate suffrage"; jobbing and hasty, crude legislation attested that "we have taken filth out of the gutter to perform our ablutions."[28] Property would increasingly come under assault from "the ten-pounders and the two-pounders."[29] Alison could only hope that this might open

25. Alison, "Experience of Democracy," 293.

26. Ibid., 294.

27. Ibid., 303. He thought only one of these had been valuable: the Poor Law Commission.

28. Ibid., 305–6.

29. Fry (*Patronage and Principle*, 34–5) notes that the Conservatives identified the "ten-pounders" – proprietors with the minimum voting qualification, such as smallholders in the countryside and tradesmen or craftsmen in the villages – as their main obstacle to regaining power. The "ten-pounders" were not so easily controlled as tenants could be. Their weight of numbers was overcome, however, by the traditional ploy of creating fictitious votes, a loophole not plugged in the poorly drafted Reform Act.

the eyes of those property-holders who had blindly supported the Whigs. Failing that, only the House of Lords remained as a barrier to democracy; "the *representatives of property, intelligence, and rational thought*" in a nation where in the great towns and in many counties, "property and knowledge are altogether unrepresented."[30]

It was not that Alison did not recognize that change was necessary. He had been extremely critical of the pre-Reform "abuse" of direct election of town councillors "out of members of the same craft which they represented." There was a political principle at stake here: the proper principle of representation in a "popular constitution" was that the "whole body" should be "chosen by the different industrial classes of society." This corporatist model, according to Alison, would have ensured "an ample representation of all the interests in the community." Instead of such a reform, there had in fact been a revolution which "overturned the old and fundamental condition of European society, the representation of classes ... trades [and] professions" and instituted the "*indiscriminate* election of the ten-pounders." Generally speaking, burgh reform seemed to Alison to violate a vital conservative principle of the balanced constitution: "*property was the directing, and numbers the watching and controlling power*."[31]

Alison's assessment ignored the strong elements of continuity in the Reform transition. Irene Maver considers the pre-Reform council of Glasgow to have been a reasonably efficient body, which itself recognized the need for change "to protect community interests." Maver concludes: "For all the legal constraints and lack of public accountability, the Council emerged after 1833 with its reputation and administration relatively intact. Moreover, despite the opening out of the electoral process, many of the personalities from the past did not disappear, but continued to play an influential part in the municipal affairs of Glasgow."[32]

---

30. Alison, "Experience of Democracy," 308.

31. Alison, "Municipal and Corporate Revolution," 967; ibid., 304.

32. Maver, "Guardianship of the Community," 270. See also Sweeney, "Municipal Administration of Glasgow," 829–35. Sweeney notes (p. 830) that "Glasgow's mercantile, manufacturing and industrial elites ... were able to collectively assert themselves against the challenge from the lower middle classes" until the rise of labour in the 1890s. Also, the town council "continued to rank alongside the Chamber of Commerce, trade associations, professional societies and voluntary organizations as an integral part of the elite social structure" (pp. 832–3). This suggests at least an informal version of the corporatist arrangement Alison posited as an ideal.

In Alison's view, the most calamitous effect of the Reform Act was the rise in the number of Irish members of parliament. (He was wrong about this: Irish representation in the House of Commons remained at 100 as set out in the Act of Union of 1801.) Alison's obsession with Ireland and with Catholicism was evident in his *Population*, where comparisons between Scotland and Ireland constantly cast Ireland in a negative light. As did many conservatives, Alison placed some responsibility for the state of Ireland on English oppression and the cupidity of absentee landlords,[33] but simple racism and religious intolerance were just as prominent in his attitude. There was, he had remarked in *Population*, "a defect in vigour or durable resolution in the native Irish race" and a propensity for violence. Alison employed the eighteenth-century stadial theory when he noted that the Irish were still in a barbarous stage and would probably benefit most from a benevolent slavery. Compounding these native defects was Catholicism, which maintained the people in superstition as well as exacerbating the growth of population.[34]

Alison did not write specifically about the Irish in Glasgow during his tenure as sheriff, but clearly he had enough clashes with Irish labourers organized in Ribbon societies and unions to reinforce his stereotype.[35] Although he was a high-ranking Freemason, this did not mean that Sher-

33. "In general, the right-wing press was far more censorious of the Irish Protestant landlord class than it was of the West Indian proprietor class of slave holders": Sack, *Jacobite to Conservative*, 167.

34. Alison, *Population*, 1: 494ff. A revealing glimpse of the private opinions of the Alisons regarding the Irish appears in a letter Alison's son wrote to him in 1849 (Alison to Alison, 2 August 1849, NLS, 4086). Young "Archy" noted that the Irish radical Smith O'Brien "has been completely defeated by 60 policemen, and deserted by his followers. If this really is the case it is a most ridiculous termination to the Irish rebellion. The great efforts of the Celtic are overthrown, not even by a company of Saxon soldiers, but by 60 of their own native police ... I think upon the whole however it will be a pity if it is put down so easily, for Paddy will never be quiet until he has had a good blood letting and been well and completely beat in the field."

35. Heavy post-famine waves of Irish migration to Scotland imposed permanent settlement on older patterns of seasonal migration. In 1841, there were 126,321 of Irish birth in west central Scotland; 5 per cent of the population, 15.93 per cent in Glasgow. By 1851, the number had risen to 207,367; 18 per cent of the Glasgow population. Contemporary perceptions that Irish took jobs from local Scots and that they lowered wage rates were strong, although this has not been definitively proven. Anti-Catholic prejudice did not preclude political co-operation between Scottish radicals and Irish workers. Numbers of Irish were identified as fraternizing with Chartists in Edinburgh, participating in bread riots in Glasgow in 1848, and taking part in Chartist demonstrations in 1849. McFarland, *Protestants First*, 101–2.

iff Alison was therefore lenient towards Orange activities. Demonstrations of any kind were threats to public order, and convicted Protestant Irish were transported as readily as their Catholic counterparts.[36] According to Alison, the two most harmful consequences of the supposed increased Irish representation ("O'Connell's tail") were "the degradation of the standard of manners" in the House of Commons and the appropriation clause, which Alison saw as the beginning of "the systematic transfer of the whole property of the church to the Catholic priesthood."[37]

Alison never came to terms with the Reform Act, and it is surely ironic that the second Reform Act – instituting household suffrage – was passed by a Conservative administration in 1867, the year he died. That the Tories carried this through would not have surprised Alison, as he had long since given up on Peelite Conservatism.

Another strand in Alison's conservatism was his support for the Church of England. His views illustrate both his defence of eighteenth-century social structure and his distance from eighteenth-century scepticism.[38] He believed that the "two greatest" historians of modern times – Hume and Gibbon – had failed to trace the real influence of religion on modern civilization. They were "tainted with the infidel spirit of the age in which they lived, and which worked out its natural and appropriate fruit in the French Revolution."[39] These historians, and "insolent and ungrateful modern liberals" generally, were guilty of an a-historical approach to the past. They applied the "feelings and information" of one age to another. Thus, they could not appreciate the role played by the church in the Middle Ages in protecting the embryonic rule of law and government. Now the established church was under attack from two sides, Catholicism and Dissent.

At stake were the whole interests of society: "the nobility, the throne, the funds, the great estates." The Church of England was "the great bond which unites the higher and the lower orders." It provided those "feelings of mutual sympathy ... perhaps the only ties of affection which, in the present artificial state of society, unite the higher and lower

36. Ibid., 54.
37. Alison, "Experience of Democracy," 299–300.
38. Despite his Enlightenment heritage, Alison seems to have shared an early-nineteenth-century Scottish Tory suspicion of the Enlightenment, certainly to the extent it was identified as a *Whig* Enlightenment. Allan, for instance, notes (*Virtue, Learning and the Scottish Enlightenment*, 17n11) John Gibson Lockhart's *Peter's Letters* as purveying "a scathing conservative critique of the Enlightenment as deviant, decadent and dangerous."
39. Alison, "Attacks on the Church," 731.

orders."[40] In the recent past, the Catholic Relief Bill and the government's commitment to support the training college for Catholic priests at Maynooth,[41] had led inexorably to the Reform Act. Now, "the Revolutionists" were demanding admission of Dissenters to Oxford and Cambridge – "those two noble seminaries" – and Alison raised the spectre of "two rival sets of theologians in one University," and a "public seminary of education" at that.[42] Alison feared the abandonment of state support for religion, for this would mean leaving the people "to choose and pay their own pastors." Human nature was such that, if left alone, people's animal passions would overwhelm their need for spirituality. In a revealing choice of words, Alison concluded that "to apply the principles of free trade and unlimited competition to religious instruction is ... to deliver both poor and rich over to the unrestrained influence of passion, sensuality and wickedness."[43]

Although not a Presbyterian, Alison had a respect for the Church of Scotland as long as it seemed to play the same stabilizing role as the Anglican Church did in England. He was distressed, therefore, by the Disruption of 1843 when those who had long opposed the imposition of ministers on unwilling congregations by patronage appointments (the non-intrusionists) left to form the Free Church of Scotland. Alison interpreted this controversy as an attempt by "fanatics" to "wrest the right of patronage from all the patrons in the kingdom who at present enjoy it." The government and opposition, neither of whom supported the non-intrusionists and neither of whom wanted the conflict to endanger their electoral fortunes, made their last attempts to find legislative solutions to this issue in 1840 and 1841.[44] In an article for *Blackwood's* late in 1840, Alison wrote that as the non-intrusionists intended to "spoliate the patrons of their property without any indemnification" and, what was more, to do this "by a general and obstinate resistance to the law," he could see no difference between their methods and those of the Jacobins and Chartists. Although the Voluntaries were opposed to non-intrusion because its supporters favoured the establishment principle, Alison

40. Ibid., 733.

41. Read, *Peel and the Victorians*, 138–9.

42. Alison had not participated in the debates over university reform in the 1820s and 1830s. In his 1839 article, "Secular and Religious Education," he claimed (p. 279) that education divorced from religious and moral instruction was totally inadequate "to check the progress of crime in the British Islands."

43. Alison, "Attacks on the Church," 734, 738.

44. Machin, "The Disruption and British Politics"; Fry, *Patronage and Principle*, 44–54; Brown and Fry, *Scotland in the Age of the Disruption*.

believed non-intrusion would nevertheless let into the church "the well-known evils of the Voluntary system." Non-intrusion would not long remain just a Scottish issue, he felt sure:

The flame of Church revolution, if it succeeds in consuming the Scotch church establishment, will infallibly spread to and destroy that of England, and thus the leaders of the violent ecclesiastical party in Scotland will have the satisfaction of thinking that they have destroyed the Protestant establishment in both ends of the island, and levelled the last bulwarks in the empire against general revolution.[45]

Alison believed that, in general, patronage was more effective when wielded by one individual, who could clearly be held responsible, thus avoiding the general evasion of responsibility which inevitably occurred in a "promiscuous body, of some hundred or thousand parishioners."[46]

Having linked radical attacks on the established church with free trade, laissez faire, and even revolution, Alison built a case for such a church as the economic foundation of the traditional landed society he wished to see maintained. An established church and the payment of its clergy by means of tithes were not simply aristocratic institutions.

Who pays the clergy in the Established Church? The landowners in the county and the houseowners in towns; that is, the richest classes in both situations. The tithe, apparently paid by the farmer, is in reality defrayed by the landlord. The clergy are in truth, *landed proprietors*, who draw their share of the produce on the condition of furnishing *gratuitous* instruction to the people in the momentous subjects of religion; while the landowner draws the remainder under no such conditions.[47]

Moreover, the clergy were truly tied economically to their locality:

Of all the classes of landed proprietors, the clergy are the one who spend their incomes most directly and immediately among the people of their own vicinity. This is a most important circumstance, especially in an age when the tendency to fly abroad, and forget the anxieties of Britain in the dissipation and luxury of foreign capitals, is so extremely prevalent in the landed proprietors.

45. Alison, "Non-Intrusion Question," 835–6, 841. Ironically, unlike the English Dissenters, the non-intrusionists "clung to the establishment principle, albeit an ideal one reformed according to their views": Machin, "The Disruption and British Politics," 20.
46. Alison, "Non-Intrusion Question," 842.
47. Alison, "Attacks on the Church," 739.

Consequently, "connected as the clergy now are with the landed proprietors, and frequently the aristocracy, by family, university education, and society, and with the poor by duty, proximity of residence, and Christian benevolence, they form a link, binding together the higher and lower orders." Alison gave his argument its final imprimatur with a quotation from Burke: " 'We are resolved to have an Established Church, an Established Monarchy, an Established Aristocracy, and an Established Democracy, each in the degree it exists and no more.' "[48]

Alison would appear to be a prime example of Jonathan Clark's argument that defence of the Anglican establishment was the over-riding obsession of the British ruling class. Actually, Alison wrote very little on the church – only three of his 171 articles for *Blackwood's*. Still, he clearly took it for granted that an established church was the foundation of the traditional order. Clark suggests that the crisis of the old regime was precipitated more immediately by the issue of Catholic Emancipation than by the Reform Act. Emancipation shattered the old order, Reform was a consequence. Whether or not one accepts Clark's broad hypothesis concerning the nature of the English "ancien regime" – and some do not[49] – Alison certainly accepted that Emancipation had opened the door to Reform.

James Sack suggests that conservatives who adopt positions of religious orthodoxy often display a general disposition towards hatred, and against (real or imagined) sexual promiscuity.[50] Alison may have appeared "gentle" to fellow members of the governing class such as Cockburn, but he was certainly a good hater as well: Jacobins, "manufac-

---

48. Ibid., 740, 742.

49. I find Innes's review of Clark's *English Society* (published in *Past and Present*) quite persuasive. Acknowledging that Clark has focused on themes – the role of the nobility, Anglicanism, conservative political philosophy – deserving of greater attention, Innes nonetheless finds his work to be seriously flawed. Methodologically, she has problems with his cavalier dismissal of the work of social historians and his concentration on "high politics" divorced from social and economic context. Substantively, Innes finds Clark's characterization of the eighteenth century as "pre-industrial," and English society as an "aristocratic" "ancien regime," with a "confessional" state, to be static and confining. Corfield ("Georgian England," 14) recently took issue with Clark's "confessional state," pointing out that "England after 1689 was not as dominated by an Anglican hegemony – either in law or in practice" as he implies. "Instead, there was a legal plurality of churches ... long before the changes of 1828–29." Clark's consequent characterization of radicalism as predominantly religious and his account of the fall of the "ancien regime" in 1832 seem similarly too narrowly conceived.

50. Sack, *Jacobite to Conservative*, 38ff.

turing rabble," unscrupulous aristocrats and landlords, and, of course, the Irish, all were regarded with "skunner." Alison was also quite convinced that members of the "lower orders" who had failed to develop civilizing "artificial wants" would inevitably succumb to drink and sexual licence. He seemed to be less prone than some conservatives to accuse Whigs of libertinism. This may have been because he feared a certain disposition in his own character, long suppressed, to prize "in a peculiar manner" "the society of elegant and superior women."[51]

Perhaps the most traumatic political event, after the Reform Act, for conservatives of Alison's stripe was Robert Peel's repeal of the Corn Laws in 1846. This split the Conservatives and led to the formation of the Protectionist Party. Alison found himself even more in the minority than usual over this issue: repeal had much more support in Scotland where agriculture was efficient enough not to need protection. Indeed, Michael Fry claims that "almost the whole country believed [the Corn Laws] ought to be drastically amended, if not abrogated entirely."[52]

Alison had somewhat of a love-hate relationship with Peel. The two were at times in quite close contact, personally and publicly: Alison arranged a public dinner for Peel and entertained him at Possil House. Peel praised Alison's *History*. Alison occasionally sent Peel political and financial information about Scotland.[53] In an overview of Peel written just after his death, Alison saw Peel's career as a thread which joined the key events of the tumultuous quarter-century since the peace of 1815. Peel's strengths, Alison thought, had to do with law and order and security of the empire – the formation of the police force, enactment of the liberal criminal law reforms of Romilly, Mackintosh, and Brougham, standing fast against the Reform Bill, and resolution in foreign policy during the Afghanistan crisis.

Peel's errors, which were all due to his "yielding to the persuasion of his political opponents," were a consequence of the first error: resumption of cash payments,[54] which had led inexorably to reform and to free

---

51. Alison, *Some Account*, 1: 233.

52. Fry, *Patronage and Principle*, 38–9.

53. Milne, "Archibald Alison," 435.

54. In times of war, the government thought it should suspend cash payments so as to save its money to meet the extreme demands of financing a war. It would resume cash payments when peace returned. Cash meant gold bullion. Alison favoured paper currency rather than bullion as a basis for government finances. In the later nineteenth century, "resumption" was viewed as favouring commerce over agriculture, but in 1819 no one really was sure what the effects would be. See Hilton, *Corn, Cash, Commerce*, 48–9, 56–9.

trade: "By vesting power in the moneyed and mercantile classes, through the Reform Act, [Peel's financial policy] brought on that series of class legislative measures, which have gone so far to endanger the colonial empire, and destroy the national independence of Great Britain."[55] Peel's defection to the "Catholic Party" in 1829, however, could not be linked to his monetary and commercial policies; Alison saw it as a surrender to political whim which caused the first crucial schism in Conservative ranks. In the final analysis, Alison put Peel's failures down to his fatal attraction to men of wealth:

He owed his greatness to commercial industry, supported by a protective policy, and an enlarged system of paper credit. But he soon forgot his origin, and was influenced in manhood in his ideas, as most men are, by his *present* position. He had no sympathy with wealth in the process of formation; but the greatest possible with it when completely formed. He was the heir of immense *realised* commercial riches, and he became its representative.[56]

Here was a specific reference to a common theme of Alison's political and economic criticism: his distrust of "formed" commercial wealth ("*realised* commercial riches") as opposed to "wealth in the process of formation." By the latter phrase he seemed to mean wealth being created by the "industrious" sort who had not risen so far above their station as to become a special interest group opposed to the national interest. This attitude harks back to Smith's attacks on mercantile interests – those "dealers" and "underling tradesmen" practising their "sneaking arts" – whose monopolizing power was disproportionate to their place in the economy.[57] Elsewhere, Alison attacked "petty traders" in the publishing business working against the "national interest."

---

55. Alison, "Sir Robert Peel," 362. See also Sack, *Jacobite to Conservative*, 184.

56. Alison, "Sir Robert Peel," 362. On Peel, see Gash, *Sir Robert Peel*, but also Hilton, "Peel: A Reappraisal." Hilton argues that Peel, while politically pragmatic, contrary to most commentators' assessments, was not flexible in his economic views but rigid and dogmatic. This doctrinal rigidity was present as early as the bullionist debate. Alison suggested a consistency to Peel's policies but also saw Peel as very much in thrall to certain financial interests.

57. Smith, *Wealth of Nations*, 1: 267, 493. In his autobiography, Alison notes that of the "three great interests in society" – producers, buyers and sellers, and consumers – the second, the shopkeepers, had interests inimical to the other two groups. The Reform Bill had vested the power of the state in the shopkeepers. *Some Account*, 2: 475.

Politics, religion, and economics – reform, attacks on the church, free trade, and a "fettered" currency – were therefore linked together by Alison as elements of an overall attack on an ordered, hierarchical, and prosperous society. As it became clear to him that the governing class was bent on concessionary reform, he narrowed his focus and took aim at free trade and currency. These two issues became his main obsessions through the 1850s.

Alison's case against free trade and for the Corn Laws was based on his analysis of two relationships: between agriculture and manufacturing; and between different nation-states. He put this case most fully in the final two chapters of *Population* and in a two-part article in *Blackwood's* in February and March of 1844. Proponents of free trade erroneously believed that the same general economic system could be applicable to nations which differed physically, economically, and politically. The reality was not co-operation between nations, all at more or less the same stage, but conflict based on the principle of self-preservation between weaker and stronger nations. England, during the past twenty years, had failed to achieve a system that was of advantage to itself. The abstract principles of free trade were based upon an international division of labour: "Banish all restrictions ... from commerce," said free traders, "let every nation apply itself to that particular branch of industry for which it is adapted by nature, and receive in exchange the produce of other countries, raised in like manner, in conformity with their natural capabilities ... each will enjoy the immense advantage of purchasing the commodities it requires at the cheapest possible rate."[58]

The main problem with this scenario, Alison claimed, was that other nations had not matched England's concessions to co-operation (such as Huskisson's repeal of the Navigation Acts). Instead, Britain had met with "increased determination on the part of the European governments to *resist the system*, and adhere more rigorously to their protecting policy."[59] Moreover, there was a double effect (a "reciprocity of evil"). The manufacturing of the younger nation would suffer a fatal blow, but so would the agriculture of the older state.[60]

58. Alison, "Free Trade and Protection," pt. 1, 260.

59. Ibid., pt. 1, 263; for instance (p. 265): "We have gained nothing by exposing our shipping interest to the ruinous competition of the Baltic vessels. The Danish, Norwegian, and Prussian ships have come into our harbours; but the British cotton and iron goods have not entered theirs. The reciprocity system has been all on one side."

60. Ibid., pt. 2, 386.

Alison's explanation and solution were based on his understanding of Smith's distinction between production in agriculture and in manufacturing in an advanced society. In manufacturing, on the one hand, the application of science, skill, capital, and machinery gave an advanced state a powerful advantage over a younger and "ruder" one, which required "fiscal regulations and heavy duties" to protect its infant manufacturing. On the other hand, relatively small, but efficient, additions to productivity in agriculture were capable "of raising food for the human race to keep far ahead of the wants of mankind." Here the younger state had the advantage over the older, especially with regard to price.[61] Alison's point was that reciprocity between such states was impossible.

Free trade, then, "in such circumstances, must lead to a destruction of important interests, and a total subversion of the balance of society in both the kingdoms subject to it."[62] Free trade was also impossible, in Alison's view, "between two nations, both manufacturing, or aspiring to be so, and in the same, or nearly the same, age and social circumstances." The only feasible policy here was "to conclude treaties, not of reciprocity, but of *commerce*," that is, negotiations which would permit goods in which one side had an advantage to enter the other on favourable terms. Under what circumstances could completely free trade be carried on?:

The only countries to which the reciprocity system is really applicable, are distant states in an early state of civilization, whose natural products are essentially different from our own, and whose stage of advancement is not such as to have made them enter on the career of manufacture, of jealousy, and of tariffs. Colonies unite all these advantages; and it is in them that the real source of our strength, and the only secure markets for our produce, are to be found.[63]

Alison's arguments for protection stemmed from his vision of a society in an advanced state with a balance between agriculture and manufacturing. England, for instance, would gain nothing by drastically increasing the "already colossal amount of its manufactures"; instead "the zone of tall chimneys, sickly faces, brick houses, and crowded jails, which at present spans across the whole of England and part of Scot-

61. Ibid., pt. 2, 386–7.
62. For instance, Alison claimed free trade had ruined the manufacturing interests of India and that it was only the great distance between India and Britain which prevented Indian agricultural production from subverting British farmers. Ibid., pt. 2, 390.
63. Ibid., pt. 1, 268.

land" would be spread even farther. "History tells us in all parts of the world," Alison concluded, "that it is in the *intermixture* of commerce and agriculture that the best security is to be found for social happiness and advancement."[64] Alison's vision was firmly based on his reading of Smith. While it was true, he admitted, that government should protect all branches of a nation's production, in the last analysis agriculture was the most vital sector. Not only did it bring in more to the national treasury, but it was not dependent for its existence on manufactures.

The historical context of Alison's discussion was the eighteenth-century "rich country–poor country" debate. Hume had transformed civic humanist pessimism about the inevitable corruption of wealthy nations into an optimistic free trade position based on the benefits of commercial society and the mutuality of markets.[65] Istvan Hont argues that by the early ninteenth century debate on the determinants of "the riches or poverty of nations ... was conducted in the language of excess accumulation, imperial markets, under-consumption, population growth, the wisdom or otherwise of the export of machinery, and the stationary state."[66]

Alison's concerns related in some way to all these problems. He was unable to share the optimism of Hume and Smith with regard to the beneficial effects of free trade and the mutuality of markets. By the 1830s he could see that the dominant fact of international commerce was the competition from other European nations which refused to cooperate and resisted the reciprocity system. Britain could have perhaps survived this situation if it were not for misguided financial policy which tied currency to gold and so risked the contraction of the currency when gold left the country. Alison put more emphasis on "the jealousy of trade" (in Hume's words) than on the mutuality of markets.

For his solutions Alison, like his political economy opponents, took from Smith what would benefit his own argument. In his case this was the insistence on agriculture as the dominant sector, which led, for Alison, to a need to protect the Corn Laws. Also, he built upon Smith's caveats regarding free trade: that in certain circumstances the "spirit of

64. Ibid., pt. 2, 397.
65. Hume, "Jealousy of Trade," *Essays*, 334. For a more detailed and nuanced discussion, see Hont, "The 'Rich Country–Poor Country' Debate."
66. Hont, "The 'Rich Country–Poor Country' Debate," 315. Hont's conclusion, that "political economy's discussion of the temporality and prospects of commercial society in the language of civic humanism had come to an end," is accurate if he is referring to the relatively narrow Whig political economy. That the language of civic humanism had certainly not disappeared is evident from this study of Archibald Alison.

system" could over-ride "public spirit" and that complete freedom of trade was utopian. As Richard Teichgraeber notes, Smith's political economy disciples, in "their significantly changed economic setting," thought that Smith had "greatly underestimated the strength of his most important argument ... law and government must be servants of economic activity; they must also give the greatest possible freedom to men who engage in trade and manufacturing."[67]

On free trade as on other questions of the applicability of Smith's ideas to the early nineteenth century, Alison tried to rationalize any discrepancy by reference to changing circumstances and to rely on what appeared to be the more timeless and fundamental parts of Smith's work. For Alison, reading Smith through Common Sense spectacles, these were the aspects infused by moral philosophy: the pernicious effects of the division of labour; the danger posed by the "man of System" and the necessity to maintain "public spirit"; and the superiority of agriculture as guardian of virtue, competency, and prudence.

One aspect of Smith's views on the role of the state was particularly agreeable to Alison and reinforced his protectionist notions. This was Smith's claim that defence was more important than concern with wealth, a claim which had led him to support the Navigation Acts.[68] Alison seized on this admission and it formed an important part of his protectionist doctrine. He devoted several pages in his chapter in *Population* entitled "On Colonization and the Reciprocity System" to detailing the ways in which Britain's naval defence had declined as well as the amount of merchant trade lost to foreign shipping. He was still at it in 1859, in his speech to the Glasgow Trades Council.[69]

Not all political economists were at one with Ricardo and Bentham in wishing to see Britain jettison its colonies. In the 1830s, Donald Winch notes, "an entirely new approach to colonies and colonization was put forward by the Colonial Reform Movement under the leadership of Edward Gibbon Wakefield."[70] Interestingly, Wakefield appealed to the

67. Teichgraeber, *"Free Trade" and Moral Philosophy*, 175. Teichgraeber also notes that Smith did not believe that all demands made in the name of free trade required the diminution of the role of the state.

68. Smith, *Wealth of Nations*, 1: 464–5.

69. Alison, *Population*, 2: chap. XV, and *Currency Laws*, 5.

70. See Winch (*Classical Political Economy and Colonies*, 44, 75) on the Ricardian case against colonies: "Colonial trade restrictions stood condemned on free-trade grounds; colonial markets were held to have no effect, beneficial or otherwise, on profits; nor were they necessary for the employment of the surplus capital of the mother country."

authority of Smith, especially the latter's view of the need for new markets to be opened up. Colonization for Wakefield, in Winch's words, "would effect the transfer of British skills and surplus capital to places where supplies of raw materials and food for the British economy could be made available more cheaply. Trade with colonies would also be more secure and less open to the interference of foreign governments."[71] Alison would have agreed wholeheartedly with that last point; indeed, he would have found himself even more in agreement with Wakefield's partner, Colonel Robert Torrens, who opposed unilateral tariff reductions by Britain and expressed fears that foreign governments might turn the terms of trade against Britain by imposing tariffs.[72]

In the end, however, these writers were free traders, and Alison's protectionism was thoroughgoing. He became a member of the Protectionist Party which first emerged in the Commons during the 1846 debate on the bill to repeal the Corn Laws.[73] Two years earlier Alison had told Blackwood of an offer he had received from J.D. Hope of the Agricultural Association of Great Britain "to do something further for them, and allow a Chapter of my Population (I presume the one on the Corn Laws) to be printed as part of [their] Tract."[74] His battle against free trade was lost, however, and his critique of Liberal policies narrowed to an almost exclusive concern with financial policy as the key to national and imperial prosperity. In his embittered old age, Alison became, in effect, a currency crank.

71. Ibid., 88.

72. Ibid., 88.

73. See Stewart, *Politics of Protection.* Alison wrote to Blackwood from London in June 1846: "I was in the House of Commons last night & saw 'justice done to Peel.' It was a somewhat different sight from the Justice done to Wellington when he received the thanks of the same House thirty two years ago." "*Everyone* here," he claimed, "seems rejoicing in Peel's fall." Alison added that he had talked to "a great many of the Protectionist party" who had given him "some very valuable documents ... which I am thinking of making into a paper ..." Alison to Blackwood, June 26 1846, NLS, Blackwood mss, 4077. This became the article on Peel, published in "Maga," September 1850.

74. Alison typically saw opportunities here: "It strikes me that if that Chapter, or rather the principle [*sic*] parts of it were *quoted* in a tract on the Subject giving the references to every quotation & to it were added some parts of the ... papers on Free Trade and Protection *also quoted* they would make a very complete treatise, and that as it will be circulated to a *great extent* among the landed & Conservative Interest it might *bring "Population"* to a great degree into notice & your Magazine also." Alison to Blackwwod, 11 March 1844, NLS, Blackwood mss, 4068.

Writing on financial policy, Alison identified the main issue since the wars as the public debt.[75] The national debt, and public finance generally, was a key focus of the attempts to grapple with the new, and to many, alarming, reality of the British economy during and immediately after the Napoleonic wars. To Alison, the growing size of the debt caused a growing deficiency of revenue. Unfortunately, the two main instruments which could have reversed this decline – indirect taxation and the sinking fund – had been respectively repealed and abandoned. William Pitt, whom Alison admired a great deal, unavoidably needed to borrow during the wars. Unfortunately, he borrowed too much. This error was redeemed by the imposition of indirect taxation on consumption goods and by setting up a sinking fund, the accumulation of which was used to reduce the principal of the debt. Alison calculated that if left alone, the sinking fund would have paid off the debt by 1847.

The standard work on the national debt had been published in 1813 by a Scot, Robert Hamilton, professor of natural philosophy at Marischal College. Hamilton took an opposite view to that which Alison was to adopt several years later. Hamilton denounced the sinking fund as a solution to the debt, claiming that a borrowed fund would in fact increase the size of the debt.[76] Most of the classical political economists followed Hamilton's line. Interestingly, Alison's bête noire, Malthus, *approved* of debt, as it involved "interest payments to the unproductive classes, thus keeping the level of unproductive consumption high" as well as positively affecting capital consumption.

Taxes on consumption (for instance, on malt, leather, tobacco) were the best source of revenue in Alison's view because they were not felt as a burden: "They were so blended with the price of commodities; their weight was so much counteracted by the effect of machinery, and the fall in prices, in consequence of the cessation of the war expenditure, that if they had been kept on, the burden would hardly have been perceptible."[77] Alison was actually close to the position of the political economists on this point, although he was more willing to accept taxes on necessaries than they were. Repealing them would not reduce the price but would instead, claimed Alison (in an argument similar to one he was to make regarding "petty trader" booksellers going against the

75. O'Brien, *Classical Economists*, 264.

76. Hamilton, *Inquiry*.

77. Alison, "British Finances," 612. For a detailed discussion of this issue see Hilton, *Corn, Cash, Commerce*.

"national interest"), enrich the dealers in those commodities "at the national expense." However, repealing direct (assessed) taxes would have "relieved all classes equally." Equally importantly,

by enabling the opulent and middling classes to augment their expenditure, it would have given a great and equal encouragement over the whole country to the industry of the poor. Nothing is so fallacious as the idea, that the only way to relieve the poor, is to diminish taxation on the articles which they individually consume. The true way to relieve them, is to augment the demand for labour, by enabling the rich to increase their expenditure.[78]

The taxation issue remained after the free trade–protectionist battle was over. In the debate over the 1859 Reform Bill, Liberals such as John Bright argued for acceleration of the gradual process by which indirect taxation was being replaced by direct taxation. A year later William Gladstone proposed to abolish the paper duty and add an extra penny to the income tax. Lord Cecil reacted by putting the taxation issue into apocalyptic class terms very much as Alison would have. The incidence of taxation was, Cecil thought,

the vital question of modern politics. It is the field upon which the contending classes of this generation will do battle … The struggle between the English constitution on the one hand, and the democratic forces that are labouring to subvert it on the other, is now, in reality … a struggle between those who have, to keep what they have got, and those who have not, to get it.[79]

Alison attacked the bullionists who, in the face of the diminution of the supply of precious metals from South America, but "driven on" in his view by the Whigs, Radicals, and political economists, contracted the currency. "Peel's" act of 1819, the resumption of cash payments, and the even worse measure of 1826 – prohibiting the circulation of small notes – ruinously reduced the "circulating medium" of England.[80] Thus followed, in Alison's opinion, a fall in prices, enhancement of debts, and the "contraction of enterprise." However, the Scots, whose banking industry was founded on secure paper currency, refused, in the face

78. Alison, "British Finances," 615.
79. Stewart, *Foundation of the Conservative Party*, 355.
80. Alison, "British Finances," 617.

of attacks by the English government and the "English Political Economists," to destroy that industry after the crisis of 1825. As a consequence Scotland prospered while England suffered.[81] Alison believed the political key to this financial mismanagement was the influence of democratic reformers and government's desire to placate popular demands. In such times of crisis, Alison insisted, government expenditure must increase, especially on a standing army.[82]

Evidence that financial policy and its relation to political reform generally remained central to Alison's position comes from a pamphlet published in 1859: *The Currency Laws: Their Effects on the Profits of Trade and Wages of Labour.* This is the text of a speech Alison gave to the Glasgow Council of United Trades. Introduced by Sir John Maxwell, who blamed the privations of the working class on the removal of gold from the country by "the Jew, and foreigner and speculating native," Alison essentially repeated his familiar message about the damage done to the country by contraction of the currency. The interest for the present discussion is the context in which this message is put. Forced to accept free trade – "I am not complaining of free trade. I take free trade as the settled, fixed policy of the country" – Alison now believed the battle to be focused on finances. Currency laws must be made "similar in a certain degree to your corn laws, or the country will be ruined."

Alison's main target was "realised capital," by which he meant the financial classes and speculators, and he was trying to rally other classes against them. It was not a question of labour against capital, he told his working-class audience, "for labour without capital is the steam engine without the coal or fire, but a question of labour, whether exerted on the part of the masses, or of the employer with his active industry, against the case of realised capital, which seeks often to make an unjust profit over both."[83] The working classes, which he believed were "on the verge of a large extension of political power," should be clear about the

81. The financial crisis of 1825 was particularly severe for the Edinburgh speculators: Alison, "British Finances," 618.

82. "Measures of severity must be resorted to; blood must be shed to extinguish the flames which have burst forth during the transports of reform": ibid., 604. Alison was referring to the riots at Bristol, unrest in Ireland, and the slave revolt in Jamaica.

83. Alison, *Currency Laws*, 1. This pamphlet contains Alison's basic argument on currency reform, one he had been making for a number of years. His previous publications in this area were: *England in 1815 and 1845* (1845), which went into three more editions in the next two years (these subsequent editions included "a postscript containing a reply to the observations of ... Sir R. Peel"); and *Free Trade and a Fettered Currency* (1847).

cause of their suffering and the means of its alleviation. The prosperity of the 1850s was caused not by "the wisdom of men" but the good providence of God: the gold discoveries in California and Australia. However, mistaken financial policy jeopardized this prosperity by making currency dependent on the retention of gold.[84] Alison admonished his apparently enthusiastic audience that, while he understood the "evils" which drove workers to strike, and while it was clear that strikes could be successful in times of prosperity, generally strikes hurt the workers far more than the masters. He recommended his audience "not to combine against your master, who is the victim merely of the currency laws, but to combine against the laws which create those great changes in the currency – and you will carry with you the whole of society."[85]

Boyd Hilton provides a useful comparison of the social visions of Liberal Tories and High Tories. Liberal Tories were concerned about commercial speculation but, unlike Samuel Coleridge for instance, they were "less mystical about the State and did not relish intervention."[86] Hilton suggests that:

Their aim in removing protections and monopolies was to strip the economy down to its natural state, based on man's appetite for profit and aversion from loss, on "goading men to be good" through fear of the consequences ... They finished up with a competitive model that in most practical essentials resembled Ricardo's. But whereas the classical economists wanted free trade in order for the economy to grow and avoid the terrors of a stationary state, the Liberal Tories like Liverpool, Huskisson, and Peel, who implemented free trade, really saw society as a stationary, self-acting, and unprogressive model, whose beneficent workings (once human excrescences had been eliminated) would illuminate the wisdom and glory and goodness of its Creator ... "High" and "Liberal" Tories shared the same social and economic vision, which was essentially retrograde, and differed mainly in their methods. Where "Highs" relied on the "spirit

84. Alison, *Currency Laws*, 12–13.

85. Ibid., 15–16. Hutchison ("Glasgow Working-Class Politics," 124–5) notes "a persisting tradition of organised working-class conservatism [in Glasgow] for much of the period between the First Reform Act and the First World War." The Glasgow Conservative Operatives' Association was formed in 1837, and lasted until 1843. In 1869 the Glasgow Workingmen's Conservative Association was established. Hutchison suggests that some of the organization behind these groups came from the middle class.

86. Hilton, *Corn, Cash, Commerce*, 312. Both Coleridge and Liberal Tories could denounce the excesses of the "commercial spirit." However, Coleridge (and no doubt Alison as well) "abhorred the callous Liberal Tory injunction to 'let things find their own level' and wanted to correct the passion for speculative excess by intervention and leadership."

of state," on contacts with the powerful, "Liberals" – who did not have such contacts – rejected "empiricism" for a belief that the economy could be self-acting, mechanical. They moved towards free trade simply as a means to get this static model working without friction. They lacked any mercantilist belief in the power of the state to organise men's lives beneficially.[87]

Discussion of Alison's conservatism would be incomplete without some comparison with Disraeli and Gladstone. British conservatism from the mid-1840s is sometimes described as Disraelian, and it is claimed that Benjamin Disraeli, acting from a social vision formed in the 1840s, led the Conservative Party to seek a reconciliation among classes, particularly between the aristocracy and the working class, and to work for social stability through applying doses of social reform. Disraeli believed, according to Paul Smith, in "a hierarchical paternalistic society, permeated by a sense of social responsibility and held together by a universal nexus of rights and duties, that would secure the contentment and docility of the labouring classes."[88] There is, however, some question about the strength of Disraeli's commitment to this view, especially when political power was at stake. In any case, Smith argues that the "basic theme in modern conservatism ... is not *rapprochement* with the masses in the spirit of the Disraelian ideal, but the assimilation of the bourgeoisie in whose image the modern party is so obviously cast – a process more in accordance with the policy of Peel."[89] P.R. Ghosh notes that the Tory style on social reform during the last few decades of the century stemmed from at least 1868 but was "broadly based, drawing especially on that mass of opinion which had been calling itself Liberal Conservative since the 1830s."[90] The party's emphasis on social reform was always cautious and watered down, and it was focused on those social issues that did not raise the spectre of class conflict. Social reform functioned for the Conservative Party as a vehicle in which to negotiate the rocky road from collapse in 1846 to being the "national" party by the end of the century. Ghosh suggests that "the measure of the success of 'Disraelian' social reform is ... paradoxically, the *absence* of social policy as a central issue before 1900 and the continued primacy of institutional questions in politics."[91]

87. Ibid., 313–14.
88. Smith, *Disraelian Conservatism*, 14–15.
89. Ibid., 3.
90. Ghosh, "Style and Substance," 62.
91. Ibid., 80–1.

A combination of political liberalism and social conservatism can also be said to have characterized the other dominating figure in mid-Victorian politics: William Ewart Gladstone. His basic social vision was of a hierarchical agrarian order. Of all kinds of property, he thought landed property most "'involved kindly and intimate relations between the higher and the lower classes.'" The privileged class must govern in a moral, disinterested way, in the tradition of Christian stewardship. Gladstone thought to bridge the gap between town and country by treating the towns "as if they were not towns at all. He desired to see in them the best features of the hierarchic rural social order: the mutual attachment of classes, the aristocracy recognized and ruling by consent and merit, the achievement of public good by the performance of private duty." Gladstone made his way to Liberalism by seeing the state "as embodying the moral effort of the upper class" as well as representing the nation against special interest groups, whether the great families, business, or labour. His social policy was based on orthodox political economy and "the morality of self-help." That meant, in practice, very little state action at all, and increasingly less as the working class began to flex its political muscles. Conveniently, "the great national overruling subjects" such as foreign policy, took precedence. Gladstone made his mark on government administratively: organizing legislation and managing the party. His main preoccupation, according to John Vincent, was "not to change the unreformed system of politics, but to establish his position in it."[92]

It is striking how closely Alison's fundamental social vision approximated those of Disraeli and Gladstone. The difference seems to have been that the latter were politicians, operating on a national stage. Their world-views could, if necessary, be relegated to the background, as practical politics dictated positions and strategies. Both of them accommodated to reform. Alison, having chosen what he saw as the less compromised callings of law enforcement and social critic, was rarely required to modify or compromise his principles. He never accepted reform. By attacking the harsher extreme of political economy, Alison cut himself off from many – Liberal Tories, Conservative Liberals, and Christian economists – who held the same fundamental agrarian world-view as himself.

92. Vincent, *Formation of the British Liberal Party*, 212–27. Alison thought Gladstone "a third rate Man, the follower of a second rate one [Peel?]. He has not vigour of mind enough to take a decided line but sense enough to see the injustice which his Policy has produced." Alison to Lady Belhaven, 26 February 1850, NLS, 5509, f. 142.

Perhaps the most interesting feature of Alison's conservatism is that his frame of reference was as much Scottish as it was British and on certain issues quite nationalistic. Since the Union of 1707, Scottish independence had been partly preserved through the institutions that were not assimilated: the kirk, the law, and the financial system. Scottish nationalism, in the sense of a movement to reclaim total political control, flickered only fitfully through the eighteenth century and well into the nineteenth. Aristocratic Scottish nationalism disappeared after the rebellion of 45. Both the bourgeoisie, which chose to link their fortunes with England's economic improvement, and the Radical movement (and later the Chartists), which chose to emphasize transnational democratic demands, were unavailable as core groups to mobilize Scottish political independence.[93] Christopher Harvie notes that class and religion cut across or even obscured Scottish nationalism. An "entente between emotive nationalism and effective unionism" had by the late nineteenth century resulted in the impotence of political nationalism. While the lack of a Scottish parliament did contribute to nationalist and devolutionist activity, it also meant the lack of a political and organizational centre for such activity.[94]

In any case, it is debatable what real possibilities there were for Scottish political independence in the late eighteenth and early nineteenth centuries. Michael Fry, in his study of the Dundas dynasty, suggests that Viscount Melville, as an astute political manager, played a major role in raising Scotland from "helpless subordination" to a more balanced relationship with England. Fry implies that this was the only realistic course. Scotland's partnership in the Union, under the guidance of Melville, resulted in an empire that was British, not just English. Patriotism in Britain was appropriated by the Conservatives.[95] However, to the extent that Whigs dominated Scottish public life in the Victorian era, Scottish affairs were decided in London. Fry's "Tory Home Rule" perspective – quite in tune with Alison's by the way – sees the Whigs dismembering Scotland's "semi-independence," eradicating "native traditions in politics and public life." Further, the Disruption, by bringing the church and the law into debilitating conflict, effectively destroyed "the only possible source of a native reforming impulse."[96] This is an overly pessimis-

93. Harvie, *Scotland and Nationalism*, 13–14.
94. Ibid., 40.
95. Fry, *Dundas Despotism*, 308–9.
96. Ibid., 383–4; Fry, *Patronage and Principle*, 54.

tic assessment, in the view of Rosalind Mitchison: a good deal of assimilation was to be expected from long overdue legislation to cope with the consequences of rapid economic and social change. Still (and particularly in those areas Alison knew well), "Scotland retained a distinctive structure of local government; educational reform followed a separate track from the English, and, as ever, the law held to its own structure and court system."[97]

Creation of a national historiography is generally considered to play a vital role in fostering national identity and nationalism. Recent writers on eighteenth- and nineteenth-century Scottish historiography see a broad Anglo-Whig framework obscuring a Scots-British perspective. Colin Kidd and Marinell Ash point to a seemingly paradoxical situation in the early decades of the nineteenth century: a simultaneous rise of interest in the Scottish past (with respect to both an antiquarian unearthing of the past for its own sake, and an attempt to establish a proper system of archives) and "an historical failure of nerve." This was true even for a figure such as Walter Scott. Kidd suggests that while Scott's patriotism did lead him to try to de-mythologize the Scottish past for his contemporaries and to resist the more extreme attempts to impose forms of English law in Scotland, in the final analysis, his was a "deconstructive" project. Scott's adherence to an Anglo-British Whig historiography which stressed the fundamental backwardness of pre-Union Scotland meant that he was not capable of using his vast historical knowledge in the service of an accurate and self-confident account of Scottish independence.[98]

Richard Finlay has recently argued that Kidd and Ash use an overly narrow definition of Scottish nationalism; one which requires independent statehood. What if, Finlay asks, we consider the ways in which Scots in the nineteenth century could "assert their nationality *within* the union" and within the empire. To the extent that they were, or thought they were, successful in doing this, they had no need to create a nationalist historiography which in other European contexts was essential for preserving the concept of nationhood.[99]

Alison's defence of Scottish institutions can be interpreted from this perspective. Examination of his arguments, moreover, points to a close connection between nationalist sentiment and political ideology.

97. Mitchison, "Dundas's Pleasure," 7.
98. Kidd, *Subverting Scotland's Past,* 256ff.; Ash, *Strange Death of Scottish History.*
99. Finlay, "Controlling the Past," 128.

Expressions of Scottish political nationalism (or at least of political an-
glophobia) seem to have become the preserve of Tories. This was, in
part, a reflection of their localist and provincial interests and, if Alison's
case is at all typical of High Tories, the defence of Scottish tradition conveniently bolstered their critique of industrialism. Alison's opinion that
the state had certain social obligations was stronger than it might have
been if he had lived in England. While economic growth was later, more
rapid, and more dislocating in Scotland, the community it affected "was
less well-endowed, more authoritarian and more collectivist than in England."[100] Alison's nationalism, qualified as it was, provided a crucial un-
derpinning for his conservatism.

It was in the mid-1820s that Alison's defence of "Scotch institutions"
first appeared in print as he attempted to combat the imposition of English practices on the Scottish criminal justice system. He expanded his
arguments in four articles which appeared in *Blackwood's* in the 1830s,
although in general there seems to have been a conscious attempt by
Alison, and perhaps by Blackwell, to avoid "provincial" topics in favour
of "national" and international ones.[101] Three of them appeared in the
two years between 1832 and 1834 and were focused on the impact of
reform on Scotland. These articles were crucial to Alison's case not only
against the Reform Bill but against reform as such and for a commercial
agrarian society. Scotland was presented as a model society of the old
type: governed by values of hierarchy and community, yet prosperous
and improving, unshaken by radicalism since the 1790s because, unlike
its southern neighbour, its legal and financial system had been built on
just foundations even before the Union. While it may not have been Alison's primary aim, he was certainly reacting to the nineteenth-century
denigration (fuelled by Enlightenment "sociology") of Scottish pre-
Union tradition and history; to what Kidd calls "the dissolution of Scottish historical confidence in the nineteenth century."[102] Alison was tak-

---

100. Morris, "Scotland, 1830–1914," 4.

101. Thus, Alison introduced a January 1832 article on Scotland by saying: "Destined as
our pages are to carry the conservative principles, and attachment to the constitution, to
the remotest quarters where the English language is spoken in the world, it is with great
reluctance that we mingle with such momentous disquisitions, anything of a local or provincial nature; and our readers must long have perceived, that our pages are, in general, as
free from the details of Scotch transactions as if they were written at Nova Zembla. But while
this is the general rule, there must be some exceptions; occasions on which the conservative
principles themselves call upon us to give publicity, and confer merited celebrity, on patri-
otic services." Alison, "State of Public Feeling in Scotland," 65.

102. Kidd, *Subverting Scotland's Past,* 7.

ing the opportunity afforded by a critique of reform and of the propensity, as he saw it, of Anglo-British Whiggism to flirt with revolution to assert the strengths of traditional Scottish society. Indeed, there was a strong sense in which, for him, local Scottish experience was exemplary.

Alison began an article written at the time of the 1831 elections, one of his series on parliamentary reform and the French Revolution, with a quotation from Lord Liverpool: " 'that there was *no part of the world so well-conditioned as Scotland.*' " Alison agreed. Scotland could boast of an unparalleled rapid progress of wealth, the spread of industriousness, and the comfort of the lower orders. While a military force of 17,000 was needed to pacify Ireland, "hardly 1200 soldiers were stationed in Scotland, whose services were never required but for parade and reviews." Despite the drastic increase of manufacturing, poor rates were nonetheless kept low. "Blessed with an admirable and stable system of paper currency," he concluded,

which her people had the firmness to rescue from the grasp of theoretical politicians – the industry and cultivation of the country had steadily and rapidly increased, even during the years of depression which followed the war; and the tempest which shook the country to its center, passed almost innocuous over the green mountains and fertile valleys of Scotland.[103]

This sketch, containing its share of emotive nationalism, prefaced a long argument against the need for reform in Scotland. The reformers had managed, for the first time since the "Jacobins," to foment class conflict, reviving the "ruinous distinction of Patrician and Plebeian." The "violence of the latter party ... roused by the prospect of political power" had caused "the happy appearance of an united people" to be "exchanged for the melancholy spectacle of one-half of the citizens armed against the other."[104]

The most threatening alliance, in Alison's eyes, was between "some of the great feudal Whig proprietors" ("Highland chieftans [*sic*]") and the "manufacturing rabble" or "democratical party" in the towns. In this, the Whigs had eschewed "their natural friends and supporters, the tenantry of their estates" and had, alarmingly, embraced "the weavers of the

103. Alison, "On Parliamentary Reform," 919.
104. Ibid., 919.

manufacturing towns in the vicinity."[105] At stake here, Alison thought, was the very existence of "the middling and useful orders of society" – "the inferior nobility, the gentry, the merchants, manufacturers, lawyers, higher tradesmen, and farmers."[106] The tenantry understood the consequences of conflict between a landlord and his farmers. They "compare their own condition with that of the English and Irish tenantry – they dread to convert the independent and prosperous Scotch cultivator into the fierce serf of the latter, or the obsequious tenant of the former country."[107]

Independence and prosperity, then, were the key words in Alison's picture of his own society. These terms could be applied not just to the various classes but also to the nation. Alison was concerned to answer the charge (made in this case by Daniel O'Connell, but also representing a clear example of the Anglo-Whig perspective described more recently by Colin Kidd) that "the original institutions of Scotland were the height of human absurdity; a compound of feudal tyranny and savage violence; and that all the prosperity which now distinguishes its surface is to be ascribed to the union with England, and the fortunate tempering of the rigour of its native customs thence arising, by the liberal intermixture of Southern freedom."[108] The proper goal of government according to Alison was civic happiness: facilitating the industry of the people, ensuring that they "enjoy all the freedom consistent with their own welfare, or the general stability of society," and protecting their persons and property. Scotland met this standard, Alison claimed, before the Whig reforms totally obliterated the "ancient Scottish constitution."

Scotland had preserved its territorial independence through three centuries of conflict with England, repulsing twenty invasions from the south; "the splendid chivalry of England ever recoiled in the end from the stubborn spearmen of Scotland."[109] Stung by the charge of the

105. Alison, "State of Public Feeling in Scotland," 65.

106. The "principal farmers" of Berwickshire, for instance, are men "superior to their brethren in any other part of the island in agricultural skill ... who pay an amount of rent which would outweigh the income of an army of radicals, and have received an education equal to that of any body of gentlemen in Great Britain": ibid., 66.

107. Ibid., 66.

108. Alison, "Old Scottish Parliament," 661.

109. Ibid., 662. Interestingly, in his *History*, Alison made much of the English yeomen, whose skill with the bow routed not only the French, but also the Scots, who had only the chivalry of the barons and the spears of the serfs.

Whig lord advocate, Francis Jeffrey, that Scotland had never displayed the spirit of genuine freedom, Alison held up the examples: Scotland's thoroughgoing Reformation, one which moreover, managed to avoid "anything like republican equality in the constitution of its General Assembly"; Scottish efforts for freedom against the Stuarts – it was the Scots who "first took up arms against the despotic authority of Charles I"; the Covenanters who resolutely opposed "the cruelties and severities of Charles II"; and the Scottish parliament which, by the act of 1701, "tied up the most dangerous powers of government" and protected the liberty of the subject more effectively than England's habeas corpus.[110]

In a number of areas, Alison argued, Scottish legislation had been either decidedly superior to, or at least prior to, that of the English. With regard to the tithe question and a proper distribution of church property (a present object of the "democratic party"), the Scottish Act of 1633 had secured an adequate provision for the clergy and settled equitably the valuation and sale of tithes. Granting credit to the attempt of the present administration at Westminster to correct the abuses of the Poor Laws, Alison nevertheless pointed out that they were merely following the example of the Scottish Poor Laws, which for 250 years "have been found equally efficacious in the relief of real suffering, and equally effective in checking the growth of fictitious pauperism."[111] In the area of criminal law, Alison repeated the comments familiar from his pamphlet of 1825 concerning the superior fairness, cheapness, and above all professionalism of the Scottish criminal justice system.[112]

Scotland had also been privileged by its education system. Alison reminded his readers that a universal system of parochial education "admirably connected with the religious institutions of the nation" was put in place in Scotland 140 years before Lord Brougham's desire to found "Universal English Education." Alison was not a believer in the powerful myth that Scottish education was democratic. However, his positive assessment of the educational system did focus on key institutional aspects

110. Alison, "Old Scottish Parliament," 662.
111. Ibid., 663. It will be remembered that one of the main arguments of Alison's *Population*, published only six years after this article, was for state-provided poor relief. The discrepancy in argument could be explained by the worsening economic and social conditions during the latter part of the 1830s and by the fact that, in 1834, Alison moved to Glasgow to take up the office of sheriff-depute and encountered a significantly different social and economic environment, one which caused him to revise his opinion of the adequacy of the Scottish Poor Laws.
112. Alison, "Old Scottish Parliament" 664, 668–9.

of the myth, particularly the ideals of universality and a national system. Further, while Alison was clearly in favour of education as a form of social control, his Scottish milieu provided a more nuanced model than the cruder English version. R.D. Anderson, noting that in Scotland "the belief in popular education took root before fears of the new factory proletariat arose," detects the emergence of "a much subtler idea of social harmony [than in England] based on common schooling or on a controlled upward mobility." This idea could carry an ethic of individual achievement while evoking "a hierarchical, paternalist society innocent of modern ideas of class, bound together ... by relationships of a personal, organic kind." Of course, the traditionalist aspects of this idea had little or no relevance to urban capitalism, but the notion of controlled upward mobility through sacrifice and hard work did, as it fitted nicely with Scots Stoicism.[113] Alison elsewhere described the Scottish education system as peculiarly suited to the middle class "with its fortune to make." However, in the nineteenth century this was a liberal, reforming middle class, not the centrepiece of a paternalist order that Alison had hoped for.

Alison believed that economic legislation had been similarly farsighted in Scotland. Its banking system, "the security of which was completely proved in the great commercial panic of 1825" and which was the foundation of Scotland's present prosperity, had been established before the Union.[114] Alison's assessment of the soundness of the Scottish banks was fair. However, in 1845 Scottish banking was remodelled on the English system, especially the rule that paper issue beyond the level of £3 million had to be covered by gold. "The vigorous expansion of the Scottish banking industry came to an abrupt halt," notes Fry, "to be replaced by a fossilised cartel."[115]

Protection of the "cultivator against the oppression of his landlord" was one of the aims of good government. Alison noted Hume's assessment of the slow progress of freedom in England in this regard. However, in Scotland, he claimed:

full and absolute protection was secured to this most important class four hundred years ago ... This act was so important in its operation, and so effectual in its protection, that Adam Smith remarks, that it is of itself sufficient, by having

113. Anderson, *Education and Opportunity,* 14–15.
114. Alison, "Old Scottish Parliament," 665–6.
115. Fry, *Patronage and Principle,* 55–6.

laid the foundation of *leases*, to account for all the subsequent agricultural prosperity of Scotland.

Alison was not very accurate here. Smith actually concluded that any
good effect of long leases in Scotland had been obscured by entails,
while the fact that leaseholds did not give a vote for Parliament resulted
in the yeomanry being thought "less respectable to their landlords than
in Europe"![116]
  Alison was at pains to point out that he did not wish to denigrate the
beneficial effects of the Union, especially internal peace and the advantages of access to the English market. Nonetheless the benefits of legislation in Scotland, Alison argued, were due almost solely to its own
practice and not to the Union. The recent changes which *were* of English origin – the Reform Act, borough reform, the introduction of trial
by jury in civil cases, and the Judicature Act – Alison clearly regarded as
unnecessary and even harmful.[117] A full explanation of the source of native Scottish wisdom required, in Alison's view, a proper historical account. This had been provided by his friend Patrick Tytler's *History of
Scotland*.[118] Kidd suggests, however, that Tytler failed to challenge the
Anglo-Whig interpretation by providing evidence for the independent
vitality of Scottish noble feudal institutions.[119]
  Alison's defence of Scottish institutions and tradition continued into
the 1850s. He was a sponsor of the National Association for the Vindication of Scottish Rights. The association was formed in May 1853, and its
Address to the People of Scotland set out eight areas in which it was claimed
Scots were either unrepresented or overly controlled by the English gov-
ernment.[120] The *Address* avoided too radical a tone, arguing that the
Union was "'a Legislative Union, but not an Administrative Union'."
Scotland should be allowed its own institutions and "'a national exist-
ence.'"[121] Regardless of how moderate the association tried to be, it was

116. Alison, "Old Scottish Parliament," 666; Smith, *Wealth of Nations*, 1: 392–3.
  117. Alison, "Old Scottish Parliament," 671.
  118. Tytler's was "the only complete History of Scotland worthy of the name which has
yet appeared, written with an antiquary's knowledge and a poet's fire": ibid., 673.
  119. Kidd, *Subverting Scotland's Past*, 273.
  120. The main grievances concerned revenue (it was argued that Scottish revenue was
spent largely in England), administrative centralization in London, inadequate parliamentary representation for Scotland, the weak municipal powers of Scottish burghs, and the
lack of a Scottish secretary of state. Also, Scottish medical degrees were not recognized in
England. Hanham, "Mid-Century Scottish Nationalism," 164–5.
  121. Ibid., 166.

an inherently unstable mix of Conservatives who tended to set the tone, such as Alison, Lord Eglinton, and William Aytoun, and Whigs and Radicals (such as James Begg). The Tories, including Alison, were feeling threatened by what they saw as extremism.[122] By late 1854 the association was in decline; its place taken by single-issue campaigns such as that for erecting a National Wallace Monument.

H.J. Hanham suggests that until the 1850s "Scottish nationalism consisted of an outpouring of emotions about the past rather than of political aspirations for the future."[123] This assumption needs revision. As early as the 1820s, Alison had set out a detailed defence of Scottish law and finance, at a time when nationalism still seemed to be expressed mainly as an emotional and diffuse nostalgia for historical cultural symbols. The kind of arguments Alison was offering at that time seem more in line with products of what Hanham identifies as a more organized movement occurring after 1850, although this later period saw attacks on the Union which Alison could not stomach. Hanham suggests that without a national literature as a foundation, it was extremely difficult for the radical nationalists to build a constituency. Scots generally, he concludes, "wanted the advantages of the Union without its disadvantages."[124] This could be an accurate description of Alison's nationalism. His pride in Scottish legislative achievements and their beneficial social consequences and his indignation at English attempts to impose reforms on Scotland coexisted with his admiration for the British empire and British power.[125] Alison often used the words "national" and "nation" in an organic, but non-ethnic sense: that is, he opposed the

---

122. "We soon found that other more ardent and hot-headed patriots were not content with this object [demanding Scotland's fair share of benefits from the union] but not obscurely aimed at a *dissolution of the Union* as the only remedy likely to be at all effectual to obviate the admitted evils of the present state of things." Alison and Eglinton agreed that the movement "should be allowed to drop, as it soon after was, on occasion of the breaking out of the Crimean war, upon the grounds that 'England's danger was not Scotland's opportunity.'" Alison, *Some Account*, 2: 31.

123. Hanham, "Mid-Century Scottish Nationalism," 147.

124. Ibid., 169–79.

125. When William Burns began a campaign to expose the language commonly used in reference to Scotland, prominent figures, such as Lord Palmerston and Alison, Hanham notes, "were found to be using the word 'England' when they meant 'Great Britain' and 'English' when they meant 'British'." Also under attack – successfully as it turned out because the press generally fell into line – was the use of "Scotch" for "Scottish." Alison certainly used the former term far more than the latter. Ibid., 162.

"national interest" (which could at any one time be British, English, or Scottish) to vested or special interests.

If it is possible, then, to see Alison as providing a more substantial defence of Scottish institutions considerably earlier than hitherto supposed, can we go farther and see Alison mounting a challenge to the Anglo-Whig orthodox interpretation of Scottish history as barbaric? Alison came close to the argument put forward in the sixteenth century by George Buchanan, that liberty was preserved in Scotland by, in Kidd's words, "preserving freedoms against external enemies and of bridling tyrannical kings." Despite his own support for monarchy and his Episcopalianism, Alison was ready to praise the Scots for their resistance to the despotism of the Stuarts in the seventeenth century and for their preservation of individual liberty in the parliament of 1701.

Alison does not, however, easily fit Kidd's Buchananite model. He was strongly influenced by the Scottish Enlightenment, especially the sceptical Whig definition of liberty, and he adopted the Whig stadial theory of progressive historical evolution. This partly explains his acceptance of the British empire as the most advanced social and political framework for Scotland's future. So his contribution was ultimately a frustrating one from a nationalist point of view. His arguments surely added to the stock from which later nationalists drew. However, he wrote relatively little on Scotland and was, in particular, a historian of Europe rather than of Scotland. Further, while a royalist or aristocratic position could very well have been progressive from a nationalist point of view before the eighteenth century, by the nineteenth it was clearly anachronistic. For besides a national literature, and a defence of the history of independence, what was necessary in any vital and enduring nationalist movement (and remains so today) was a strong collective democratic component. But that was a road the High Tory Archibald Alison would not take.

Conclusion

Sir Archibald Alison died on 23 May 1867, the year of the second Reform Act. According to his obituary in *Blackwood's Magazine*, an estimated 100,000 to 150,000 people lined the three-mile route his coffin took from Possil House to the railway station. The obituary also claimed that a good three-quarters of the crowd were workers – particularly mill girls and iron workers – who had given up half a day's work to attend.[1] Even allowing for some exaggeration, this account does suggest that Alison had achieved the kind of power and respectability he had always craved. Whether most of those present saw him simply as an old-fashioned paternalist who had helped keep the region free from "insurrection" and knew little, if anything, of his intellectual endeavours and his wish to be taken seriously as a political philosopher, is impossible to say.

Most of what Alison did and wrote did not survive his passing. In many respects he was a transitional figure in a transitional age, an age grappling with the effects of capitalism and political reform. The ingredients of his Toryism illustrate not only this transitional stage in the evolution of British society, but also the more rapid and dislocating change occurring in Scotland. Alison insisted on the survival of the landed aristocracy, yet criticized its corruption, idleness, and selfishness. The Scottish Enlightenment profoundly influenced his values, but he also regarded its thought as too lacking in respect for religion and God's work. He had respect for commercial wealth and (unlike many High Tories) for the use of machinery, yet he saw commercial groups, especially financial interests, as inimical to the national interest. He was appalled by the suffering of the poor, and did not condemn trade com-

---

1. The obituary is reprinted in Alison, *Some Account*, 2: 528.

binations, yet he sought for the labouring classes only a comfortable material existence, not any share in political power or intellectual achievement. He believed government had an obligation to alleviate social problems yet that it should not direct economic development as such. Alison's attitudes had a certain consistency which came from a combination of his sense of local Scottish experience as exemplary, his overall vision of an agrarian capitalism, and his defence of Anglicanism. However, his conservatism, for all its intensity, seemed rather pedestrian alongside, say, the fierce populism of Cobbett, the powerful myths of Coleridge's clerisy, or Carlyle's heroes.

In his historical writing, Alison looked to the great eighteenth-century philosophical historians for his models, but he also tried to incorporate newer methods such as the use of original sources. Alison's *History of Europe* gave him his contemporary reputation as much as anything save his exploits as sheriff of Lanarkshire. But it did not satisfy him intellectually; it did not give him the recognition as a "political philosopher" that he desired.

As a critic of what he saw as the heartless and calculating methods of political economy, he preferred in his *Principles of Population* a Smithian utopia based on the "middling and useful ranks." Social harmony was to be achieved through a combination of relief and small landholdings for the poor and emigration and transportation for those whom the system could not accommodate. But he also tried to bolster this anachronistic vision with the statistics and analysis of early-nineteenth-century social science. This work was published far too late to have any effect in the Malthus debate. It received a small and predictable response along ideological lines. It is, however, of considerable historical and intellectual interest, as a prime example of a High Tory social vision.

Alison's prolific output as a critic for *Blackwood's* played a not insignificant role in the continued vitality of the right-wing press in the first half of the nineteenth century. The importance of this press (and *Blackwood's* was arguably its most influential journal) lay not so much in its anti-Irish, anti-Catholic, anti-reform, and protectionist aspects as in its continued assault on the social effects of capitalism, urbanization, and the market. James Sack, for instance, argues: "that certain humanitarian and political reforms did occur in nineteenth-century Britain no doubt owes something to their espousal by literary, political and press forces of the Right." However, he also cautions that, no matter how much more profound their diagnoses of social misery were than those offered by utilitarians and liberals, Tory humanitarians had virtually no influence with Tory politicians.[2] Further, Alison's Tory humanitarianism was High not radical. His pity, even sympathy, for the poor never translated into a desire to see any kind of working-class political representation beyond that of "numbers." Alison could not acknowledge that the artisans and labourers from whom he expected great things in the area of moral stoicism were also capable of deciding their own place in the new society which was coming into being all around them. They had more faith than Alison in the capacity of ordinary human beings for creativity and struggle.

Ironically, a work that Alison did not rate so highly in a philosophical sense has survived and remained of practical use to this day: Alison's attempts to improve and rationalize the framework of the Scottish criminal justice system – his *Principles* and *Practice of the Criminal Law of Scotland* – were a solid achievement because they were informed by a depth of knowledge and experience that was not present in his other writing. Most of his work resulted from voluminous but rapid and superficial reading, fuelled by an obsession with the danger of mass politics and revolution. Alison was a practical man who wished to be the intellectual conscience of his age. But it was arguably as a practical man – as lawyer and sheriff – that he made the most impact on his contemporaries.

It could be argued that the most important, indeed the unifying, theme in Alison's intellectual development was that, like eighteenth-century Scottish intellectuals, he lacked any sense of being provincial. Scottish experience was regarded as "exemplary so long as it was rigorously defined against the background of the general historical development which they thought to have uncovered." That development "everywhere revealed itself in the local and particular, so that no special precedence was to be accorded to the metropolitan, to the experience of, say, London or Paris as compared to that of Scotland." Alison too, it could be said, saw the problems of his own Scottish society, and the need to protect its traditions from or adapt them to a rapidly changing world, as exemplary.[3] This indeed was an important aspect of Alison's outlook. However, his perspective was more complicated. Alison did have a sense of being provincial. A clear illustration of this was his prefacing a major defence of Scottish institutions with an apology for introducing "provincial" topics into *Blackwood's*. Further, we should not obscure the British aspects of Alison's outlook, his pride in the power

2. Sack, *Jacobite to Conservative*, 160, 187.
3. I am grateful to an anonymous reader for this argument.

and civilizing mission of the British empire and, especially, his recognition that England was the leading force in that empire. Scotland's local experience may have been representative in many respects, but real power was metropolitan.

While Alison was comfortable in the new world of political parties after 1832, he could not adapt to the new kind of politics this development required. His ideological identification with the landed interest (at least with the "middling" part of it) rendered him incapable of understanding Peel's decision to recognize the claims of industrial property and force the Conservative Party to appeal across a broader spectrum of interests than just landed property. Peelite conservatism most successfully dealt with the question of how conservatism was to adapt to the social changes of the nineteenth century without destroying the old social order. Its solution, especially from the 1850s on, was to eschew social reform and to build some kind of bridge to the middle class. Alison espoused the politics of One Nation, but in the sense of the old constitution under which paternal landed property "represented" commerce and the propertyless. This refusal to bend with the times – to moderate his fierce insistence that under the old constitution, property and liberty were in the best and only possible relationship – effectively denied him an intellectual voice. Disraeli's One Nation, in contrast, was designed to attract the *votes* of the propertyless working class. Political pragmatism and flexibility overcame ideological purity. And met with success.

Had he been able to look into the future, Alison might have been gratified to see the Conservative Party become, in the twentieth century, the normal party of government. But his response would have been half-hearted: *his* party had long ago compromised its fundamental principles on the altar of power. The "oldest of the Tories" would have much preferred to gaze into the past, probably "to many an expedition with the yeomanry by moonlight, with Sir Norman Lockhart, their colonel, riding by my side, and the long line of the Clyde, marked by a white mist along its course, visible in the distance."[4]

4. Alison, *Some Account,* 1: 494.

Bibliography

ARCHIVAL SOURCES

Edinburgh University, Edinburgh
Special Collections

Mitchell Library, Glasgow
Relevant issues of *Glasgow Chronicle, Glasgow Post, Glasgow Saturday Post, Glasgow Saturday Post and Paisley and Renfrewshire Reformer,* and *Scots Times*

National Library of Scotland, Edinburgh (NLS)
Blackwood MSS
Constable Collection

Public Record Office, London (PRO)
Home Office Papers (HO)

Scott Library, York University, Toronto
Northern Star

Scottish Record Office, Edinburgh (SRO)
Lord Advocate's Department Papers

PRINTED SOURCES

Ahmad, Syed. "Adam Smith's Four Invisible Hands." *History of Political Economy* 22 (1990): 137–44.
Alison, The Reverend Archibald. *Essays on Taste.* 2 vols. Edinburgh: Archibald Constable 1790.

– *Sermons, Chiefly on Particular Occasions.* 2 vols. Edinburgh: Archibald Constable 1814 and 1815.

– "Memoir of the Life and Writings of the Honourable Alexander Fraser Tytler, Lord Woodhouselee." *Transactions of the Royal Society of Edinburgh* (1818).

Alison, Sir Archibald. *The Currency Laws, Their Effects on the Profits of Trade and Wages of Labour.* [Edinburgh] 1859.

– *England in 1815 and 1845: or, a Sufficient and a Contracted Currency.* London 1845.

– *Essays, Political, Historical, and Miscellaneous.* 3 vols. Edinburgh: Blackwood 1850.

– *Free Trade and a Fettered Currency.* Edinburgh: Blackwood 1847.

– *History of Europe from the Commencement of the French Revolution in 1789 to the Restoration of the Bourbons in 1815.* 10 vols. Edinburgh: Blackwood 1833–42.

– *History of Europe from the Fall of Napoleon in 1815 to the Accession of Louis Napoleon in 1852.* 8 vols. Edinburgh: Blackwood 1852–9.

– *The Military Life of John, Duke of Marlborough.* Edinburgh: Blackwood 1848.

– *Practice of the Criminal Law of Scotland.* Edinburgh: Blackwood 1833.

– *Principles of the Criminal Law of Scotland.* Edinburgh: Blackwood 1832.

– *Principles of Population and Their Connection with Human Happiness.* 2 vols. Edinburgh: Blackwood 1840.

– *Remarks on the Administration of Criminal Justice in Scotland and the Changes Proposed to be Introduced into It.* Edinburgh: Blackwood 1825.

– *Some Account of My Life and Writings: An Autobiography by the late Sir Archibald Alison.* Edited by Lady Jane Alison. 2 vols. Edinburgh: Blackwood 1883.

– "Attacks on the Church." *Blackwood's Magazine* (May 1834): 731–42.

– "The British Finances." *Blackwood's Magazine* (April 1832): 598–621.

– "British History during the Eighteenth Century." *Blackwood's Magazine* (March 1845): 353–68.

– "The Copyright Question." *Blackwood's Magazine* (January 1842): 107–21.

– "Duties of the Conservative Party." *Blackwood's Magazine* (July 1832): 139–43.

– "Experience of Democracy – The Prospects of the Constitution." *Blackwood's Magazine* (September 1836): 293–303.

– "The Fall of Rome." *Blackwood's Magazine* (June 1846): 693–718.

– "Free Trade and Protection." *Blackwood's Magazine* (February 1844): 259–68; (March 1844): 385–400.

– "The Historical Romance." *Blackwood's Magazine* (September 1845): 341–56.

– "How to Disarm the Chartists." *Blackwood's Magazine* (June 1848): 341–56.

– "The Increase of Crime." *Blackwood's Magazine* (May 1844): 533–45.

– "M. de Tocqueville," *Blackwood's Magazine* (May 1847): 523–40.

– "Municipal and Corporate Revolution." *Blackwood's Magazine* (June 1835): 964–77.

- "The Non-Intrusion Question." *Blackwood's Magazine* (December 1840): 833–42.
- "The Old Scottish Parliament." *Blackwood's Magazine* (November 1834): 661–73.
- "On the Instances in which the Law of England has been Borrowed from that of Scotland." *Scottish Law Magazine and Sheriff Court Reporter* 1 (January 1862): 5–15.
- "On Parliamentary Reform and the French Revolution," Parts I–VI. *Blackwood's Magazine* (January 1831–June 1831).
- "Policy of the Protectionists." *Blackwood's Magazine* (June 1852): 643–68.
- "Practical Workings of Trades' Unions." *Blackwood's Magazine* (March 1838): 281–303.
- "Restoration of the Parthenon." *Edinburgh Review* (February 1823): 126–44.
- "Secular and Religious Education." *Blackwood's Magazine* (February 1839): 275–86.
- "Sir Robert Peel." *Blackwood's Magazine* (September 1850): 354–72.
- "Social and Moral Condition of the Manufacturing Districts in Scotland." *Blackwood's Magazine* (November 1841): 659–73.
- "State of Public Feeling in Scotland." *Blackwood's Magazine* (January 1832): 65–76.
- "The Transportation Question." *Blackwood's Magazine* (November 1849): 517–37.

Alison, William Pulteney. *Further Illustrations of the Practical Operation of the Scotch System of Management of the Poor etc.* London 1842.
- *Observations on the Famine of 1846–7 in the Highlands of Scotland and in Ireland, as Illustrating the Connection of the Principle of Population with the Management of the Poor.* Edinburgh 1847.
- *Observations on the Management of the Poor in Scotland, and its Effects on the Health of the Great Towns.* Edinburgh 1840.
- *Observations on the Reclamation of Waste Lands and Their Cultivation by Croft Husbandry etc.* Edinburgh 1840.
- "Remarks on the Review of Mr. Stewart's Dissertation in the *Quarterly Review.*" *Blackwood's Edinburgh Review* (October 1817): 57–65; (November 1817): 159–65.

"Alison's French Revolution – Conclusion." *Dublin University Magazine* 20 (November 1842): 583–97.

Allan, David. *Virtue, Learning and the Scottish Enlightenment.* Edinburgh: Edinburgh University Press 1993.

Anderson, R.D. *Education and Opportunity in Victorian Scotland: Schools and Universities.* Oxford: Clarendon 1983.

Andrew, Donna T. *Philanthropy and Police: London Charity in the Eighteenth Century.* Princeton NJ: Princeton University Press 1989.

Ash, Marinell. *The Strange Death of Scottish History.* Edinburgh: Ramsay Head 1980.

Aughey, Arthur, Greta Jones, and W.T.M. Riches. *The Conservative Political Tradition in Britain and the United States.* Rutherford NJ: Fairleigh Dickinson University Press c. 1992.

Bailey, Victor, ed. *Policing and Punishment in Nineteenth-Century Britain.* London: Croom Helm 1981.

Barfoot, Michael. "James Gregory (1753–1821) and Scottish Scientific Metaphysics, 1750–1800." Doctoral dissertation, University of Edinburgh, 1983.

Barnes, James John. *Authors, Publishers and Politicians: The Quest for an Anglo-American Copyright Agreement, 1815–1854.* London: Routledge 1974.

Beattie, John. *Crime and the Courts in England, 1660–1800.* Princeton NJ: Princeton University Press 1986.

Bellamy, Richard, ed. *Victorian Liberalism.* London: Routledge 1990.

Benedict, Barbara. " 'Service to the Public': William Creech and Sentiment for Sale." In Dwyer and Sher, eds., *Sociability and Society,* 119–46.

Ben-Israel, Hedva. *English Historians on the French Revolution.* Cambridge: Cambridge University Press 1968.

Berg, Maxine. *The Machinery Question and the Making of Political Economy, 1815–1848.* Cambridge: Cambridge University Press 1980.

Berg, Maxine, Pat Hudson, and Michael Sonenscher, eds. *Manufacture in Town and Country before the Factory.* Cambridge: Cambridge University Press 1983.

Berry, J. "The Nature of Wealth and the Origins of Virtue: Recent Essays on the Scottish Enlightenment." *History of European Ideas* 7 (1986): 85–99.

Blain, Virginia, Isobel Grundy, and Patricia Clements, eds. *The Feminist Companion to Literature in English.* London: Batsford 1990.

Blair, Hugh. *Lectures on Rhetoric and Belles Lettres.* Edited by H.F. Harding and D. Potter. 2 vols. Carbondale: Southern Illinois University Press 1965.

Bowler, Peter J. "Malthus, Darwin and the Concept of Struggle." *Journal of the History of Ideas* 37 (1976): 631–50.

Brash, J.I. "The New Scottish County Electors in 1832: An Occupational Analysis." In *The Scots and Parliament,* edited by Clyve Jones, 120–39. Special edition of *Parliamentary History.* Edinburgh: Edinburgh University Press 1996.

Brown, Stewart J. *Thomas Chalmers and the Godly Commonwealth in Scotland.* Oxford: Oxford University Press 1982.

Brown, Stewart, and Michael Fry. *Scotland in the Age of the Disruption.* Edinburgh: Edinburgh University Press 1993.

Brundage, Anthony. *The Making of the New Poor Law: The Politics of Inquiry, Enactment, and Implementation, 1832–39.* London: Hutchinson 1978.

Bryson, Gladys. *Man and Society: The Scottish Inquiry of the Eighteenth Century.* Princeton NJ: Princeton University Press 1945.

Bumsted, J.M. "Introduction." *The Collected Writings of Lord Selkirk, 1799–1809.* Volume 1. Winnipeg: Manitoba Record Society 1984.

Burke, Edmund. *A Philosophical Inquiry into the Origins of Our Ideas of the Sublime and Beautiful.* Volume 1 of *The Writings and Speeches of Edmund Burke.* Boston: Little, Brown 1901.

– *Reflections on the French Revolution.* Volume 8 of *The Writings and Speeches of Edmund Burke,* edited by L.G. Mitchell. Oxford: Clarendon 1989.

Burrow, John. *Gibbon.* Oxford: Oxford University Press 1985.

Cage, R.A. *The Scottish Poor Law.* Edinburgh: Scottish Academic Press 1981.

– ed. *The Working Class in Glasgow 1750–1914.* London: Croom Helm 1987.

Camic, Charles. *Experience and Enlightenment: Socialization for Cultural Change in Eighteenth-Century Scotland.* Edinburgh: Edinburgh University Press 1983.

Campbell, Alan B. *The Lanarkshire Miners: A Social History of Their Trade Unions, 1775–1974.* Edinburgh: John Donald 1979.

Campbell, R.H. "The Landed Classes." In Devine and Mitchison, eds., *People and Society in Scotland,* 91–108.

Campbell, R.H., and T.M. Devine. "The Rural Experience." In Fraser and Morris, eds., *People and Society in Scotland,* 46–72.

Cannon J.P. *Parliamentary Reform, 1640–1832.* Cambridge: Cambridge University Press 1973.

Carson, Kit, and Hilary Idzikowska. "Social Production of Scottish Policing, 1795–1900." In Hay and Snyder, eds., *Policing and Prosecution in Britain.*

Carson, W.G. "Policing the Periphery: The Development of Scottish Policing, 1795–1900." *Australia and New Zealand Journal of Criminology* 17 (1984): 207–32; 18 (1985): 3–16.

Carter, Jennifer J., and Joan H. Pittock, eds. *Aberdeen and the Enlightenment.* Aberdeen: Aberdeen University Press, 1981.

Checkland, Olive. "Chalmers and William Pulteney Alison: A Conflict of Views on Scottish Social Policy." In *The Practical and the Pious: Essays on Thomas Chalmers,* edited by A.C. Cheyne, 130–9. Edinburgh: St Andrew's Press 1985.

Checkland, Olive and Sydney. *Industry and Ethos: Scotland 1832–1914.* Edinburgh: Edinburgh University Press 1989.

Chisick, Harvey. "The Wealth of Nations and the Poverty of the People in the Thought of Adam Smith." *Canadian Journal of History* 25 (1990): 325–44.

Chitnis, Anand C. *The Scottish Enlightenment: A Social History.* London: Croom Helm 1976.

– *The Scottish Enlightenment and Early Victorian English Society.* London: Croom Helm 1986.

Claeys, Gregory. *Citizens and Saints: Politics and Anti-Politics in Early British Social-ism.* Cambridge: Cambridge University Press 1989.

- *Machinery, Money and the Millennium: From Moral Economy to Socialism, 1815–60.* Cambridge: Polity 1987.

- "The French Revolution Debate and British Political Thought." *History of Political Thought* 11 (1990): 59–80.

- "A Utopian Tory Revolutionary at Cambridge: The Political Ideas and Schemes of James Bernard, 1834–1839." *Historical Journal* 25 (1982): 583–603.

Clark, J.C.D. *English Society 1688–1832: Ideology, Social Structure and Political Practice during the Ancien Regime.* Cambridge: Cambridge University Press 1985.

Clarke, Tony. "Early Chartism in Scotland: A 'Moral Force' Movement?" In *Conflict and Stability in Scottish Society 1700–1850*, edited by T.M. Devine, 106–21. Edinburgh: John Donald 1990.

Cockburn, Henry. *Circuit Journeys.* Edinburgh: Mercat Press 1975.

- *Memorials of His Time.* Edinburgh: T.N. Foulis 1910.

- *Journal of Henry Cockburn: Being a Continuation of the Memorials of His Time.* Vol. 2. Edinburgh: Edmonston and Douglas 1874.

- "Criminal Law of Scotland." *Edinburgh Review* (January 1825): 450–64.

- "Nomination of Scottish Juries." *Edinburgh Review* 36 (October 1821): 174–219.

- "Nomination of Scottish Juries." *Edinburgh Review* 38 (February 1823): 226–34.

- "Office of Lord Advocate of Scotland." *Edinburgh Review* 39 (January 1824): 363–92.

Collini, Stefan, Donald Winch, and John Burrow. *"That Noble Science of Politics".* Cambridge: Cambridge University Press 1983.

Connolly, S.J. "Albion's Fatal Twigs: Justice and Law in the Eighteenth Century." In *Economy and Society in Scotland and Ireland 1500–1939*, edited by Rosalind Mitchison and Peter Roebuck, 117–25. Edinburgh: John Donald 1988.

Cooper, David D. *The Lesson of the Scaffold.* London: Allen Lane 1974.

Corfield, Penelope. "Georgian England: One State, Many Faiths." *History Today* (April 1995): 14–21.

Crowther, M.A. "Poverty, Health and Welfare." In Fraser and Morris, eds., *People and Society in Scotland*, 265–89.

- "Response: North of the Border." *Scottish Historical Review* 73 (April 1994): 100–2.

Davis, Jennifer. "The London Garrotting Panic of 1862: A Moral Panic and the Creation of a Criminal Class in Mid-Victorian London." In Gatrell, Lenman, and Parker, eds., *Crime and the Law*, 190–213.

Davis, J. Ronnie. "Adam Smith on the Providential Reconciliation of Individual and Social Interests: Is Man Led by an Invisible Hand or Misled by a Sleight of Hand?" *History of Political Economy* 22 (1990): 341–52.

Devine, T.M. "Glasgow Colonial Merchants and Land, 1770–1815." In *Land and Industry: The Landed Estate and the Industrial Revolution*, edited by J.T. Ward and R.G. Wilson, 205–44. Newton Abbott: David and Charles 1971.

– "Urbanisation and the Civic Response: Glasgow, 1800–1830." In *Industry, Business and Society in Scotland since 1700*, edited by A.J.G. Cummings and T.M. Devine. Edinburgh: Edinburgh University Press 1994.

Devine, T.M., and Gordon Jackson. *Glasgow.* Volume 1: *Beginnings to 1830*. Manchester: Manchester University Press 1995.

Devine, T.M., and Rosalind Mitchison, eds. *People and Society in Scotland.* Volume 1: *1760–1830*. Edinburgh: John Donald 1988.

Diamond, Peter J. "Rhetoric and Philosophy in the Social Thought of Thomas Reid." In Dwyer and Sher, eds., *Sociability and Society*, 57–80.

Dickinson, H.T. *Liberty and Property.* New York: Hackett 1971.

– ed. *Britain and the French Revolution, 1789–1815*. New York: St. Martin's 1989.

Dickson, Tony, ed. *Capital and Class in Scotland.* Edinburgh: John Donald 1982.

– *Scottish Capitalism: Class, State and Nation from before the Union to the Present.* London: Lawrence and Wishart 1980.

Disraeli, Benjamin. *Coningsby, or The New Generation.* Edited by Sheila M. Smith. Oxford: Oxford University Press 1982.

Donajgrodzki, A.P., ed. *Social Control in Nineteenth Century Britain.* London: Croom Helm 1977.

Donnelly, F.K. "The Scottish Rising of 1820: A Reinterpretation." *Scottish Tradition* 6 (1976): 27–37.

Duman, Daniel. *The English and Colonial Bars in the Nineteenth Century.* London: Croom Helm 1983.

– *The Judicial Bench in England 1727–1875: The Reshaping of a Professional Elite.* London: Royal Historical Society 1982.

– "Pathway to Professionalism: The English Bar in the Eighteenth and Nineteenth Centuries." *Journal of Social History* 13 (1980): 615–28.

Dunkley, Peter. *The Crisis of the Old Poor Law in England 1795–1834: An Interpretive Essay.* New York: Garland 1982.

– "Whigs and Paupers: The Reform of the English Poor Laws, 1830–1834." *Journal of British Studies* (1981): 124–49.

Dwyer, John. *Virtuous Discourse: Sensibility and Community in Late Eighteenth Century Scotland.* Edinburgh: John Donald 1987.

– "Property and Propriety: The Ideological Context of Adam Smith's Ethics." I am grateful to Dr. Dwyer for a copy of this unpublished manuscript.

Dwyer, John, and Alexander Murdoch. "Paradigms and Politics: Manners, Morals and the Rise of Henry Dundas 1770–1784." In Dwyer, Mason, and Murdoch, eds., *New Perspectives*, 210–48.

Dwyer, John, Roger A. Mason, and Alexander Murdoch, eds. *New Perspectives on the Politics and Culture of Early Modern Scotland.* Edinburgh: John Donald c. 1982.

Dwyer, John, and Richard B. Sher, eds. *Sociability and Society in Eighteenth Century Scotland,* a special issue of *Eighteenth Century Life* 15 (February and May 1991).

Eastwood, David. "Robert Southey and the Intellectual Origins of Romantic Conservatism." *English Historical Review* 104 (1989): 308–31.

Eccleshall, Robert. *English Conservatism since the Restoration: An Introduction and Anthology.* London and Boston: Unwin Hyman 1990.

– "English Conservatism as Ideology." *Political Studies* 25 (1977): 62–83.

Edsall, Nicholas C. *The Anti-Poor Law Movement, 1834–44.* Manchester: Manchester University Press 1971.

Ellis, Peter Beresford, and Seumas Mac a' Ghobhainn. *The Scottish Insurrection of 1820.* London: Pluto 1989.

Emerson, Roger. *Professors, Patronage and Politics: The Aberdeen Universities in the Eighteenth Century.* Aberdeen: Aberdeen University Press 1992.

– "Lord Bute and the Scottish Universities 1760–1792." In *Lord Bute: Essays in Re-interpretation,* edited by Karl Schweizer, 453–74. Leicester: Leicester University Press 1988.

– "Science and the Origins and Concerns of the Scottish Enlightenment." *History of Science* 26 (1988): 333–66.

– "Scottish Universities in the Eighteenth Century, 1690–1800." *Studies on Voltaire and the Eighteenth Century* 167 (1977): 453–74.

Emsley, C. *English Police: A Political and Social History.* New York: Longman 1996.

– *Policing and Its Context, 1750–1850.* New York: Schocken 1984.

Engell, James. *The Creative Imagination: Enlightenment to Romanticism.* Cambridge MA: Harvard University Press 1981.

Engels, Frederick. *The Condition of the Working Class in England.* London: Panther 1972.

Epstein, James, and Dorothy Thompson, eds. *The Chartist Experience: Studies in Working-Class Radicalism and Culture, 1830–60.* London: Macmillan 1982.

Evans, E.J. *The Forging of the Modern State: Early Industrial Britain 1783–1870.* Harlow: Longman 1983.

Evans, D. Gareth. *A History of Wales, 1815–1906.* Cardiff: University of Wales Press 1989.

Feather, John. *A History of British Publishing.* London: Croom Helm 1988.

– "Publishers and Politicians: The Remaking of the Law of Copyright in Britain 1775–1842. Part II: The Rights of Authors." *Publishing History* 25 (1989): 45–72.

Ferguson, Adam. *Essay on the History of Civil Society.* Edited by Duncan Forbes. Edinburgh: Edinburgh University Press 1966.

Ferguson, W. "The Reform Act (Scotland) of 1832: Intention and Effect." *Scottish Historical Review* 45 (1966): 105–14.

Fetter, Frank Whitson. "The Economic Articles in *Blackwood's Edinburgh Magazine*, and Their Authors, 1817–1853." *Scottish Journal of Political Economy* 7 (1960): 55–107; 213–31.

– "The Rise and Decline of Ricardian Economics." *History of Political Economy* 1 (1969): 67–84.

Finlay, Richard J. "Controlling the Past: Scottish Historiography and Scottish Identity in the 19th and 20th Centuries." *Scottish Affairs* 9 (autumn 1994): 127–42.

Fontana, Biancamaria. *Rethinking the Politics of Commercial Society: The Edinburgh Review 1802–1832.* Cambridge: Cambridge University Press 1985.

Forbes, Duncan. *Hume's Philosophical Politics.* Cambridge: Cambridge University Press 1975.

– "Sceptical Whiggism, Commerce, and Liberty." In *Essays on Adam Smith*, edited by Andrew S. Skinner and Thomas Wilson, 179–201. Oxford: Oxford University Press 1975.

Fraser, W. Hamish. *Conflict and Class: Scottish Workers, 1700–1838.* Edinburgh: John Donald 1988.

Fraser, W. Hamish, and R.J. Morris, eds. *People and Society in Scotland.* Volume 2: *1830–1914.* Edinburgh: John Donald 1990.

Fry, Michael. *The Dundas Despotism.* Edinburgh: Edinburgh University Press 1992.

– *Patronage and Principle: A Political History of Modern Scotland.* Aberdeen: Aberdeen University Press 1987.

Gallacher, Geraldine. "The First Glasgow Police." Dissertation, Department of History, University of Strathclyde, 1987.

Gash, Norman. *Politics in the Age of Peel: A Study in the Technique of Parliamentary Representation 1830–1850.* London: Longman 1960.

– *Sir Robert Peel: The Life of Sir Robert Peel after 1830.* 2nd ed. London: Longman 1986.

Gatrell, V.A.C., Bruce Lenman, and Geoffrey Parker, eds. *Crime and the Law: The Social History of Crime in Western Europe since 1500.* London: Europa 1988.

Ghosh, P.R. "Style and Substance in Disraelian Social Reform, c. 1860–80." In *Politics and Change in Modern Britain: Essays Presented to A.E. Thompson*, edited by P.J. Waller, 59–90. Brighton: Harvester; New York: St. Martin's 1987.

Gordon, Barry. *Economic Doctrine and Tory Liberalism 1824–1830.* London: Macmillan 1979.

Greenleaf, W.H. *The British Political Tradition.* Volume 2: *The Ideological Tradition.* London: Routledge 1983.

Haakonssen, Knud. "Introduction." *Practical Ethics,* by Thomas Reid. Princeton
    NJ: Princeton University Press 1990.

– *The Science of a Legislator: The Natural Jurisprudence of David Hume and Adam
    Smith.* Cambridge: Cambridge University Press 1981.

– "John Millar and the Science of the Legislator." *Juridical Review* (June 1985):
    41–68.

– "The Science of a Legislator in James Mackintosh's Moral Philosophy." *History
    of Political Theory* 5 (1984): 245–80.

– "Jurisprudence and Politics in Adam Smith." In *Traditions of Liberalism: Essays
    on John Locke, Adam Smith, and John Stuart Mill,* edited by K. Haakonssen, 107–
    15. Sydney: CIS 1988.

– "Natural Law and Moral Realism: The Scottish Synthesis." In *Studies in the Phi-
    losophy of the Scottish Enlightenment.* Volume 1 of *Oxford Studies in the History of
    Philosophy,* edited by M.A. Stewart, 61–85. Oxford: Clarendon 1990.

Hamilton, Robert. *Inquiry Concerning the Rise and Progress, the Redemption and
    Present State of the National Debt of Great Britain.* Edinburgh 1813.

Hammond, J.L., and Barbara Hammond. *The Village Labourer.* London: Long-
    man 1978.

Hamowy, Ronald. *The Scottish Enlightenment and the Theory of Spontaneous Order.*
    Carbondale: Southern Illinois University Press 1987.

Hanham, H.J. "Mid-Century Scottish Nationalism: Romantic and Radical." In
    Ideas and Institutions of Victorian Britain, edited by Robert Robson, 143–79.
    London: G. Bell 1967.

Harvie, Christopher. *Scotland and Nationalism: Scottish Society and Politics 1707–
    1994.* London and New York: Routledge 1994.

Hay, Douglas. "Property, Authority and the Criminal Law." In Douglas Hay,
    Peter Linebaugh, John G. Rule, E.P. Thompson, and Cal Winslow, *Albion's
    Fatal Tree: Crime and Society in Eighteenth-Century England.* New York: Pantheon
    1975.

Hay, Douglas, and Francis Snyder, eds. *Policing and Prosecution in Britain 1750–
    1850.* Oxford: Clarendon 1989.

Hill, R.L. *Toryism and the People, 1832–46.* London: Constable 1929; reprinted in
    1975 by Porcupine Press, Philadelphia.

Hilton, Boyd. *The Age of Atonement: The Influence of Evangelicalism on Social and
    Economic Thought, 1795–1865.* Oxford: Oxford University Press 1988.

– *Corn, Cash, Commerce: The Economic Policies of the Tory Governments, 1815–1830.*
    Oxford: Oxford University Press 1977.

– "Peel; A Reappraisal." *Historical Journal* 22 (1979): 585–614.

Himmelfarb, Gertrude. *The Idea of Poverty: England in the Early Industrial Age.* New
    York: Knopf 1984.

Hipple, Walter John. *The Beautiful, the Sublime, and the Picturesque in Eighteenth Century British Aesthetic Theory.* Carbondale: Southern Illinois University Press 1957.

Hirschman, Albert O. *The Passions and the Interests: Political Arguments for Capitalism before its Triumph.* Princeton NJ: Princeton University Press 1977.

Holmes, Geoffrey. *Augustan England: Professions, State and Society, 1600–1730.* London and Boston: Allen 1982.

Honderich, Ted. *Conservatism.* London: Hamish Hamilton 1990.

Hont, Istvan, "The 'Rich Country–Poor Country' Debate." In Hont and Ignatieff, eds., *Wealth and Virtue,* 271–315.

Hont, Istvan, and Michael Ignatieff, eds. *Wealth and Virtue: The Shaping of Political Economy in the Scottish Enlightenment.* Cambridge: Cambridge University Press 1983.

Hope, Vincent, ed. *Philosophers of the Scottish Enlightenment.* Edinburgh: Edinburgh University Press 1984.

Hopfl, H.M. "From Savage to Scotsman: Conjectural History in the Scottish Enlightenment." *Journal of British Studies* 17 (1978): 19–40.

Houghton, Walter and Esther, eds. *Wellesley Index to Victorian Periodicals.* Toronto: University of Toronto Press 1972.

Hume, David. *Essays: Moral, Political and Literary.* Oxford: Clarendon 1963.

Hutchison, I.G.C. *A Political History of Scotland, 1832–1924: Parties, Elections and Issues.* Edinburgh: John Donald 1986.

– "Glasgow Working-Class Politics." In Cage, ed., *The Working Class in Glasgow,* 98–141.

Ignatieff, Michael. *A Just Measure of Pain: The Penitentiary in the Industrial Revolution 1750–1850.* London: Penguin 1989.

Innes, Joanna. "Jonathan Clark, Social History and England's 'Ancien Regime'." *Past and Present* 115 (May 1987): 165–200.

Jaggard, Edward. "Political Behaviour in England's Small Boroughs: A Cornwall Case Study." Paper presented at the Pacific Coast Conference on British Studies, University of California, Los Angeles, March 1996.

James, Patricia. "Introduction." *An Essay on the Principle of Population,* by T.R. Malthus. Vol. 1. Cambridge: Cambridge University Press 1989.

– *Population Malthus: His Life and Times.* London: Routledge 1979.

Johnson, Edgar. *Sir Walter Scott: The Great Unknown.* Vol. 1. London: Hamish Hamilton 1970.

Jones, David V.J. *The Newport Insurrection of 1839.* Oxford: Clarendon 1985.

– *Rebecca's Children: A Study of Rural Society, Crime and Protest.* Oxford: Clarendon 1989.

Kenyon, J.P. *The History Men: The Historical Profession in England since the Renaissance.* London: Weidenfeld 1983.

Keohane, Nannerl O. *Philosophy and the State in France: The Renaissance to the Enlightenment.* Princeton NJ: Princeton University Press 1980.

Kettler, David. "History and Theory in Ferguson's *Essay on the History of Civil Society:* A Reconsideration." *Political Theory* 5 (1977): 437–60.

Kidd, Colin. *Subverting Scotland's Past: Scottish Whig Historians and the Creation of an Anglo-British Identity 1689–c.1830.* Cambridge: Cambridge University Press 1993.

Kolbert, C.F., and N.A.M. Mackay. *History of Scots and English Land Law.* Berkhamstead: Geographical Pub., 1977.

Langer, Gary. *The Coming of Age of Political Economy, 1815–1825.* New York: Greenwood 1987.

Langford, Paul. *A Polite and Commercial People: England 1727–1783.* Oxford: Clarendon 1989.

Larson, Margali Sarfatti. *The Rise of Professionalism: A Sociological Analysis.* Berkeley: University of California Press 1977.

Lehmann, W.C. *John Millar of Glasgow, 1735–1801: His Life and Thought and His Contribution to Sociological Analysis.* Cambridge: Cambridge University Press 1960.

LeMahieu, D.L. "Malthus and the Theology of Scarcity." *Journal of the History of Ideas,* 40 (1979): 467–74.

Lenman, Bruce P. *An Economic History of Modern Scotland, 1660–1976.* Hamden CT: Archon 1977.

– *Integration, Enlightenment, and Industrialization: Scotland 1746–1832.* Toronto: University of Toronto Press 1981.

– "The Teaching of Scottish History in the Scottish Universities." *Scottish Historical Review,* 52 (1973): 165–90.

Lenman, Bruce P., and Geoffrey Parker, "Crime and Control in Scotland 1500–1800." *History Today* 30 (January 1984): 13–17.

Levitt, Ian, and Christopher Smout. *The State of the Scottish Working Class in 1843.* Edinburgh: Scottish Academic Press 1979.

Lieberman, David. "The Legal Needs of a Commercial Society: The Jurisprudence of Lord Kames." In Hont and Ignatieff, eds., *Wealth and Virtue,* 203–34.

Lindgren, J. Ralph. *The Social Philosophy of Adam Smith.* The Hague: Nijhoff 1973.

Lockhart, John Gibson. *Memoirs of the Life of Sir Walter Scott, Bart.* Vol. 2. Edinburgh: Cadell 1887.

Lough, John, "Reflections on Enlightenment and Lumières," *British Journal for Eighteenth-Century Studies* 8 (1985).

McConville, Sean. *A History of English Prison Administration.* Volume 1: *1750–1877.* London: Routledge 1981.

McElroy, Davis D. "A Century of Scottish Clubs." 1951–2. Transcript in NLS.

McFarland, E.W. *Protestants First: Orangeism in Nineteenth Century Scotland.* Edinburgh: Edinburgh University Press.

McGowen, Randall. "The Image of Justice and Reform of the Criminal Law in Early Nineteenth-Century England." *Buffalo Law Review* 32 (1983): 89–125.

Machin, G.I.T. "The Disruption and British Politics 1834–43." *Scottish Historical Review* 51 (1972): 20–51.

McLaren, A.A. "Patronage and Professionalism: The 'Forgotten Middle Class' 1760–1860." In *The Making of Scotland: Nation, Culture and Social Change,* edited by David McCrone, Stephen Kendrick, and Pat Straw, 123–42. Edinburgh: Edinburgh University Press 1989.

Macmillan, Duncan. *Painting in Scotland: The Golden Age.* Oxford: Phaidon 1986.

McNally, David. *Political Economy and the Rise of Capitalism: A Reinterpretation.* Berkeley: University of California Press 1990.

Mandler, Peter. *Aristocratic Government in the Age of Reform: Whigs and Liberals, 1830–1852.* Oxford: Clarendon 1990.

– "Tories and Paupers: Christian Political Economy and the Making of the New Poor Law." *Historical Journal* 33 (1990): 81–103.

Mather, F.C. *Public Order in the Age of the Chartists.* Manchester: Manchester University Press 1959.

Maver, Irene. "Guardianship of the Community: Civic Authority prior to 1833." In Devine and Jackson, eds., *Glasgow,* 239–77.

Meek, Ronald. *Marx and Engels on the Population Bomb.* Berkeley CA: Ramparts 1971.

– "The Scottish Contribution to Marxist Sociology." In *Democracy and the Labour Movement,* edited by J. Saville, London 1954.

– "Smith, Turgot, and the 'Four-Stages Theory.'" *History of Political Economy* 3 (1971): 9–27.

Meikle, Henry W. *Scotland and the French Revolution.* New York: Kelley 1969.

Mill, J.S. *Collected Works of John Stuart Mill.* Vol. 20. Edited by John M. Robson. Toronto: University of Toronto Press 1985.

– *Principles of Political Economy.* Edited by Donald Winch. Harmondsworth: Penguin 1970.

Miller, Karl. *Cockburn's Millennium.* Cambridge MA: Harvard University Press 1976.

Miller, Wilbur. *Cops and Bobbies: Police Authority in New York and London, 1830–1870.* Chicago: University of Chicago Press 1977.

Milne, Maurice. "Archibald Alison: Conservative Controversialist." *Albion* 27 (fall 1995): 417–43.

Mitchison, Rosalind. "Dundas's Pleasure." *Times Literary Supplement* (1 January 1993): 7.

– "Nineteenth Century Scottish Nationalism: The Cultural Background." In *The Roots of Nationalism: Studies in Northern Europe*, edited by Rosalind Mitchison, 131–42. Edinburgh: John Donald 1980.

– "North and South: The Development of the Gulf in Poor Law Practice." In *Scottish Society 1500–1800*, edited by R.A. Houston and I.D. Whyte, 199–224. Cambridge: Cambridge University Press 1989.

– "The Poor Law." In Devine and Mitchison, eds., *People and Society in Scotland*, 252–67.

Montgomery, Fiona A. "Glasgow and the Struggle for Parliamentary Reform, 1830–1832." *Scottish Historical Review* 61 (October 1982): 130–45.

Moody, Susan R., and Jacqueline Tombs. *Prosecution in the Public Interest*. Edinburgh: Scottish Academic Press 1982.

Moore, David Cresop. *The Politics of Deference: A Study of the Mid-Nineteenth Century English Political System*. Hassocks: Harvester 1976.

– "Concession or Cure: The Sociological Premises of the First Reform Act." *Historical Journal* 9 (1966): 39–59.

– "The Other Face of Reform." *Victorian Studies* 5 (1961–2): 7–34.

Moore, James, and Michael Silverthorne. "Gershom Carmichael and the Natural Jurisprudence Tradition in Eighteenth-Century Scotland." In Hont and Ignatieff, eds., *Wealth and Virtue*, 73–85.

Morris, R.J. "Scotland, 1830–1914: The Making of a Nation within a Nation." In Fraser and Morris, eds., *People and Society in Scotland*, 1–7.

Murdoch, Alexander. "The Advocates, the Law and the Nation in Early Modern Scotland." In *Lawyers in Early Modern Europe and America*, edited by Wilfred Prest. New York: Holmes and Meir 1981, 147–61.

Nenadic, Stana. "The Rise of the Urban Middle Class." In Devine and Mitchison, eds., *People and Society in Scotland*.

Nicholes, Joseph. "Revolutions Compared: The English Civil War as Political Touchstone in Romantic Literature." In *Revolution and English Romanticism*, edited by Keith Hanley and Raman Selden. Hemmel Hempstead: Harvester/Wheatsheaf 1990.

Nisbet, Robert. *Conservatism: Dream and Reality*. Minneapolis: University of Minnesota Press 1986.

Normand, W.G. "The Public Prosecutor in Scotland." *Law Quarterly Review* 215 (July 1938): 345–57.

Nowell-Smith, Simon. *International Copyright Law and the Publisher in the Reign of Queen Victoria*. Oxford: Oxford University Press 1968.

O'Brien, D.P. *The Classical Economists.* Oxford: Clarendon 1975.

O'Gorman, Frank. *British Conservatism: Conservative Thought from Burke to Thatcher.* New York: Longman 1986.

Oliphant, Margaret. *Annals of a Publishing House: William Blackwood and His Sons, Their Magazine and Friends.* 3rd ed. 2 vols. Edinburgh: Blackwood 1897.

O'Sullivan, Noel. *Conservatism.* New York: St. Martin's 1976.

Paterson, Audrey. "The Poor Law in Nineteenth-Century Scotland." In *The New Poor Law in the Nineteenth Century,* edited by Derek Fraser, 171–203. London: Macmillan 1976.

Patten, Robert L. *Charles Dickens and His Publishers.* Oxford: Clarendon 1978.

Perkin, Harold. *The Origins of Modern English Society 1780–1880.* London: Routledge 1972.

– "Land Reform and Class Conflict." In *The Victorians and Social Protest,* edited by J. Butt and I.F. Clarke. Newton Abbott: David and Charles 1973.

Philips, D. *Crime and Authority in Victorian England: The Black Country 1835–1860.* London: Croom Helm 1977.

– "'A New Engine of Power and Authority': The Institutionalisation of Law-Enforcement in England, 1780–1830." In Gatrell, Lenman, and Parker, eds., *Crime and the Law.*

Phillips, John A., and Charles Wetherell. "The Great Reform Act of 1832 and the Political Modernization of England." *American Historical Review* 100 (April 1995): 411–36.

Phillips, Mark. "Macaulay, Scott, and the Literary Challenge to Historiography." *Journal of the History of Ideas* 50 (1989): 117–33.

Phillipson, Nicholas. *Hume.* London: Weidenfeld 1989.

– *The Scottish Whigs and the Reform of the Court of Session 1785–1830.* Dissertation, University of Cambridge, 1967. Edinburgh: Stair Society 1990.

– "Culture and Society in the Eighteenth-Century Province: The Case of Edinburgh and the Scottish Enlightenment." In *The University in Society,* edited by L. Stone, 407–48. 2 vols. Princeton NJ: Princeton University Press 1974.

– "Lawyers, Landowners, and the Civic Leadership of Post-Union Scotland." In *Lawyers in their Social Setting,* edited by D.N. McCormick, 171–94. Edinburgh: Green 1976.

– "The Pursuit of Virtue in Scottish University Education: Dugald Stewart and Scottish Moral Philosophy." In *Universities, Society and the Future,* edited by N.T. Phillipson, 82–101. Edinburgh: Edinburgh University Press 1983.

– "The Social Structure of the Faculty of Advocates in Scotland 1661–1840." In *Law-Making and Law-Makers in British History,* edited by A. Harding, 146–56. London: Royal Historical Society 1980.

– "Towards a Definition of the Scottish Enlightenment." In *City and Society in the Eighteenth Century*, edited by P. Fritz and D. Williams, 125–49. Toronto: Hakkert 1973.

Pinkerton, John M. "Cockburn and the Law." In *Lord Cockburn: A Bicentenary Commemoration 1779–1979*. Edinburgh: Scottish Academic Press 1979.

Pocock, J.G.A. "Introduction." *Reflections on the Revolution in France*, by Edmund Burke. Indianapolis and Cambridge: Hackett 1987.

– *The Machiavellian Moment: Florentine Political Thought and the Atlantic Republican Tradition*. Princeton NJ: Princeton University Press 1975.

– *Politics, Language and Time: Essays on Political Thought and History*. New York: Atheneum 1971.

– *Virtue, Commerce, and History*. Cambridge: Cambridge University Press 1985.

– "Between Machiavelli and Hume: Gibbon as Civic Humanist and Philosophical Historian." In *Edward Gibbon and the Decline and Fall of the Roman Empire*, edited by G.W. Bowersock, John Clive, and Stephen R. Graubard, 103–19. Cambridge MA: Harvard University Press 1977.

– "Clergy and Commerce: The Conservative Enlightenment in England." In *L'Eta dei Lumi. Studi Storico sul Settecento Europeo in Honore di Franco Ventura*. Vol. 1. Naples 1985.

– "Conservative Enlightenment and Democratic Revolutions: The American and French Cases in British Perspective." *Government and Opposition* 24 (1989): 81–105.

– "Gibbon's Decline and Fall and the World View of the Late Enlightenment." *Eighteenth Century Studies* 10 (1977): 287–303.

– "The Political Economy of Burke's Analysis of the French Revolution." *Historical Journal* 25 (1982): 331–49.

Polanyi, Karl. *The Great Transformation: The Political and Economic Origins of Our Time*. Boston: Beacon 1957.

Poor Law Inquiry Scotland. Vols. 20–25 in United Kingdom, Parliamentary Papers, Reports from Commissioners, 1844.

Porter, Roy. *Edward Gibbon: Making History*. London: Weidenfeld 1988.

Poynter, J.R. *English Ideas on Poor Relief, 1795–1834*. London: Routledge 1969.

– *Society and Pauperism: English Ideas on Poor Relief, 1795–1834*. London: Routledge/Toronto: University of Toronto Press 1969.

Prest, Wilfred, ed. *The Professions in Early Modern England*. London: Croom Helm 1987.

Pullen, J.M. "Malthus's Theological Ideas and Their Influence on His Principle of Population." *History of Political Economy* 13 (1981): 39–54.

Quayle, Eric. *The Ruin of Sir Walter Scott*. London: Rupert Hart-Davis 1968.

Quinton, Anthony. *The Politics of Imperfection: The Religious and Secular Traditions of Conservative Thought in England from Hooker to Oakeshott.* London and Boston: Faber 1978.

Radzinowicz, L. "New Departures in Maintaining Public Order in the Face of Chartist Disturbances." *Cambridge Law Journal* (1960): 51–80.

Raphael, D.D., and A.L. Macfie. "Introduction." *The Theory of Moral Sentiments,* by Adam Smith. Oxford: Oxford University Press 1976.

Rashid, Salim. "David Robinson and the Tory Macroeconomics of *Blackwood's Edinburgh Magazine.*" *History of Political Economy* 10 (1978): 258–70.

Read, Donald. *Peel and the Victorians.* Oxford: Blackwell 1987.

Reid, Christopher. *Edmund Burke and the Practice of Political Writing.* Dublin: Gill and Macmillan 1985.

Reid, Thomas. *Essays on the Active Powers of Man.* Vol. 2 of *Philosophical Works.* Edited by Sir William Hamilton. Hildesheim: G. Olms 1967.

– *Essays on the Intellectual Powers of Man.* Vol. 1 of *Philosophical Works.* Edited by Sir William Hamilton. Hildesheim: G. Olms 1967.

– *Practical Ethics.* Edited & introduced by Knud Haakonssen. Princeton NJ: Princeton University Press 1990.

Rendall, Jane. "Virtue and Commerce: Women in the Making of Adam Smith's Political Economy." In *Women in Western Political Philosophy,* edited by Ellen Kennedy and Susan Mendus, 44–77. Brighton: Wheatsheaf 1987.

Roach, W.M. "Alexander Richmond and the Radical Reform Movements in Glasgow in 1816–17." *Scottish Historical Review* 51 (1972): 1–19.

Roberts, David. *Paternalism in Early Victorian England.* London: Croom Helm 1979.

– "The Social Conscience of the Tory Periodicals." *Victorian Periodicals Newsletter* 10 (1977): 154–69.

Robertson, J. Charles. "A Bacon-Facing Generation: Scottish Philosophy in the Early Nineteenth Century." *Journal of the History of Philosophy* 14 (1976): 37–49.

Robertson, John. *The Scottish Enlightenment and the Militia Issue.* Edinburgh: John Donald 1985.

– "The Legacy of Adam Smith: Government and Economic Development in the *Wealth of Nations.*" In Bellamy, ed., *Victorian Liberalism,* 15–41.

Rosner, Lisa. *Medical Education in the Age of Improvement: Edinburgh Students and Apprentices 1760–1826.* Edinburgh: Edinburgh University Press 1991.

Sack, James J. *From Jacobite to Conservative: Reaction and Orthodoxy in Britain, c. 1760–1832.* Cambridge: Cambridge University Press 1993.

Samuel, Ralph. "Workshop of the World: Steam Power and Hand Technology in Mid-Victorian Britain." *History Workshop* 3 (1977): 6–72.

Santurri, Edmund N. "Theodicy and Social Policy in Malthus' Thought." *Journal of the History of Ideas* 43 (1982): 315–30.

Saville, John. *1848: The British State and the Chartist Movement.* Cambridge: Cambridge University Press 1987.

Schofield, T.P. "Conservative Political Thought in Britain in Response to the French Revolution." *Historical Journal* 29 (1986): 601–22.

Senior, Hereward. *Orangeism in Ireland and Britain, 1795–1836.* New York: Hilary House 1966.

Shaw, A.G.L. *Convicts and the Colonies.* London: Faber 1966.

Sher, R.B. *Church and University in the Scottish Enlightenment: The Moderate Literati of Edinburgh.* Princeton NJ: Princeton University Press 1985.

Silver, Alan. "The Demand for Order in Civil Society: A Review of Some Themes in the History of Urban Crime, Police and Riot." In *The Police: Six Sociological Essays*, edited by D. Bordua, 1–24. New York 1967.

– "Social and Ideological Bases of British Elite Reactions to Domestic Crisis in 1829–1832." *Politics and Society* 1 (1971): 179–201.

Simpson, A.W.B. "Entails and Perpetuities." *Juridical Review* 24 (1979): 1–21.

Simpson, J. "Scottish Enlightenment Studies: Three Routes through a Busy Place." *Scottish Journal of Political Economy* 34 (1987): 97–103.

"Sir Archibald Alison." *Scottish Law Magazine and Sheriff Court Reporter,* new series, 6 (1867). An abridgment of the obituary in the *North British Daily Mail.*

Smail, John. "New Languages for Labour and Capital: The Transformation of Discourse in the Early Years of the Industrial Revolution." *Social History* 12 (1987): 49–71.

Smith, Adam. *The Correspondence of Adam Smith.* Edited by Ernest Campbell Mossner and Ian Simpson Ross. Oxford: Clarendon 1971.

– *An Inquiry into the Nature and Causes of the Wealth of Nations.* 2 vols. Edited by R.H. Campbell and A.S. Skinner. Oxford: Oxford University Press 1976; Indianapolis: Liberty 1981.

– *Lectures on Jurisprudence.* Edited by R.L. Meek, D.D. Raphael, and P.G. Stein. Oxford: Oxford University Press 1978.

– *The Theory of Moral Sentiments.* Edited by D.D. Raphael and A.L. Macfie. Oxford: Oxford University Press 1976; Indianapolis: Liberty 1982.

Smith, J. Irvine. "Introduction." *Principles of the Criminal Law of Scotland,* by Archibald Alison. Edinburgh: Blackwood 1832; Law Society of Scotland/Butterworths 1989.

Smith, Kenneth. *The Malthusian Controversy.* London: Routledge 1951; Ann Arbor MI: University Microfilms 1971.

Smith, Paul. *Disraelian Conservatism and Social Reform.* London: Routledge; Toronto: University of Toronto Press 1967.

Smout, T.C. *The Social Condition of Scotland in the 1840s*. Dundee: University of Dundee Press 1981.

– "The Landowner and the Planned Village in Scotland, 1730–1830." In *Scotland in the Age of Improvement*, edited by N.T. Phillipson and Rosalind Mitchison, 73–102. Edinburgh: Edinburgh University Press 1970.

– "Problems of Nationalism, Identity and Improvement in Later Eighteenth-Century Scotland." In *Improvement and Enlightenment*, edited by T.M. Devine, 1–21. Edinburgh: John Donald 1989.

Spring, Eileen. "Landowners, Lawyers, and Land Law Reform in Nineteenth-Century England." *American Journal of Legal History* 21 (1977): 40–59.

Steedman, Carolyn. *Policing the Victorian Community: The Formation of English Provincial Police Forces, 1856–80*. London/Boston: Routledge 1984.

Stein, Peter. "Adam Smith's Theory of Law and Society." In *Classical Influences on Western Thought, AD 1650–1870*, edited by R.R. Bolgar, 263–73. Cambridge: Cambridge University Press 1978.

– "The Legal Philosophy of the Scottish Enlightenment." In *Rechtsphilosophie der Aufklärung*, edited by R. Brandt, 61–78. Berlin: De Gruyter 1982.

Steuart, Sir James. *The Works, Political, Metaphysical and Chronological, of Sir James Steuart*. New York: Kelley 1967.

Stevenson, A.G. "Walter Scott at the Bar," *Juridical Review* (1993, Part 1): 74–82.

Stewart, Dugald. *Lectures on Political Economy*. Edited by Sir William Hamilton. 2 vols. New York: Kelley 1968.

– *The Philosophy of the Active and Moral Powers of Man*. 9th ed. Revised by James Walker. Philadelphia: E.H. Butler 1866.

Stewart, Robert. *The Foundation of the Conservative Party 1830–1867*. New York: Longman 1978.

– *Party and Politics, 1830–1852*. London: Macmillan 1989.

– *The Politics of Protection: Lord Derby and the Protectionist Party, 1841–42*. Cambridge: Cambridge University Press 1971.

Storch, R.D. "The Plague of the Blue Locusts: Police Reform and Popular Resistance in Northern England, 1840–57." *International Journal of Social History* 20 (1975): 61–90.

Sunter, Ronald. *Patronage and Politics in Scotland, 1707–1832*. Edinburgh: John Donald 1986.

Sutherland, J.A. *Victorian Novelists and Publishers*. London: Athlone 1976.

Sweeney, Irene E. "The Municipal Administration of Glasgow, 1833–1912: Public Service and the Scottish Civic Identity." Doctoral dissertation, Strathclyde University, 1990.

Teichgraeber, Richard, III. *"Free Trade" and Moral Philosophy: Rethinking the Sources of Adam Smith's "The Wealth of Nations"*. Durham NC: Duke University Press 1986.

Thomson, Alexander. *Punishment and Prevention.* London: Nisbet 1857.

Thompson, Dorothy. Review of Saville, *1848. In History Workshop Journal* (1989): 165.

Thompson, F.M.L. "Land and Politics in England in the Nineteenth Century." *Transactions of the Royal Historical Society* 15 (1965): 23–44.

Tocqueville, Alexis de. *Democracy in America.* Edited by J.P. Mayer; translated by George Lawrence. Garden City NY: Anchor-Doubleday 1969.

– *The Old Regime and the French Revolution.* Translated by Stuart Gilbert. Garden City: Anchor-Doubleday 1955.

Townsend, Dabney. "Archibald Alison: Aesthetic Experience and Emotion." *British Journal of Aesthetics.* 28 (1988): 132–44.

Vickers, Daniel. "Competency and Competition: Economic Culture in Early America," *William and Mary Quarterly* 47 (1990): 3–29.

Vincent, John. *The Formation of the British Liberal Party.* New York: Scribner's 1966.

Wallech, Steven. " 'Class Versus Rank': The Transformation of Eighteenth Century English Social Terms and Theories of Production." *Journal of the History of Ideas* 47 (1986): 409–31.

Waller, P.J. *Democracy and Sectarianism: A Political and Social History of Liverpool 1868–1939.* Liverpool: Liverpool University Press 1981.

Ward, J.T. *The Factory Movement 1830–1855.* London: Macmillan 1962.

Waterman, A.M.C. "The Ideological Alliance of Political Economy and Christian Theology 1798–1833." *Journal of Ecclesiastical History* 34 (1983): 321–44.

Wells, Roger A.E. *Insurrection: The British Experience, 1795–1803.* Gloucester: Alan Sutton 1983.

Whatley, Christopher A. "Labour in the Industrialising City, c. 1660–1830." In Devine and Jackson, eds., *Glasgow,* 360–401.

Whetstone, A.E. *Scottish County Government in the Eighteenth and Nineteenth Centuries.* Edinburgh: John Donald 1981.

– "The Reform of the Scottish Sheriffdoms in the Eighteenth and Nineteenth Centuries." *Albion* 9 (1977): 61–71.

Wilks, Ivor. *South Wales and the Rising of 1839: Class Struggle as Armed Struggle.* Urbana: University of Illinois Press 1984.

Williams, Gwyn A. *The Merthyr Rising.* London: Croom Helm 1978.

Williams, Raymond. *Cobbett.* Oxford; New York: Oxford University Press 1983.

– *Keywords.* Glasgow: Fontana 1976.

Wilson, Alexander. *The Chartist Movement in Scotland.* New York: Kelley 1970.

Winch, Donald. *Classical Political Economy and Colonies.* London: London School of Economics and Political Science 1965.

– *Malthus.* Oxford: Oxford University Press, 1987.

– "The Smith-Burke Problem and Late Eighteenth-Century Political and Economic Thought." *Historical Journal* 28 (1985): 231–47.

Withers, Charles W.J. "Improvement and Enlightenment: Agriculture and Natural History." In *Philosophy and Science in the Scottish Enlightenment*, edited by Peter Jones. Edinburgh: John Donald 1988.

Withrington, Donald J., "What was Distinctive about the Scottish Enlightenment?" In Carter and Pittock, eds., *Aberdeen and the Enlightenment*, 9–19.

Womersley, D.J. "The Historical Writings of William Robertson." *Journal of the History of Ideas* 47 (1986): 497–506.

Wood, Paul. "The Hagiography of Common Sense: Dugald Stewart's Account of the Life and Writings of Thomas Reid." In *Philosophy, Its History and Historiography*, edited by A.J. Holland, 305–22. Dordrecht, Holland/Boston: D. Reide 1983.

Young, James D. *The Rousing of the Scottish Working Class*. London: Croom Helm 1979.

Index

McGill-Queen's Studies in the History of Ideas